Contents

List of figures, maps and tables   iv

List of contributors and acknowledgements   ix

Introduction   x

Section 1: Articles   1

1   Ageing across the UK   2
2   Portrait of the North East   29
3   Portrait of the South West   43
4   Regional health inequalities in England   60
5   Understanding income at small area level   80

Section 2: Regional and Country Profiles   95

Statistical Regions of the United Kingdom (map)   96
6.1   North East   97
6.2   North West   98
6.3   Yorkshire and The Humber   99
6.4   East Midlands   100
6.5   West Midlands   101
6.6   East of England   102
6.7   London   103
6.8   South East   104
6.9   South West   105
6.10a Wales   106
6.10b Cymru   107
6.11 Scotland   108
6.12 Northern Ireland   109

Section 3: Data   111

7   Maps   112
8   Tables   119
9   Directory of Online Tables   124

Section 4: Reference   129

Useful websites   130
Boundary maps   132
Glossary   141
Symbols and conventions   146

Figures, maps and tables

The latest regional data on a wide range of topics can be accessed through the Directory of Online Tables on the ONS website at: www.statistics.gov.uk/regionaltrends/data

The 'Type' column provides information on the status of the statistics included in this edition: National Statistics (NS), Non-National Statistics (Non-NS) or Mixed. Statistics accredited as 'National Statistics' are fully compliant with the Code of Practice for Official Statistics and carry the National Statistics kitemark. Statistics labelled as 'Non-National Statistics' follow many of the best practice principles set out in the Code but have not been accredited as fully compliant.

Page number refers to the page on which the figure, map or table can be found in *Regional Trends 42*.

			Type	Page
Section 1: Articles				
1 Ageing across the UK				
Map	1.1	Percentage of the population aged 50 and over: by local authority, 2008	NS	4
Figure	1.2	Percentage of total population in key age groups, 2008	NS	5
Figure	1.3	Population by Rural/Urban Definition at MSOA level, England, 2008	Non-NS	6
Figure	1.4	Population by Rural/Urban Definition at MSOA level, Wales, 2008	Non-NS	6
Figure	1.5	Population by Urban Rural Classification at Data Zone level, Scotland, 2008	Non-NS	6
Figure	1.6	Population by Urban-Rural Classification: by Settlements, Northern Ireland, 2001	Non-NS	6
Figure	1.7	Projected population for men and women aged 50 and over, 2006 to 2031	Non-NS	8
Figure	1.8	Projected population for men and women aged 75 and over, 2006 to 2031	Non-NS	9
Figure	1.9	Age-specific death rates: by age group, 2008	NS	10
Figure	1.10	Net internal migration of people aged 50 and over, mid-2007 to mid-2008	Non-NS	10
Figure	1.11	Legal marital status for men and women aged 65 and over, 2008	Non-NS	11
Figure	1.12	Percentage of population aged 50 and over who are not White British, 2007	Non-NS	11
Figure	1.13	Percentage of people aged 60 and over in low-income households, 2005/06 to 2007/08	NS	13
Figure	1.14	Beneficiaries of Pension Credits as a percentage of population aged 60 and over, 2008	NS	13
Figure	1.15	Population aged 60 and over in the 10 per cent most deprived LSOAs in England, 2008	Mixed	13
Figure	1.16	Population aged 60 and over: by IDAOPI decile and Rural/Urban Definition, England, 2008	Mixed	14
Figure	1.17	Urban population aged 60 and over: by IDAOPI decile by region of England, 2008	Mixed	15
Map	1.18	The 10 per cent most and least deprived LSOAs, North West, 2007	NS	16
Map	1.19	The 10 per cent most and least deprived LSOAs, South East, 2007	NS	17
Figure	1.20	Percentage of households with one or more persons aged 60 or over in fuel poverty, England, 2007	Non-NS	17
Figure	1.21	Life expectancy, healthy life expectancy and disability-free life expectancy at age 65: by sex and UK country, 2004 to 2006	NS	18
Map	1.22	Life expectancy at age 65: by sex and local authority, 2005 to 2007	NS	19
Figure	1.23	Breast and cervical cancer screening: by country and strategic health authority, 31 March 2008	NS	20
Figure	1.24	Percentage of people aged 65 and over, immunised against influenza: by country and strategic health authority, 2007/08	NS	21

DATA

Hover and click over tables and graphs on the online pdf of Regional Trends and you can download them in Microsoft Excel. It's as simple as that.

www.statistics.gov.uk/regionaltrends42

Figure	1.25	Rates of hip and knee replacements for 65 year-olds and over: by strategic health authority, 2008/09	Non-NS	21
Figure	1.26	Percentage of people aged 65 and over living at home after discharge from hospital, 31 October 2008 to 31 December 2008	Non-NS	21
Figure	1.27	Rate of adults aged 65 and over assisted to live independently, 2008/09	Non-NS	22
Figure	1.28	Percentage of people aged 60 and over receiving Disability Living Allowance, 2008	NS	22
Figure	1.29	Percentage of people aged 65 and over receiving Attendance Allowance, 2008	NS	22
Figure	1.30	Percentage of people aged 60 and over receiving Carer's Allowance, 2008	NS	23
Figure	1.31	Employment, unemployment and economic inactivity rates for people aged 50 to state pension age, 2008	NS	23
Figure	1.32	Percentage of employed men and women aged 50 to state pension age that are in full- or part-time employment, 2008	NS	24
Figure	1.33	Housing tenure for people aged 65 and over, 2008	Non-NS	25
Figure	1.34	Highest qualification level achieved for people aged 50 to state pension age, 2009 Q2	Non-NS	26
Figure	1.35	Percentage of people aged 50–64 undertaking adult learning in the last year, April 2008 to March 2009	Non-NS	26
Figure	1.36	Uptake of concessionary bus fare schemes for people aged 60 and over, 2006 to 2008	NS	27

2 Portrait of the North East

Map	2.1	North East: physical features	Non-NS	30
Map	2.2	North East: local or unitary authority, NUTS 2 sub-regions and Rural/Urban Definition	Non-NS	30
Figure	2.3	Population: by local authority, North East, mid-2008	NS	31
Table	2.4	Components of population change: by local authority, mid-2007 to mid-2008	NS	32
Figure	2.5	Net migration: by region, 2008	NS	32
Figure	2.6	Mid-year population estimates by 5 year age band and sex, North East, 2008	NS	32
Figure	2.7	Household estimates and projections: by household type, 2001 to 2026	NS	33
Figure	2.8	Median dwelling prices: by local authority, North East, 2008	Non-NS	33
Figure	2.9	Proportion of working age population with no qualifications: by region, 2009 Q2	NS	34
Map	2.10	Employment rate: North East, 1992 Q4 to 2009 Q4	NS	35
Table	2.11	Claimant count: by sex, North East, January 2006 to January 2010	NS	35
Figure	2.12	Reasons for economic inactivity: North East, 2004 to 2009	NS	35
Figure	2.13	Labour productivity: gross value added per hour worked, by region, 2008	NS	36
Table	2.14	Percentage employed in manufacturing: by local authority, North East, 2007	NS	37
Figure	2.15	Business enterprise research and development expenditure as a proportion of gross value added: by region, 2007	NS	37
Table	2.16	Distribution of LSOA rankings on the 2007 Index of Multiple Deprivation: by region	Non-NS	38
Figure	2.17	Distribution of LSOA rankings on the 2007 Index of Multiple Deprivation, for local authorities in the North East	Non-NS	39
Figure	2.18	Difference in life expectancy at birth between the regions and the UK average, 2006 to 2008	NS	39
Figure	2.19	Alcohol drunk on 5 or more days in week, men and women aged 16 or over: by region, 2007	NS	40
Figure	2.20	Usual method of travel to work: by region of residence, 2008 Q4	NS	40
Figure	2.21	CO_2 emissions per resident: by region, 2007	NS	41
Figure	2.22	Crimes committed against households: by region, 2007 to 2008	NS	41

3 Portrait of the South West

Map	3.1	South West: physical features	Non-NS	44
Map	3.2	South West: local or unitary authority, NUTS 2 sub-regions and Rural/Urban Definition	Non-NS	44
Figure	3.3	Population: by county and unitary authority, South West, mid-2008	NS	45

Map	3.4	Percentage change in population by local or unitary authority, 2003 to 2008	NS	46
Figure	3.5	Components of population change: by county and unitary authority, South West, mid-2007 to mid-2008	NS	47
Figure	3.6	Net internal migration into the South West: by region of origin, mid-2007 to mid-2008	NS	47
Figure	3.7	Mid-year population estimates: by five-year age band and sex, South West, 2008	NS	47
Figure	3.8	Household estimates and projections: by household type, South West, 2001–2026	NS	48
Map	3.9	Ratio of lower quartile house price to lower quartile earnings by local or unitary authority, 2009	Non-NS	49
Figure	3.10	Second homes: by region, average 2005/06 to 2007/08	NS	50
Figure	3.11	Population of working age: by level of highest qualification, 2009 Q2	NS	50
Figure	3.12	Employment rate, South West, 1992 Q4 to 2009 Q4	NS	51
Figure	3.13	Economic inactivity by reason: by region, 2008	NS	52
Figure	3.14	Median gross weekly pay for full-time employees, workplace-based: by region, April 2009	NS	52
Figure	3.15	Labour productivity: gross value added per hour worked: per region, 2008	NS	53
Figure	3.16	Employee jobs: by industry, South West, September 2009	NS	53
Figure	3.17	Expenditure on research and development: by sector and region, 2007	NS	53
Figure	3.18	Distribution of LSOA rankings in the 2007 Index of Multiple Deprivation: by South West county and unitary authority	Non-NS	55
Figure	3.19	Indices of deprivation 2007: South West population living in LSOAs in the 10 per cent most deprived in England, by domain of deprivation	Non-NS	55
Figure	3.20	Workless households, by county and unitary authority, South West, 2008	NS	55
Figure	3.21	Difference in life expectancy at birth between counties and unitary authorities and the UK average, South West, 2006 to 2008	NS	56
Figure	3.22	Age-standardised mortality rates: by cause and region, 2008	NS	56
Figure	3.23	Usual method of travel to work: by region of residence, 2008	NS	57
Figure	3.24	Household recycling rates: by region, 2003/04 and 2008/09	NS	58
Figure	3.25	Crimes committed against households: by type and region, 2008/09	NS	59

4 Regional health inequalities in England

Table	4.1	An example – prevalence of childhood obesity in reception years	NS	61
Figure	4.2	Health indicator spine charts by region – standardised values	NS	63
Figure	4.3	Health indicator spine charts by indicator– standardised values	NS	64
Table	4.4	England indicators	NS	62
Figure	4.5	Spine chart for North East	NS	65
Table	4.6	North East indicators	NS	65
Figure	4.7	Spine chart for North West	NS	66
Table	4.8	North West indicators	NS	66
Figure	4.9	Spine chart for Yorkshire and The Humber	NS	67
Table	4.10	Yorkshire and The Humber indicators	NS	67
Figure	4.11	Spine chart for East Midlands	NS	68
Table	4.12	East Midlands indicators	NS	68
Figure	4.13	Spine chart for West Midlands	NS	69
Table	4.14	West Midlands indicators	NS	69
Figure	4.15	Spine chart for East of England	NS	70
Table	4.16	East of England indicators	NS	70
Figure	4.17	Spine chart for London	NS	71
Table	4.18	London indicators	NS	71
Figure	4.19	Spine chart for South East	NS	72
Table	4.20	South East indicators	NS	72

Figure	4.21	Spine chart for South West	NS	73
Table	4.22	South West indicators	NS	73
Figure	4.23	Life expectancy at birth in the North East and England, 1991–93 to 2006–08	NS	75
Figure	4.24	Infant mortality rate, England, West Midlands and South East, 1996 to 2008	NS	76
Table	4.25	Age-standardised mortality rates, selected causes, England, 2008	NS	76
Figure	4.26	Prevalence of cigarette smoking by sex and for all people, England, 1998 to 2008	NS	77

5 Understanding income at small area level

Table	5.1	Average weekly household net income (equivalised BEFORE housing costs)	NS	82
Table	5.2	Average weekly household net income (equivalised AFTER housing costs)	NS	82
Figure	5.3	Distribution of MSOA average household net income BHC, model-based estimates, 2007/08	Non-NS	83
Table	5.4	Thresholds and ratios for MSOA BHC net income estimates, model-based estimates 2007/08	Non-NS	84
Map	5.5	High and low levels of average household net income BHC, England and Wales, 2007/08	Non-NS	85
Map	5.6	High and low levels of average household net income AHC, England and Wales, 2007/08	Non-NS	86
Map	5.7	High and low levels of average household net income BHC, London, 2007/08	Non-NS	87
Map	5.8	High and low levels of average household net income AHC, London, 2007/08	Non-NS	88
Map	5.9	High and low levels of average household net income within the North West, 2007/08	Non-NS	88
Table	5.10	BHC net income distributions from MSOAs in Manchester and Liverpool, 2007/08	Non-NS	89
Map	5.11	Local patterns of average household net income for Manchester and Liverpool by MSOA, 2007/08	Non-NS	90
Table	5.12	Changes in net income before housing costs	Non-NS	90
Figure	5.13	Regional distributions of change in BHC income	Non-NS	91
Figure	5.14	Scatter plot showing MSOA level BHC income in 2004/05 and 2007/08: by region	Non-NS	92
Table	5.15	Differences in within-region percentile thresholds and ratio for BHC income, 2004/05 to 2007/08	Non-NS	93

Section 2: Region and Country Profiles

Map		Statistical Regions of the United Kingdom	N/A	96
Map	6.1	North East – population density: by local or unitary authority, 2008	NS	97
Map	6.2	North West – population density: by local or unitary authority, 2008	NS	98
Map	6.3	Yorkshire and The Humber – population density: by local or unitary authority, 2008	NS	99
Map	6.4	East Midlands – population density by local or unitary authority, 2008	NS	100
Map	6.5	West Midlands – population density by local or unitary authority, 2008	NS	101
Map	6.6	East of England – population density by local or unitary authority, 2008	NS	102
Map	6.7	London – population density by London borough, 2008	NS	103
Map	6.8	South East – population density by local or unitary authority, 2008	NS	104
Map	6.9	South West – population density by local or unitary authority, 2008	NS	105
Map	6.10a	Wales – population density by unitary authority, 2008	NS	106
Map	6.10b	Cymru – dwysedd y boblogaeth: yn ôl awdurdod unedol, 2008	NS	107
Map	6.11	Scotland – population density by council area, 2008	NS	108
Map	6.12	Northern Ireland – population density by district council area, 2008	NS	109

Section 3: Data

7 Maps

Map	7.1	Population change: by county or unitary authority, 2003 to 2008	NS	113
Map	7.2	Projected population change: by county or unitary authority, 2006 to 2026	NS	113
Map	7.3	Population density: by county or unitary authority, 2008	NS	114
Map	7.4	Population under 16: by county or unitary authority, 2008	NS	114
Map	7.5	Population: state pension age, 2008	NS	114
Map	7.6	Percentage of population of working age claiming key social security benefit: by local authority, August 2009	NS	115
Map	7.7	Unemployment rates: by unitary and local authority, July 2008 to June 2009	NS	116
Map	7.8	Percentage claiming for more than 12 months: by local authority, December 2009	NS	117
Map	7.9	Carbon dioxide emissions per resident: by local authority, 2005 to 2007	NS	118

8 Tables

Table	8.1	Key statistics: population, health and welfare	NS	120
Table	8.2	Key statistics: labour market and education	NS	121
Table	8.3	Key statistics: economy	NS	122
Table	8.4	Key statistics: housing, transport, environment and crime	Mixed	123

Section 4: Reference

Boundary maps

Counties and unitary authorities in England, 1998 and 2009	N/A	133
NUTS levels 1, 2 and 3 in England, 2008	N/A	134
Unitary authorities in Wales, 2005/Awdurdodau unedol yng Nghymru, 2005	N/A	135
NUTS levels 1, 2 and 3 in Wales, 2008/NUTS lefelau 1, 2 a 3 yng Nghymru, 2008	N/A	135
Councils in Scotland, 1996	N/A	136
NUTS levels 1, 2 and 3 in Scotland, 2008	N/A	136
Geographical classifications in Northern Ireland	N/A	137
Police areas, United Kingdom	N/A	138
Health areas, England, 2006	N/A	139
Environment Agency regions, England and Wales, 1996	N/A	139
Regions of the National Rivers Authority, England	N/A	139
Education authorities in England	N/A	140

Contributors and acknowledgements

The Editor would like to thank article authors and other colleagues in ONS, contributing Departments and other organisations for their generous support and helpful comments, without which this edition of *Regional Trends* would not have been possible.

Production editor:	Cliff Thornton
Production team:	Robert Adams
	Iain Wilson
	Bernadette Perry
	Pam Johnston
	Gaynor Andrews
Lead reviewers:	Judith Jones
	Paul Vickers
Design:	ONS Design
Typesetting:	Curran Publishing Services Ltd
Publishing management:	Phil Lewin
	Rod Tonge
Maps:	Nick Richardson
	Deborah Rhodes

Introduction

Welcome to the 42nd edition of *Regional Trends*. This is the second to be based around articles aimed at a wide range of readers including policy makers in both central and local government, academics and students, the media and the general public. In addition, a short profile for each region and country is included in Section 2, towards the back of the book. Section 3 provides summary tables and maps covering the UK.

The tables and profiles are supplemented online by a broader range of tables and longer regional profiles, which are updated periodically at:

www.statistics.gov.uk/regionaltrends/data
www.statistics.gov.uk/regionalprofiles

Chapter 9 of this edition provides a comprehensive directory of the online tables. Because of relatively long lead times, some of the data used in the articles, tables and maps will not be the most recent available when *Regional Trends* is published. The online tables may be more up to date but for the latest data please check with source websites or the Publication Hub at: www.statistics.gov.uk/hub. This provides the latest news on releases of all UK National Statistics, no matter where they are produced.

This is the last edition of *Regional Trends* that will be available in print. The Office for National Statistics (ONS) is utilising online access to offer better value for money and to open up statistics to a wider audience. For more information see the 26 November 2009 ONS News Release at: www.statistics.gov.uk/mediareleases/currentreleases.asp. *Regional Trends* will be developed online over the coming months to deliver articles as soon as they are ready for publication. You will also see other changes to the way *Regional Trends* is presented on the website. We encourage you to look out for developments at:

www.statistics.gov.uk/regionaltrends

This edition includes five articles:

- Ageing across the UK

- Portrait of the North East

- Portrait of the South West

- Regional health inequalities in England

- Understanding income at small area level

Ageing and older people

The lead article in this year's *Regional Trends* is 'Ageing across the UK'. This follows on from the National Statistician's 2008 article on the population, which focused on ageing and mortality in the UK, and an article in *Economic and Labour Market Review*, April 2009 on 'Employment of the older generation'.

The increasing numbers of people living and remaining healthy at older ages gives cause for celebration but also presents a new set of challenges, for example: housing, health and access to local and welfare services. The article explores regional and sub-regional variations in the concentration of older people, projected trends and regional measures of their wellbeing. London and Northern Ireland have the lowest proportions of older people and the South West and Wales have the highest proportions. Local authority level data show a greater concentration of older people in many coastal and rural areas. Using the Rural/Urban Definition for Middle Layer Super Output Areas confirms that higher proportions of older people live in rural areas than for the whole population. In England, for example, about 75 per cent of older people (whether defined as 50 and over or 65 and over) live in urban areas with populations over 10,000, compared with 80 per cent of the population of all ages.

The population aged 65 and over is projected to grow steadily in all regions between 2006 and 2031. The greatest percentage increases are expected in Northern Ireland, the East Midlands and the East of England and are likely to be greatest among the 'oldest old' (those aged 85 and over) The population aged 50 to 64 is projected to grow less rapidly, or even decrease in a few regions. This age group is expected to increase most in London, although the population aged 65 and over is projected to rise less than in all other regions.

The article also investigates how the health and quality of life of the older population vary geographically. Life expectancy at age 65 and age-specific death rates illustrate the patterns in mortality that underpin the population projections. Life expectancy was found to be generally higher in the south and midlands, although there was considerable variation within regions. Some data were also obtained showing, for example, frequency of hip and knee operations, social care to help older people live independently, marital status, housing tenure and take-up of concessionary bus passes.

Highest levels of income deprivation among older people were generally found in the North East, North West and London. Much of the variation between and within regions appears to reflect the rurality of the areas where older people live. The article includes case studies of income deprivation (in terms of the proportion of people aged 60 and over receiving state benefits) at Lower Layer Super Output Area level in the North West and the South East regions. These demonstrate that older people living in urban areas (population over 10,000) were more likely to live in the most income-deprived areas than those living in small towns, urban fringe and rural areas. However, in the South East only 1 per cent of the older population lived in areas that were among the 10 per cent most deprived in England, compared with 17 per cent in the North West.

The article also examines the employment, qualifications and learning activities of people aged 50 to state pension age (SPA). Northern Ireland, Wales and the North East had the highest percentages of their population aged 50 to SPA who were economically inactive in 2008. However, Northern Ireland and the North East (and also Scotland) had the highest percentages among those men aged 50 to 64 that were in employment who were working full-time.

Regional portraits

These articles focus on what it is like to live and work in the North East and South West regions of England.

The **North East** has the slowest rate of population increase among the regions of England, with the lowest fertility rates and the highest death rates for men aged 55 and over. The region has relatively high rates of unemployment and of economic inactivity due to long-term sickness. It has the lowest rates of pay of all English regions and the lowest average house prices.

The **South West** has more people living in villages, hamlets and isolated dwellings than any other English region and has the highest proportion of people of state pension age and above. It has more second homes than any other English region, receives more domestic tourists and has a larger hotel and restaurant sector relative to the whole regional economy than any other UK region or country. It has among the highest proportions of self-employed workers, part-time workers and people with more than one job and has the highest regional life expectancy at birth for females and second highest for males.

Regional health inequalities in England

This article brings together a range of health indicators for each of the nine government office regions and makes comparisons across regions and against England as a whole. Indicators include life expectancy, alcohol consumption, smoking, drug usage, child obesity and mortality rates by cause. Bringing these indicators together in this manner provides a fuller picture of health differences between regions, instead of looking at each indicator in isolation. The article confirms other studies showing that the north–south divide between regions persists. However, it also reveals some health indicators that do not fit in with this trend.

Small area income estimates

ONS has produced experimental model-based estimates of average household income for Middle Layer Super Output Areas in England and Wales. The article 'Understanding income at small area level' looks at spatial disparities in average income within regions and local authorities. The article finds wide variation in patterns of average household income, in particular London had the widest spread while Wales had the narrowest spread. Wales had the largest increase in average household income between 2004/05 and 2007/08 with the North West and South West having the smallest. The article also examines whether the gap between the richest and poorest areas was decreasing. The article should be of interest to planners and regeneration specialists, and those who want to understand local economies.

Available to download

We hope you enjoy this edition of *Regional Trends* and that it encourages more investigation of the wealth of data that are available on the website to inform debate and policy. The full report is available on the Office for National Statistics website:

www.statistics.gov.uk

The interactive PDF includes links to spreadsheets containing the data used and supplementary analysis. More local area data for England and Wales can be accessed from the Neighbourhood Statistics web pages:

www.statistics.gov.uk/neighbourhood

In *Regional Trends* and the online data tables we aim to include data that cover the entire UK where that is possible. However, there will often be more data on the websites of the constituent countries as well as those of other government departments that produce statistics. A list of useful websites can be found in Section 4 at the end of the book.

The *Regional Trends* team welcome your views on this edition, the online content and the development of *Regional Trends* as an online publication. Please email your comments to: regional.trends@ons.gsi.gov.uk

RT Editorial Team

Articles

1   **Ageing across the UK**   2

By James Bayliss and Frances Sly,
Office for National Statistics

2   **Portrait of the North East**   29

By Allan Worthy and Ian Gouldson,
Office for National Statistics

3   **Portrait of the South West**   43

By Eddie Smith,
Office for National Statistics

4   **Regional health inequalities in England**   60

By Amy Ellis and Robert Fry,
Office for National Statistics

5   **Understanding income at small area level**   80

By Stephen Bond and Cecilia Campos,
Office for National Statistics

DATA

Download data by
clicking the online pdf

www.statistics.gov.uk/
regionaltrends42

Ageing across the UK

By James Bayliss and Frances Sly, Office for National Statistics

Abstract

The wellbeing of the older population in the UK is a priority to local and national government and health authorities, as well as to people themselves. The population aged over 65 is progressively becoming a larger percentage of the nation's population. The effects of falling mortality rates are especially visible among the 'oldest old'. At the same time, however, the older population is supported by a shrinking labour force.

This article explores regional and sub-regional variations in the concentration of older people. The populations of London and Northern Ireland have smaller proportions of older people than other regions. The South West and Wales have higher proportions and local authority level data suggest a pattern of settlement in coastal and rural areas. Population projections indicate, on the basis of past trends, the expected future growth in the population at older ages.

The article also investigates measures of wellbeing of the ageing population including benefits and income deprivation, life expectancy, aspects of health and social care, older workers, and qualifications and learning. At local authority and small area level, variations in the older population often appear to correspond to the rural or urban nature of the areas concerned. The article includes case studies of income deprivation of older people at Lower Layer Super Output Area (LSOA) level in the North West and the South East regions.

Notes

Unless otherwise stated the data used in this article were those available at the time of writing. In particular, mid-year population estimates were those released in August 2009.

The authors would like to thank colleagues in contributing departments and organisations for their generous support and helpful comments without which this article would not have been possible.

Introduction

The population of the UK is becoming increasingly older. This is a cause for celebration but population ageing also presents a new set of challenges, for example: access to local services, housing, health and welfare services. Over the last 25 years, the number of people aged 65 and over in the UK has increased by 18 per cent, from 8.4 million to 9.9 million in 2008. In the same period, the population aged 16–64 increased by 11 per cent while the under 16 population decreased by 5 per cent.

Decreases in infant and childhood mortality and, from the middle of the 20th century, mortality at older ages contributed to larger numbers of people surviving to old age. Most striking is the growth in the number of very old people. Since 1983 the numbers of people aged 85 and over (sometimes described as the 'oldest old') have more than doubled, to reach 1.3 million in 2008. As a proportion of the total population, they have increased from 1.1 per cent to 2.2 per cent over the past 25 years. There were 410,000 people aged 90 and over in 2008, of whom over 10,000 were centenarians.

The post-World War II 'baby boom' generation has started to reach retirement age and the 1960s baby boom generation will be another boost to the older population in future decades. Fertility levels declined after the mid-1960s, reaching their lowest levels in the mid-1970s; they have been increasing since 2001 but are still below replacement level (the level at which a couple has only enough children to replace themselves). Thus the younger cohorts contain fewer people than those aged around 40, and hence there are likely to be fewer people working to help support the retired population in future, unless steps are taken such as raising the retirement age.

Population ageing is an important issue facing planners and service providers at national, regional and local levels across the UK. The older population is becoming an ever-larger focus of UK government policy. Provision of health and social care, the raising of retirement ages, and incentives for more people aged over 50 (termed 'older workers') to remain in employment are among the many issues facing the government. The demographic changes will be different and will have a range of effects on services in the various countries and regions, as well as in different types of local area.

This article examines the differences between the UK countries and English regions in the current age structure of the population and the projected ageing of the population up to 2031. The article goes on to describe a number of key statistics relevant to the older working-age and retired populations in the early 21st century. The devolution of most areas of policy-making and service provision mean that comparable statistics are not available for all topics across the whole of the UK and in some cases data are considered for England or England and Wales only.

Broadly speaking, the article considers the population aged 50 and over. Those currently aged 50 and over in the regions are a very good guide to what their populations aged 65 and over will be in 15 years time, subject only to relatively low rates of death and (mainly inter-regional) migration.

The most commonly used definition of old age is the age at which a person becomes entitled to receive state pension benefits – state pension age (SPA), currently 65 for men and, until 2009, 60 for women. From 2010 the pension age for women is being gradually increased until it reaches 65 in 2020 (Box 1). The majority of population statistics in this article are divided into two groups therefore, above and below the age of 65. The group aged under SPA or under 65 can be described as 'young older people'. Those aged 65 and over (or sometimes 60 and over) may be referred to in this article simply as 'old', although it is recognised that subjectively many people in their sixties do not feel 'old'.

Labour market data are shown for young older people, aged 50 to SPA (known also as 'older workers'); the numbers of people above SPA in employment is too small to be identified accurately at regional level. The majority of policy issues relate to provision for the increasing numbers of people aged 65 and above, so projections of population growth are also considered for this age group. Some datasets are available only for those aged 65 and over, for example hip and knee replacements, social care and influenza vaccination take-up.

Box 1: State pension age

By the time this article is published in June 2010, the definition of state pension age for women will have started to change from that previously adopted. As this article uses population and pension data for 2008, statistics have been presented with reference to the definition of State Pension Age that was in use in 2008; 60 for women and 65 for men.

The change in female state pension age starts from 6 April 2010. From that point, the state pension age for females will increase by 1 month every 2 months for the next 10 years; this will result in a total 5-year increase from 60 to 65 by April 2020. So, in April 2010, it will become 60 years 1 month, in June 2010 it becomes 60 years 2 months and so on.

Phased increases in the state pension age for men and women are due to be introduced by the UK government between 2024 and 2046.

Many of the key 'life events' (for example, loss of a spouse or partner or retirement) are now occurring at older ages than in the past. It is therefore useful to divide the population aged 65 and over into smaller age bands, for example, 65–74, 75–84 and 85 and over. The latter are known as the 'oldest old'. However, at a regional level many data are difficult to obtain for these smaller age groups and issues of disclosure control and statistical uncertainties become more prominent.

Information on levels of poverty and income deprivation is presented for the population aged 60 and over using data on receipt of key government benefits, fuel poverty and households below 60 per cent of median income. The Income Deprivation Affecting Older People Index (IDAOPI) provides insight into smaller geographic areas which have the largest numbers of the most deprived people aged 60 and over. IDAOPI also allows the incidence of income deprivation among the over 60s to be examined by the Rural/Urban Definition of the area.

Population

All countries of the UK and English regions show evidence of population ageing, but the change has not occurred evenly across the country and the concentration of older people varies. Regional differences may be smaller than differences between urban and rural areas as a result of geographic, economic and social factors that have shaped communities over time.

Geographic distribution of the older population

People aged 50 and over made up at least one-quarter of the population in each region and country of the UK in 2008. Most regions had proportions close to the UK average of 34 per cent. The lowest percentages were found in London at 26 per cent and Northern Ireland at 31 per cent. The highest percentages were found in the South West (39 per cent) and Wales (37 per cent).

The region with the largest population aged 50 and over was the South East (2.9 million), also the region with the largest total population. But while London had the next largest total population, it ranked fifth on population aged 50 and over, at 2.0 million.

The UK population aged 50 and over increased by 5.1 per cent in the five years between 2003 and 2008, from 20 million to just over 21 million. In comparison the population of all ages increased by 3.1 per cent over the same five-year period. All UK countries and English regions saw increases in the population aged 50 and over; in most, the increases were close to the average. The largest percentage increase was in Northern Ireland (8.7 per cent). In England, the largest regional increases were in the East (6.6 per cent) and the East Midlands (6.4 per cent). The smallest percentage increases occurred in London and the North West, at 2.5 and 3.3 per cent respectively.

Map 1.1   Percentage of the population aged 50 and over: by local authority, UK, 2008

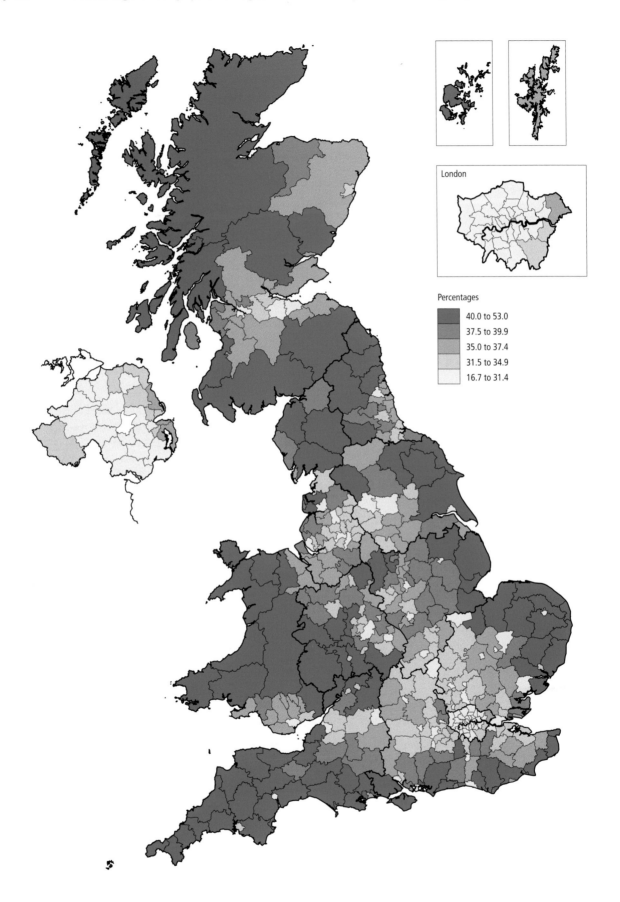

London

Percentages

- 40.0 to 53.0
- 37.5 to 39.9
- 35.0 to 37.4
- 31.5 to 34.9
- 16.7 to 31.4

Source: Office for National Statistics

Map 1.1 shows the percentage of the population aged 50 and over at local authority and district level. Coastal and rural areas had the highest percentages of population aged 50 and over, except such areas in Northern Ireland. The highest percentages were seen in West Somerset (53 per cent), North Norfolk (51 per cent), Rother (East Sussex; 50 per cent) and Christchurch (50 per cent). These are the only local authorities with more than 50 per cent of their population aged 50 and over. These higher percentages were partly because of internal migration of people of retirement age within the UK over a period of many years.

The higher percentage of older people in the coastal and rural areas of Great Britain contrasts with lower levels found in London (for example, Tower Hamlets, 17 per cent; Lambeth, 20 per cent; Newham, 20 per cent), and around urbanised areas of central England, most notably Nottingham, 25 per cent; Manchester and Oxford both 23 per cent. The lowest levels in Wales, Scotland and Northern Ireland were equivalent to some others in the midlands and north of England. Cardiff (29 per cent); City of Edinburgh (31 per cent); and Glasgow (30 per cent) compare to Leeds, Bradford, Coventry (all 30 per cent); Blackburn and Darwen, Milton Keynes (both 29 per cent); and Birmingham (28 per cent). The majority of Northern Ireland districts had similar levels and the lowest value was 27 per cent in Dungannon, Newry and Mourne, Derry and Magherafelt.

Population by age

One of the features of population ageing is the increasing numbers in the oldest age groups. Although much smaller in number, they are important because this is where most growth is projected to take place in the future. These age groups also tend to be those that are heavily reliant on health and care services. The age distribution varies between regions for a variety of reasons including historical differences in fertility, mortality and migration (Online tables 10.9. 10.10, 10.6 respectively). Figure 1.2 shows the proportions of the total population represented by the age groups 50–64, 65–74, 75–84 and 85 and over.

The South West consistently had the largest percentages in each age group considered. For the two oldest age groups (75–84 and 85 and over), the South West stands out as having markedly higher percentages than all other regions (6.7 per cent compared with 5.6 per cent for the UK and 2.8 compared with 2.2 per cent respectively). Wales had the second largest percentages except among the oldest old (85 and over), where the South East (2.5 per cent) ranked second, with Wales close behind (2.4 per cent).

London and Northern Ireland consistently had the lowest percentages in each group, with each having only 1.6 per cent of their population aged 85 and over. For the three younger age groups considered, London's percentages were lower than any other region or country: 14.2 per cent for age 50–64 (compared with 18.0 per cent for the UK); 5.9 per cent (UK 8.4 per cent) for 65–74; and 4.1 per cent (UK 5.6 per cent) for 75 to 84.

In Scotland, the percentages of the population in the three age groups covering ages 50 to 74 were at, or above, the UK averages but for the oldest old the percentage was lower in Scotland (1.9 per cent) than in the UK (2.2 per cent).

Figure 1.2

Percentage of total population in key age groups, 2008

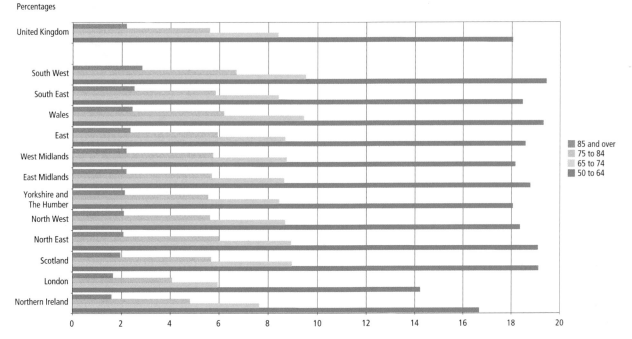

Source: Office for National Statistics

Box 2: Defining areas by rurality

The constituent countries of the UK define their geographic small areas in terms of rurality in different ways. Each country does, however, use definitions based upon a small area's proximity to major urban areas and/or its population size as a means to defining it as rural or urban. However, different thresholds to the physical distance to settlements, and/or population size may be adopted.

England and Wales – Rural/Urban Definition (www.statistics.gov.uk/geography/nrudp.asp; www.defra.gov.uk/evidence/statistics/rural/rural-definition.htm#defn)

The full definition uses settlements with a population of 10,000 persons, and population density in 1 hectare squares across both countries to define land areas into six different levels of rurality.

MSOA-level population estimates used to create Figure 1.3 and Figure 1.4 are experimental statistics. These do not yet meet the quality standards for designation as National Statistics.

Scotland – Urban Rural Classification (www.scotland.gov.uk/Publications/2004/06/19498/38784)

The full definition uses population thresholds at 3,000, 10,000 and 125,000 people and a drive-time threshold of 30 minutes to a settlement for classifying their Data Zones into six categories of rurality.

Scottish small area population estimates used to create Figure 1.5 are not National Statistics.

Northern Ireland – Urban–Rural Classification (www.nisra.gov.uk/geography/default.asp10.htm)

Rurality is based upon proximity to areas defined as settlements, and a general consensus that divide between urban and rural lines among settlements whose populations are between 3,000 and 5,000 persons.

Northern Ireland small area population estimates defined at a Settlement level and used to create Figure 1.6 are not National Statistics.

Population by Rural/Urban Definition

Figure 1.3 shows the estimated percentages of people aged under 50, 50–64 and 65 and over by Rural/Urban Definition at Middle Layer Super Output Area (MSOA) level in England in 2008 (Box 2). About 76 per cent of the population in the 50–64 and 65 and over age groups lived in areas defined as 'Urban over 10,000 [population]'. The remaining population in these age groups was divided approximately equally between 'Town and Fringe' areas (10 per cent) and 'Village,

Figure 1.3

Population: by Rural/Urban Definition at MSOA level, England, 2008

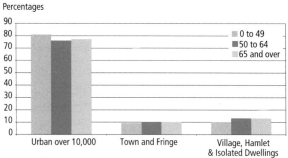

Source: Office for National Statistics

Figure 1.4

Population: by Rural/Urban Definition at MSOA level, Wales, 2008

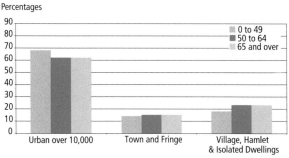

Source: Office for National Statistics

Figure 1.5

Population: by Urban Rural Classification[1] at Data Zone level, Scotland, 2008

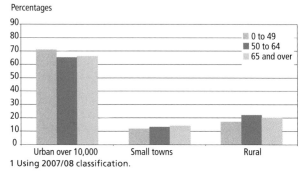

1 Using 2007/08 classification.

Source: Scottish Government

Figure 1.6

Population: by Urban–Rural Classification by settlements, Northern Ireland, 2001[1]

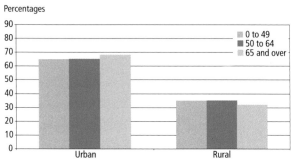

1 2001 Northern Ireland Census estimates.

Source: Northern Ireland Statistics and Research Agency

Hamlets and Isolated Dwellings' (13 per cent). This compares with 81 per cent, 9 per cent and 10 per cent respectively for the population of England aged under 50.

Using the same Rural/Urban Definition as England, the age 50 and over population of Wales (Figure 1.4) is divided into 62 per cent in 'Urban over 10,000 [population]', 15 per cent in 'Town and Fringe' and 23 per cent in 'Village, Hamlets and Isolated Dwellings' compared with 68 per cent, 14 and 18 per cent respectively of Wales' population aged under 50.

Figure 1.5 illustrates Scotland's 2008 population divided into the same age groups, and classified using its own 2007/08 Urban Rural Classification by its Data Zone small area geography (Box 2). Again, the majority of the 50 and over population lived in urban areas (66 per cent, compared with 71 per cent for the under 50 population).

Northern Ireland uses a different method again for small area Urban–Rural Classification (Box 2). However, population estimates for Northern Ireland classified in this way have not been made since the 2001 Census, and so are seven years out

Figure 1.7

Projected[1] population for men and women aged 50 and over, 2006 to 2031

Percentages

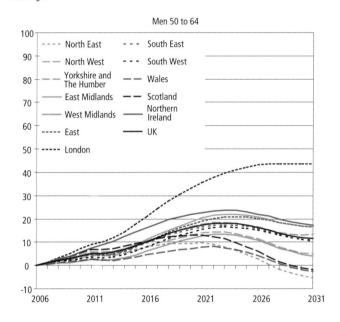

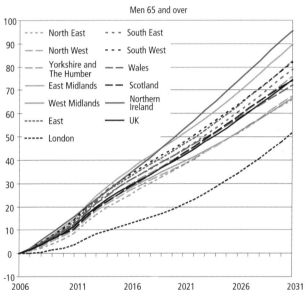

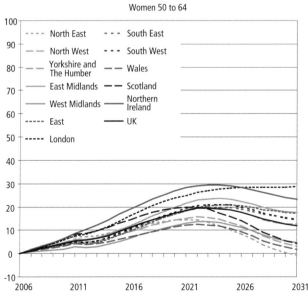

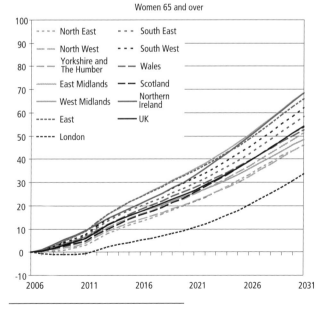

1 Based on 2006 population estimates.

Source: Office for National Statistics

3 Although 2008-based National Population Projections (NPP) have been published, 2008-based Subnational Population Projections (SNPP) were not available at the time of writing. The projections for UK countries shown here are 2006-based NPP to be consistent with the regional projections.

Figure 1.8

Projected[1] population for men and women aged 75 and over, 2006 to 2031

Percentages

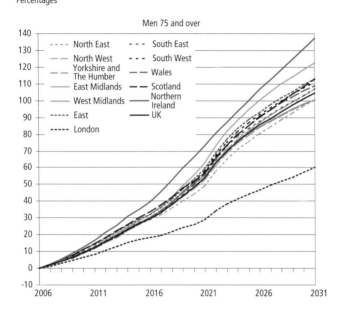

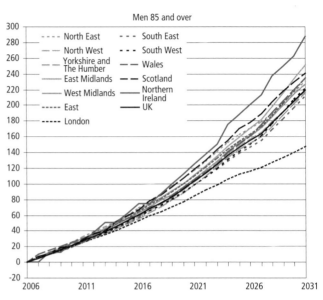

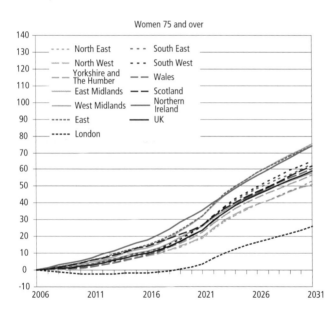

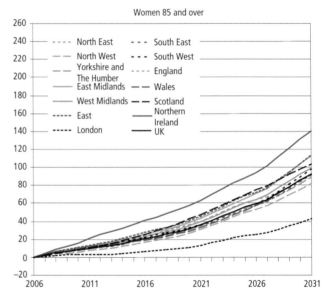

1 Based on 2006 population estimates.

Source: Office for National Statistics

of date relative to the three other countries of the UK. These are given in terms of level of rurality at output area level in Figure 1.6. Two-thirds of Northern Ireland's population lived in these urban areas in 2001 and this did not vary between the age groups shown.

Population projections

Population ageing is projected to continue, with the number of people in the UK aged 65 and over increasing by nearly two-thirds to reach 15.8 million by 2031. By this time, those aged 65 and over will account for 22 per cent of the UK population.

The greatest population increases are projected for the oldest of the older age groups. By 2031 a 77 per cent increase is expected in the number of those aged 75 and over and a 131 per cent increase in those aged 85 and over.

Projected increases in the number of old people, together with past falls in fertility rates, mean the average age of the UK population is also expected to continue to rise (www.statistics.gov.uk/ageingintheuk/default.htm).

Women in older age groups outnumber men because, on average, women have a greater life expectancy. However, with improvements in male life expectancy this differential is projected to decrease. By 2031 the number of women aged

Figure 1.9

Age-specific death rates: by age group, 2008

Deaths per 1,000 population

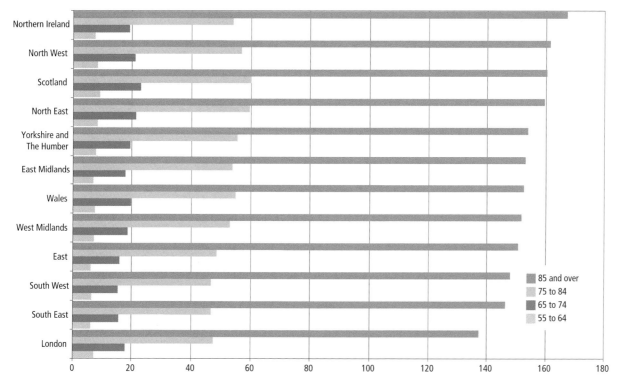

Source: Office for National Statistics; General Register Office for Scotland; Northern Ireland Statistics and Research Agency

65 and over is projected to increase by 54 per cent compared with a 74 per cent increase in men of this age. This effect is even more pronounced for the oldest old with projected increases of 93 per cent in women aged 85 and over, compared with a 220 per cent increase in men aged 85 and over by 2031.[3]

Figures 1.7 and 1.8 illustrate regional population projections for men and women aged 50–64, 65 and over, 75 and over and 85 and over in terms of percentage increase in the population from 2006. The data for each region are available as a supplementary table on the ONS website.

London is projected to experience markedly different patterns of population growth from the other regions and countries. For the 50–64 age band, this region is projected a greater population increase than other regions; growth of its more elderly age groups is projected to be slower than other regions.

Between 2006 and 2031 the projected increase in the London population aged 50–64 is 44 per cent for men and 29 per cent for women (compared with the UK average of a 12 per cent for both sexes in this age band). Outside London, Northern Ireland, the East and the East Midlands show the largest projected increases in this age group between 2006 and 2031. For men, the projected increase is 17 per cent in all three areas and for women 24 per cent in Northern Ireland and 18 per cent in the East and the East Midlands.

Wales, Scotland, and the North East show little change in the population aged 50–64 between 2006 and 2031. The 50–64 male populations of Wales and Scotland are projected to reduce in size by about 2 per cent on 2006 population sizes, the North East by about 5 per cent. The female populations in this age group are expected to increase by 2 to 4 per cent on 2006 estimates in the two countries and to reduce by 1 per cent in the North East.

For those aged 65 and over, London has the lowest projected increases between 2006 and 2031; a 52 per cent increase in men and 34 per cent increase in women. These projected increases are notably below the UK average of 74 per cent and 54 per cent respectively. Northern Ireland, the East Midlands and the East are projected to have the highest increases in this age group, 96 per cent for men and 69 per cent for women in Northern Ireland and for the East Midlands and the East 90 per cent and 83 per cent respectively for men, and 69 per cent and 66 per cent respectively for women.

The 65 and over age group is narrowed down into older sub-groups – 75 and over, and 85 and over – in Figure 1.8. Projected growth in each of these age groups is close to the UK average in most regions. In London, the number of men aged 75 and over is projected to increase by 60 per cent in this 25-year period and the number of women aged 75 and over by 26 per cent. Northern Ireland is projected markedly

Figure 1.10

Net internal migration of people aged 50 and over, mid-2007 to mid-2008

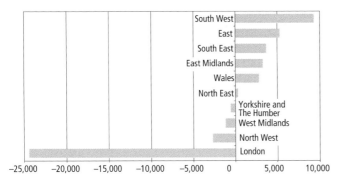

Source: Office for National Statistics

greater than average population increases of 137 per cent and 74 per cent for men and women respectively.

In the 85 and over age group, Northern Ireland continues the trend shown for the other age groups considered, exhibiting a noticeably greater projected increase than all other UK regions and countries (291 per cent for men and 139 per cent for women). At the other extreme, in London the projected increases are 147 per cent and 42 per cent respectively.

Factors affecting population change

Age-specific death rates are available for 10-year age bands by English region and UK country. Figure 1.9 presents age-specific death rates per 1,000 people aged 55–64, 65–74, 75–84 and 85 and over in 2008. Generally, excluding London from consideration, age-specific death rates increased in the regions of England from south to north, regardless of the age group considered. London had the lowest rate for those aged 85 and over (137 per 1,000 compared with the UK average of 152 deaths per 1,000), below other southern regions (146 in the South East, 148 in the South West and 151 in the East). For the two lowest age groups considered, the death rates in London equalled the UK and England averages and were above those of the other southern regions. Death rates in Scotland were the highest in all age groups, closely followed by the North West and the North East, except for those aged 85 and over, where Northern Ireland had the highest rate (Online table 10.10).

Figure 1.10 presents net internal migration for those aged 50 and over between mid-2007 and mid-2008 between the English regions and Wales. These data are not National Statistics, but are presented as an example of annual movements between regions to aid understanding of the different regional patterns of population growth for older people. In net terms (after subtracting those entering from those leaving), almost 25,000 people aged 50 and over left London in this annual period. This was by far the highest net internal migration, 10 times the net out-migration for the next highest region (the North West, 3,000 people).

The regions with the greatest increase from internal migration of those aged 50 and over were the South West (net internal in-migration of 9,000) and the East, the South East, the East Midlands and Wales (net in-migration ranging from 5,000 down to 2,000 people respectively).

Demographic characteristics

In 2008, 71 per cent of men in the UK aged 65 and over were married and living with their spouse. The equivalent proportion for women aged 65 and over was much lower at 46 per cent. Conversely, the proportion of women aged 65 and over who were widowed was much higher than the equivalent proportion of widowed men, (40 per cent and 16 per cent respectively) (Figure 1.11). These differing patterns for older men and women are a result of the tendency for women to live longer than men and also to marry men older than themselves.

The proportions of single, never-married men and of single never-married women aged 65 and over were very similar (6 per cent and 5 per cent respectively) as were the proportions of men and women of this age group who were divorced or separated (8 per cent and 9 per cent respectively).

The pattern of marital status described for men and women aged 65 and over in the UK was broadly mirrored across the UK countries and English regions; there were a few regional variations, however. These may well be due to slightly differing age profiles within the population aged 65 and over across the regions and countries. The biggest marital status variations from the average were for London and Northern Ireland.

London had higher proportions of men and women aged 65 and over who were single and never married than other regions, at 11 per cent for men (compared with the UK average of 6 per cent) and 9 per cent for women (compared with 5 per cent). In this age group, London also had the highest proportions of divorced and separated people – 10 per cent of men and 12 per cent of women; these proportions were slightly above the respective UK averages of 8 per cent and 9 per cent. London had the lowest proportions of men and women aged 65 and over who were married and living with their partner, 63 per cent of men (compared with the UK average of 71 per cent) and 37 per cent of women (compared with 46 per cent).

Northern Ireland also had relatively high proportions of men and women aged 65 and over who were single and never married, at 9 per cent for both sexes. However, Northern Ireland had the lowest proportions of men and women aged 65 and over who were divorced and separated, 4 per cent of men (compared with the UK average of 8 per cent) and 5 per cent of women (compared with 9 per cent). It also had relatively low proportions of men and women who were married and living with their spouse.

Figure 1.11

Legal marital status for men and women[1] aged 65 and over, 2008

Percentages

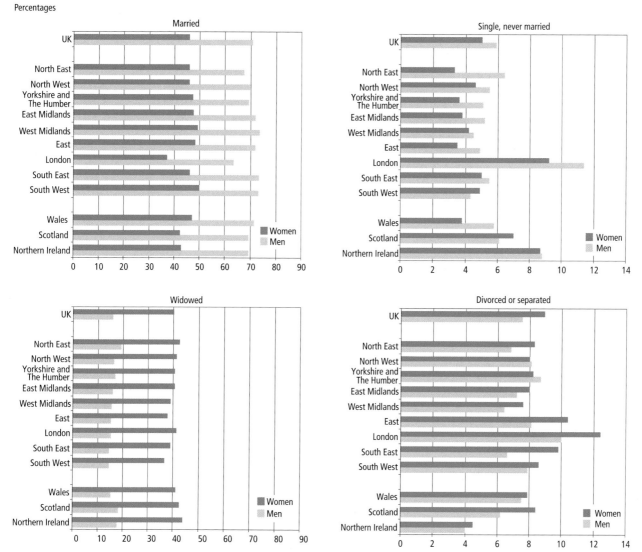

1   Married, living with husband/wife includes civil partnerships; Divorced or separated includes separated civil partnerships and legally dissoved civil partnerships; Widowed includes surviving civil partners.

Source: Annual Population Survey, Office for National Statistics

The distribution of the population aged 50 and over by ethnic group mirrors the ethnic make-up of the population of all ages (Online table 10.4). However, the older population has a higher proportion of White British than the population of all ages. Figure 1.12 uses experimental statistics to show the percentages of the population aged 50 and over who consider themselves to belong to any other ethnic group than White British. London had a significantly larger percentage of people in all other ethnic groups (31 per cent) than the other regions of England, although this was a lower percentage than for the population as a whole (42 per cent). About 10 per cent of the West Midlands older population was of other ethnicities than White British, compared with 17 per cent of the region's total population. This was the only other region where the proportion of the older population that was not White British was above the England average of 9 per cent. The North East (3 per cent) and the South West (4 per cent) had the lowest percentages (6 and 8 per cent respectively for all ages).

Figure 1.12

Population aged 50 and over who are not White British, England, 2007

Percentages

Source: Office for National Statistics, Experimental Statistics

Poverty and deprivation

There are regional variations in the proportion of over 60s who live on low incomes, and even greater differences at small area level. A number of measures of poverty are available at regional level, including household income and benefit receipt (Box 3) and the regional patterns vary according to which measure is used. Regional and also rural/urban differences mask variations in deprivation at small area level, which are explored using the Income Deprivation Affecting Older People Index, which is part of the Indices of Deprivation.

Households Below Average Income

Households Below Average Income is a standard measure of poverty that is available at region and country level across the

UK. At this geographic level, data have to be averaged over three years. Figure 1.13 illustrates the percentage of people aged 60 and over living in households where the household income was below 60 per cent of median household income (after housing costs) for 2005/06 to 2007/08. The highest percentages were found in London, the East Midlands and Northern Ireland (22 per cent, 21 per cent and 20 per cent respectively) compared with a UK average of 18 per cent. The lowest level of poverty on this measure was 16 per cent in the East of England, the South East and Scotland.

Pension Credits

Pension Credit data give another measure of poverty that is available across the whole of Great Britain (but not Northern Ireland). Pension Credits are available to people aged 60 and

---

Box 3: Measures of poverty and deprivation in the ageing population

Three currently available measures that enable assessment of the levels of poverty and income deprivation of the older population of the UK are detailed below.

Households Below Average Income

Households Below Average Income (HBAI) uses household disposable incomes, after adjusting for the household size and composition, as a proxy for material living standards. More precisely, it is a proxy for the level of consumption of goods and services that people could attain given the disposable income of the household in which they live. In order to allow comparisons of the living standards of different types of households, income is adjusted to take into account variations in the size and composition of the households in a process known as equivalisation, which is explained in more detail below. A key assumption made in HBAI is that all individuals in the household benefit equally from the combined income of the household. This enables the total equivalised income of the household to be used as a proxy for the standard of living of each household member.

This section includes results only for those individuals above state pension age. Thus, any working-age partners will be excluded from results for pensioner couples.

Statistics presented in this section have been equivalised by the Department of Work and Pensions (DWP) before publication in their annual report. Income is adjusted, or equivalised, to take into account variations in both the size and composition of the household. This reflects the idea that a family of several people needs a higher income than a single person in order for both households to enjoy a comparable standard of living. The reference point, conventionally, is a couple with no children.

Pension Credits

Pension Credit (PC) was introduced on 6 October 2003 and replaced the Minimum Income Guarantee (MIG). It is paid to people aged 60 and over who are living on low incomes and guarantees all pensioners a certain level of income. There are two parts to Pension Credit: the Guarantee Credit (GC) and the Savings Credit (SC). The Guarantee Credit ensures a guaranteed level of income by providing financial help for people aged 60 and over whose income is below a given threshold. The Savings Credit is an extra amount for people aged 65 or over who have made modest provision for their retirement above the level of the basic state pension (such as savings or a second pension). Entitlement to the Guarantee Credit and the Savings Credit is calculated separately, and as a result, pensioners can receive both or either elements of Pension Credit.

Income Deprivation Affecting Older People Index

The Income Deprivation Affecting Older People Index (IDAOPI) was developed by Communities and Local Government (CLG) as part of the Indices of Deprivation (see Understanding the Indices of Deprivation in Regional Trends 41). IDAOPI represents income deprivation affecting adults aged 60 and over living in pension credit (guarantee) households. This comprises claimants of Income Support, Job Seekers Allowance, Incapacity Benefit, Pension Credit or Council Tax Credit, and their partners (if also aged 60 or over). The IDAOPI score is the percentage of adults aged 60 and over living in such households as a percentage of all adults aged 60 and over. The index is not a National Statistic although the underlying data are.

IDAOPI is calculated at Lower Layer Super Output Area (LSOA) level. LSOAs are ranked on their IDAOPI score according to their position relative to all other LSOAs in England. They can be divided into 10 equal-sized groups (deciles), with decile 1 being the most deprived and 10 being the least deprived.

Figure 1.13

Percentage of people aged 60 and over in low-income households,[1] 2005/06 to 2007/08

Percentages

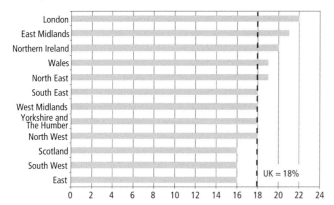

1 Households below 60 per cent of median income; after housing costs. See Notes and Definitions Online.

Source: Family Resources Survey, Department for Work and Pensions

over and guarantee a minimum income by topping up weekly income. Those receiving Pension Credit are also eligible for other benefits such as Council Tax Benefit. However, as a measure of low income, it has the disadvantage that take-up by those who are eligible is relatively low (estimated at between 61 and 70 per cent in 2007/08, and a little lower for pensioner couples compared with single pensioners (DWP, 2009)). Those who do not claim may suffer greater hardship than those receiving credits. Figure 1.14 illustrates the percentage of people aged 60 and over who were claiming Pension Credit at a regional level in 2008.

In 2008 approximately a quarter of the 60 and over population in Great Britain were either claiming Pension Credit or benefiting from it by being related to someone who did claim. The North East (33 per cent) had the highest percentage of the 60 and over population receiving this benefit, while the South East (18 per cent) had the lowest.

Figure 1.14

Beneficiaries[1] of Pension Credits as a percentage of population aged 60 and over,[2] 2008

Percentages

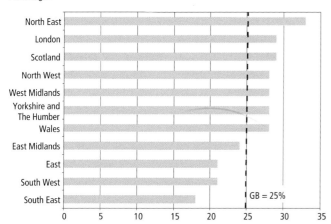

1 Beneficiaries are claimants and their partners for whom Pension Credit is received and are on the administrative system at the reference date.
2 Claimant partners who may be aged under 60.

Source: Department for Work and Pensions; Office for National Statistics

Income Deprivation Affecting Older People Index

The Income Deprivation Affecting Older People Index (IDAOPI) – part of Communities and Local Government's (CLG's) Indices of Deprivation – provides a measure of poverty for small areas. It is defined as those adults aged 60 and over living in Pension Credit (guarantee) households as a percentage of all those aged 60 and over (Box 3). This measure is available for Lower Layer Super Output Areas (LSOAs), which only apply to England. Northern Ireland has also produced a similar index measure – the Income Deprivation Affecting Older People (IDAOP) – as part of the Northern Ireland Multiple Deprivation Measure 2005 (NIMDM, 2005).

Figure 1.15 illustrates the percentage of adults aged 60 and over in 2008 living in the 10 per cent most deprived LSOAs in

Figure 1.15

Population aged 60 and over in the 10 per cent most deprived LSOAs[1] in England, 2008

Percentages

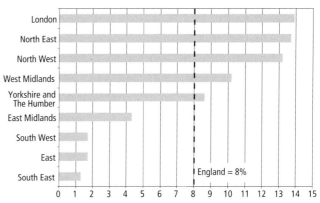

1 As defined in the Income Deprivation Affecting Older People Index (IDAOPI; See Box 3).

Source: Communities and Local Government; Office for National Statistics

each English region measured using IDAOPI. Except for London, which has the highest percentage at nearly 14 per cent, all the other regions above the England average of 8 per cent are found in the midlands or north of England (with the highest being the North East, also nearly 14 per cent and the North West, 13 per cent). The South East, the South West and the East of England were the lowest, each at between 1 and 2 per cent. Although the geographic distribution (that is, the order of regions) is broadly similar to that shown in Figure 1.14 – illustrating Pension Credit take-up – the variation is much more dramatic between the maximum and minimum values, as it focuses solely upon the 10 per cent most deprived areas. In 2008 less than 800,000 people aged 60 and over lived in the 10 per cent most deprived LSOAs compared with 1.4 million people in the 10 per cent least deprived LSOAs.

Older people in deprived areas by the Rural/Urban Definition

Just over 8.6 million people aged 60 and over lived in urban areas (with a population over 10,000), with a further

Figure 1.16

Population aged 60 and over: by IDAOPI[1] decile and Rural/Urban Definition,[2] England, 2008

Thousands

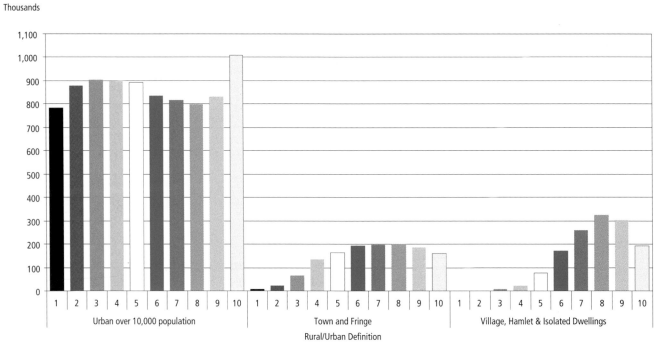

1   Income Deprivation Affecting Older People Index. See Box 3. Decile 1 (bottom 10 per cent of IDAOPI) is 'most deprived';Decile 10 (top 10 per cent of IDAOPI) is 'least deprived'.

2   Categorised at Lower Layer Super Output Area level.

Source: Communities and Local Government; Office for National Statistics

1.3 million living in town and fringe areas, and the remaining 1.4 million of this demographic group living in villages, hamlets and isolated dwellings. Figure 1.16 compares the distribution of the population aged 60 and over by IDAOPI for these main settlement types in the Rural/Urban Definition for England.

Those living in town and fringe or the most rural areas were more likely to live in the less deprived LSOAs than the more deprived areas. Urban areas exhibited a more uniform spread, although a relatively high percentage of the older population was found in the least deprived decile (12 per cent). This is the outcome of a wide variety of distributions of deprivation across the regions. In areas deemed 'Town and Fringe' and 'Village, Hamlet and Isolated Dwelling' the distribution of the older population across the 10 deciles of IDAOPI was similar in all regions of England.

Figure 1.17 shows the different regional distributions of the 60 and over population by the IDAOPI deciles, in areas defined as 'Urban over 10,000 [population]' of the Rural/ Urban Definition.

It shows that the South East had a different distribution of deprivation levels from the other eight regions. The urban LSOAs in the South East that appeared in the least deprived 10 per cent of LSOAs in England included 18 times more people aged 60 and over than the urban LSOAs in the region that were among England's 10 per cent most deprived areas. This pattern is reflected in the high percentage of the population found in urban least-deprived areas shown in Figure 1.16.

Like the South East, the South West, the East Midlands and the East of England show relatively small percentages of their older urban population living in the more deprived areas However, unlike the South East, each of these regions shows a levelling off or reduction in the proportions that are in the two or three least deprived deciles.

In contrast, London, the North East and the North West had more of their older (urban) population living in LSOAs in the more deprived half of England's LSOAs than in the less deprived half.

The other regions – the West Midlands and Yorkshire and The Humber – had relatively uniform spreads of their age 60 and over urban populations across the IDAOPI distribution.

Regional case studies

Maps 1.18 and 1.19 illustrate the geographical distribution, at LSOA level, of the areas of highest and lowest deprivation among the older population, for the North West and the South East respectively. These maps each highlight the LSOAs present within the top and bottom 10 per cent of IDAOPI and are selected to illustrate the variation in geographic distribution of the extremes of older people deprivation.

The **North West** exhibited a broad spread across the deprivation deciles of IDAOPI. Each decile contained between 9 and 13 per cent of the North West's population aged 60 and over. There was an approximately equal split between the five most and five least deprived deciles; 796,000 people

Figure 1.17

Urban[1] population aged 60 and over: by IDAOPI decile[2] by region of England, 2008

Percentages

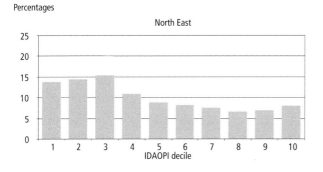

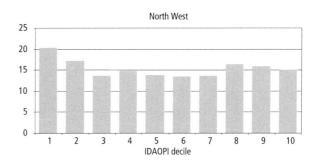

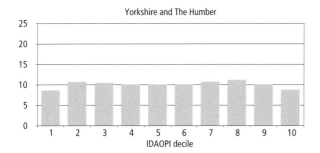

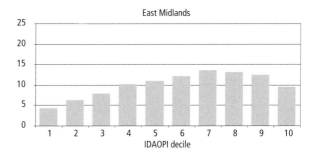

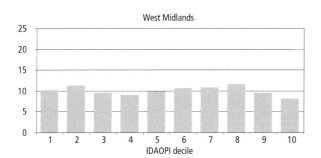

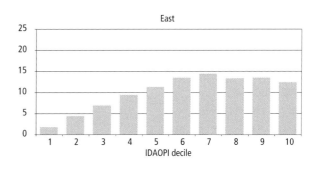

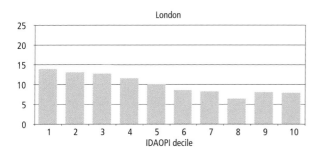

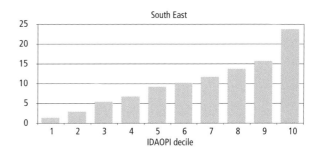

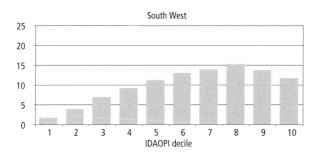

1 Urban over 10,000 population according to the Rural/Urban Definition. Categorised at Lower Layer Super Output Area level.
2 Income Deprivation Affecting Older People Index. See Box 3. Decile 1 (bottom 10 per cent of IDAOPI) is 'most deprived'; decile 10 (top 10 per cent of IDAOPI) is 'least deprived'.

Source: Communities and Local Government; Office for National Statistics

Map 1.18   The 10 per cent most and least deprived LSOAs,[1] North West, 2007

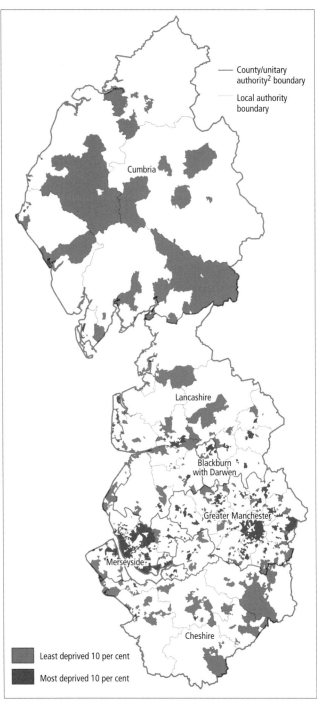

County/unitary authority[2] boundary

Local authority boundary

Cumbria

Lancashire

Blackburn with Darwen

Greater Manchester

Merseyside

Cheshire

Least deprived 10 per cent

Most deprived 10 per cent

1 Most or least deprived in England according to the Income Deprivation Affecting Older People Index. See Box 3.
2 Unitary authorities not labelled: Blackpool, Halton and Warrington.

Source: Communities and Local Government, Office for National Statistics

Map 1.18 shows that the North West's LSOAs in the least deprived decile of IDAOPI were roughly evenly spread throughout the region. The most deprived LSOAs, however, were more concentrated in inner city Liverpool and Manchester, and also Blackburn and Preston. They were also scattered through outer areas of the conurbations and some coastal areas. The least deprived LSOAs were located in the suburban and rural areas surrounding these cities, and large portions of the Lake District National Park, Cumbria and rural Cheshire.

Map 1.19 illustrates the **South East** region, which contained the largest percentage of the UK's 60 and over population of any region in 2008, at 17 per cent (1.9 million people). As the South East is the most affluent region in England (see article 'Understanding income at small area level' on pages 80 to 94), it is perhaps unsurprising that a very large percentage of this region's population aged 60 and over (75 per cent or 1.4 million) and LSOAs (70 per cent or 3,725) were found in the five least deprived deciles (as illustrated in Figure 1.17). This compares with nearly 0.5 million people and 1,594 LSOAs in the five most deprived deciles.

The stark contrast between most and least deprived areas in the South East is highlighted further when comparing only the most and least deprived deciles. Nearly 0.5 million (24 per cent) of the region's population and 1,129 (21 per cent) of the LSOAs were found in the least deprived decile, compared with just over 1 per cent (25,000) of the population and 91 (2 per cent) of the LSOAs in the most deprived decile.

The least deprived LSOAs were geographically distributed across the entire region, although none were present on the Isle of Wight, and few were found east of Maidstone in Kent, or in the west of the region. The small numbers of most deprived LSOAs were located in small pockets throughout the region, mainly in inner city areas of Southampton and Portsmouth, and towns such as Brighton, Margate, Ramsgate, Gravesend, Rochester, Reading and Milton Keynes.

This case study analysis showed that the South East had a small proportion of its older population living in deprived areas, but these areas were concentrated in certain urban areas, both on the coast and in large inland towns. In contrast, the North West had a larger proportion of its older population living in more deprived areas. The most deprived areas, while more widespread than in the South East, were also located mostly in inner city areas, other large towns and in towns on the coast.

Fuel poverty

Income deprivation also contributes to fuel poverty. Being in fuel poverty means being unable to afford to keep warm. A household – not specifically the pensioner – is considered to be in fuel poverty if 10 per cent or more of its income is spent on fuel for adequate heating (usually 21 degrees Celsius for the main living area, and 18 degrees for other occupied rooms).

Living in cold homes can damage people's health and affect their quality of life. The elderly and those with a disability or long-term illness are among the population subgroups that are especially vulnerable.

aged 60 or over lived in the five most deprived LSOA deciles, compared with 744,000 in the five least deprived deciles.

However, about one-third more people aged 60 and over lived in the most deprived 10 per cent of LSOAs in England than in the least deprived 10 per cent (203,000 compared with 150,000). The least deprived decile contained under half the number of LSOAs compared with the most deprived decile (8 per cent and 17 per cent respectively).

Map 1.19   The 10 per cent most and least deprived LSOAs,[1] South East, 2007

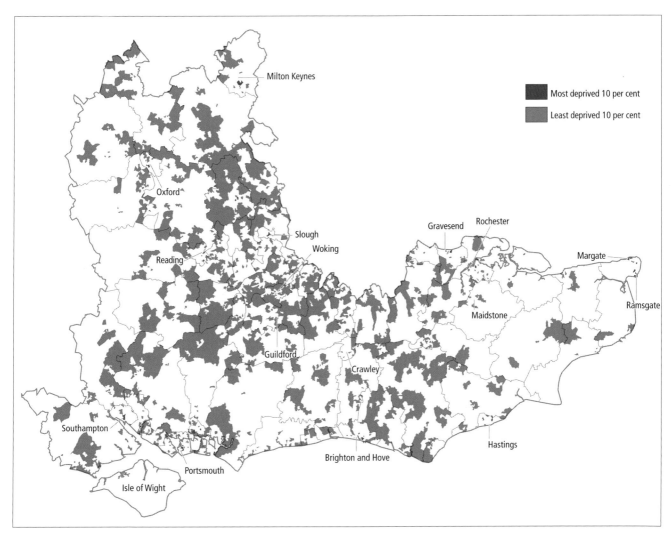

Most deprived 10 per cent

Least deprived 10 per cent

Milton Keynes

Oxford

Slough

Woking

Reading

Gravesend

Rochester

Margate

Ramsgate

Maidstone

Guildford

Crawley

Southampton

Hastings

Brighton and Hove

Portsmouth

Isle of Wight

1   Most or least deprived in England according to the Income Deprivation Affecting Older People Index. See Box 3.

Source: Communities and Local Government, Office for National Statistics

There are three main causes of fuel poverty:

- Poor energy efficiency in the home

- High energy prices

- Low household income

The Department of Energy and Climate Change (DECC) produces annual statistics (which are not National Statistics) for England detailing the number of households considered to be in fuel poverty. Figure 1.20 illustrates these statistics for 2007 with respect to the number of households with at least one adult aged 60 and over living within it, as a percentage of all households of this type.

These data show there is an obvious geographic pattern to where people aged 60 and over are most likely to be living in fuel poverty. All northern and midland regions of England are above the English average of 18 per cent. The North East (24 per cent), the West Midlands (23 per cent) and Yorkshire and The Humber (22 per cent) had the highest percentages in 2007.

Figure 1.20

Percentage of households with one or more persons aged 60 or over in fuel poverty,[1] England, 2007

Percentages

North East	
West Midlands	
Yorkshire and The Humber	
East Midlands	
North West	
East of England	
South West	
London	
South East	

England = 18%

0 2 4 6 8 10 12 14 16 18 20 22 24

1 Not a National Statistic.

Source: English Housing Survey; Department of Energy and Climate Change

17

southerly regions exhibited lower percentages of
useholds in fuel poverty containing one or more persons
aged 60 and over. The South East had the lowest percentage
at 15 per cent, followed by London and the South West at
16 per cent.

Health

While life expectancy has increased, the extra years are not
necessarily lived in good health. Well-established health care
provision for older people includes vaccination against
influenza, breast and cervical cancer screening, and hip and
knee replacements. Other data are not available readily by
age group or at regional level.

Life expectancy

Life expectancy (LE) estimates the average expected
lifespan, in this case, that remains at age 65. Healthy life
expectancy (HLE) divides the total LE into years spent in
good and 'not good' health; disability-free life expectancy
(DFLE) divides LE into years lived with and without a
chronic illness or disability.

Figure 1.21 compares estimates of life expectancy, health life
expectancy and disability-free life expectancy at age 65 by
sex and UK country in 2004–2006. (Although 2006–08 life
expectancy statistics are currently available, DFLE and HLE
statistics will only be available towards the end of 2010,
preventing them from being illustrated together in

Figure 1.21). Women were consistently estimated to have
longer life expectancies – of all forms – than men in all
countries of the UK between 2004 and 2006, with the
exception of DFLE in Northern Ireland. On average in the UK,
women at age 65 were expected to live for approximately
another 20 years, three years more than men. Lowest
estimates for both sexes were in Scotland, while England had
the highest values for both sexes.

People at age 65 were expected to have an average of 13
years of healthy life ahead of them, but the gap between
women and men dropped to less than 2 years. The largest
difference was 2 years in Scotland.

The UK average was further reduced to about 10 years for
DFLE regardless of the sex in 2004–2006, with Northern
Ireland exhibiting the lowest values at individual country level
for both men (9.1 years) and women (9.0 years). England and
Scotland showed the highest single country levels for DFLE, at
10.7 years for women.

More recent estimates of total life expectancy (LE) at age
65 are, however, available for lower UK geographies. Map
1.22 illustrates life expectancy at age 65 by sex at local
authority level across the UK in 2005–2007. The majority
of LADs exhibit differences in life expectancy between men
and women close to the UK average. However, 25 LADs
had female life expectancies at least 3.5 years greater than
men. These are spread geographically across the UK. In six
local authorities, the male/female difference was 1.5 years
or less.

Figure 1.21

Life expectancy, healthy life expectancy and disability-free life expectancy at age 65: by sex and UK country, 2004 to 2006

Years

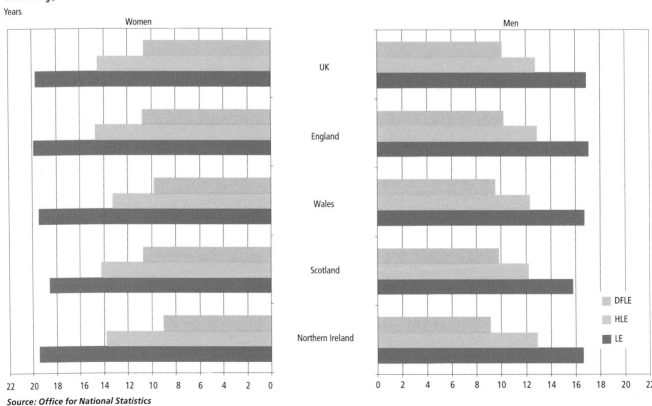

Source: Office for National Statistics

Map 1.22   Life expectancy at age 65: by sex and local authority, UK, 2005 to 2007

Men[1]

	24.0 and over
	22.0 to 23.9
	20.0 to 21.9
	18.0 to 19.9
	16.0 to 17.9
	15.9 or under

London

Women[1]

	24.0 and over
	22.0 to 23.9
	20.0 to 21.9
	18.0 to 19.9
	16.0 to 17.9
	15.9 or under

London

1 No data available for City of London and Isles of Scilly.

Source: Office for National Statistics

ig men, the local authority districts with the highest LE
ge 65 were Kensington and Chelsea (22.7 years),
Westminster (21.2 years) and Crawley (20.3 years). In a
further 24 LADs, men at age 65 had between 19 and
20 years of life expectancy, with the majority located in the
South East, and none further north than Rutland and
Leicester in the East Midlands. This trend was also seen in
LADs in the East of England, Wales, the West Midlands and
the South West. The local authorities with the lowest life
expectancy at age 65 for men were Glasgow City
(13.9 years) and North Lanarkshire (14.9 years), while
Manchester, Hartlepool and Liverpool had the lowest in
England, all at 15.5 years for men.

In more than half of all local authorities in the UK
(255 out of 434), women at age 65 were expected to live,
on average, another 20 or more years. The highest life
expectancy at age 65 for women was seen in Kensington
and Chelsea at 25.2 years. Life expectancy for women at
age 65 was also high in Rutland, East Dorset (both
22.7 years) and Westminster (22.6 years).

Only three local authorities had life expectancies of over
20 years for both men and women (Kensington and Chelsea,
22.7 years and 25.2 years; Westminster, 21.2 years for men
and 22.6 years for women; and Crawley, 20.3 years and
21.1 years).

Breast and cervical cancer screening

Cervical and breast cancer may be treated successfully in a
suitable treatment programme if identified early enough by
screening programmes. Generally, breast screening
programmes target the 50 and over female population, while
cervical screening programmes target a wider age range,
down to 25 years of age. Figure 1.23 (Online table 6.7)
presents the percentages of women aged 50–64 who had
been screened for cervical and breast cancer in the period
before March 2008 by the English strategic health authorities
(SHAs), Wales and Northern Ireland.

In the three years before March 2008 an average of 71 per cent
of women aged 50–64 across the whole of the UK attended a
breast cancer screening. Women of this age in Scotland had the
highest participation in breast cancer screening (76 per cent).
London had the lowest percentage participation in the breast
screen programme, at 58 per cent. This is well below the next
lowest percentage seen among women of this age group in the
North West (69 per cent). All other countries and regions of the
UK had coverage of 70 per cent or greater.

In England, 79 per cent of women aged 50–64 participated
in cervical cancer screening in the five years before March
2008. The percentage of women of this age participating in
cervical cancer screening was highest in the East Midlands,
the South West and the South East Coast SHAs, all with over
80 per cent participation. Of the countries for which
comparable data are available, Northern Ireland had the
lowest percentage of women of this age group (72 per cent)
participating in the cervical cancer screening programme.
Scotland has been excluded because the screening
programme ends at age 59.

Figure 1.23

Breast[1] and cervical[2] cancer screening: by country and strategic health authority, 31 March 2008

Percentages

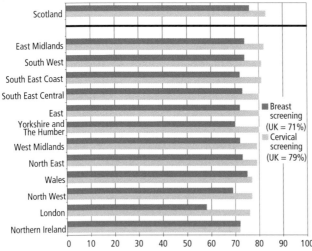

1 Percentage of target population aged 50 to 64 screened in the previous three years. See Online Notes and Definitions.
2 Percentage of women aged 50 to 64 years screened in the previous five years. For Scotland, women aged 55 to 59 screened in the previous five and a half years. See Online Notes and Definitions.

Source: Office for National Statistics; Department of Health; Welsh Assembly Government; General Register Office for Scotland; Information and Statistics Division, NHS Scotland; Northern Ireland Statistics and Research Agency; Department of Health, Social Services and Public Safety, Northern Ireland

Figure 1.24

Percentage of people aged 65 and over, immunised against influenza: by country and strategic health authority, 2007/08[1]

Percentages

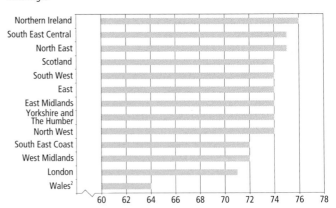

1 England and strategic health authorities, persons aged 65 and over immunised against influenza between October 2007 and January 2008.
2 Wales figure aggregated from GP practice systems which was received by 8 August 2008. See Online Notes and Definitions.

Source: Health Protection Agency, The NHS Information Centre for health and social care; Health Statistics and Analysis Unit, Welsh Assembly Government; Information Services Division (ISD) Scotland; Department of Health, Social Services, Northern Ireland

Flu vaccinations

In recent years, the government has put great effort into providing older people with free influenza vaccinations. The highest flu vaccination uptake between October 2007 and January 2008 was in Northern Ireland (76 per cent of the people aged 65 and over) (Figure 1.24; Online table 6.7). A further five regions (the South West, the East, the East Midlands, Yorkshire and The Humber, and the North West) as well as Scotland had 74 per cent of their population aged 65 and over vaccinated against influenza. People aged 65 and over in Wales had the lowest percentage of vaccination take up, at 64 per cent.

Hip and knee replacements

Figure 1.25 presents rates per 10,000 population aged 65 and over for hip and knee replacements completed in England and Wales in 2008/09 using non-National Statistics data from Hospital Episode Statistics (HES). Of the English regions, the South West (173 per 10,000) had the highest rate, and was the only region with a level above 170 per 10,000 population, while London (118 per 10,000) had the lowest rate of completed admissions for these procedures.

Figure 1.25

Rates of hip and knee replacements for 65 year-olds and over: by strategic health authority, 2008/09

Rate per 10,000 people aged 65 and over

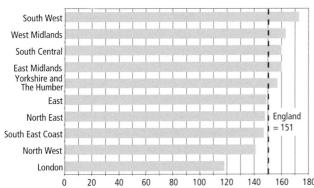

Source: The NHS Information Centre for health and social care; Office for National Statistics

Social care

The growing numbers of older people living to advanced years but with poor health increases the demand for social care. Some statistics are available on care organised or supported by local government social services departments to enable people aged 65 and over to live independently. However, this is likely to understate the total care provision since families may provide care themselves or pay for private care services. Many people with disabilities or needing some sort of care are entitled to government benefits such as Disability Living Allowance and Attendance Allowance. Some of the informal carers are themselves older people but they are identifiable only if they claim Carer's Allowance. Other old

people are unable to live independently and move into residential care homes; these are not identified here.

Care at home

The government aims to achieve independence for older people through rehabilitation/intermediate care either in hospitals, care homes or private homes. One indicator (not National Statistics) in England is 'the percentage of older people aged 65 and over discharged from hospital to intermediate care/rehabilitation/re-ablement who are still living "at home" three months after the date of their discharge from hospital'.

Figure 1.26 presents this percentage for those discharged from hospital to intermediate care during the period 1 October to 31 December 2008 and who were still living at

Figure 1.26

Percentage of people aged 65 and over living at home after discharge from hospital,[1] 31 October 2008 to 31 December 2008[2]

Percentages

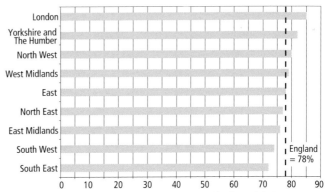

1 Who are still living 'at home' three months after the date of their discharge.
2 The collection of the denominator was for a three month period (1 October 2008 to 31 December 2008) with a three month follow-up for the numerator.

Source: The NHS Information Centre for health and social care

Figure 1.27

Rate of adults aged 65 and over assisted to live independently, 2008/09[1]

Rate per 100,000 people aged 65 and over

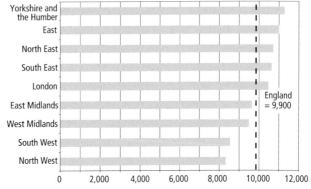

1 Provisional.

Source: The NHS Information Centre for health and social care

1.28

...centage of people aged 60 and over receiving Disability Living Allowance,[1] 2008

Percentages

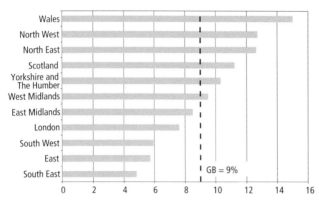

1 Disability Living Allowance is a tax-free benefit for those who need help with personal care or have walking difficulties because they are physically and/or mentally disabled, who were aged under 65 at the time of claiming. Those aged 65 or over who are already receiving DLA may continue to receive it.

Source: Department for Work and Pensions; Office for National Statistics

home three months later. During this period in England, 78 per cent of people aged 65 and over were living at home three months after being discharged from hospital. London had the highest percentage of people aged 65 and over (85 per cent) living at home three months after being discharged from hospital. The South East had the lowest percentage at 72 per cent.

The NHS also monitors the levels and type of social care of people aged 65 and over. Figure 1.27 presents provisional estimates (not National Statistics) for the 'number of people aged 65 and over per 100,000 population [aged 65 and over] that are assisted directly through social services assessed/care planned, funded support to live independently, plus those supported through organisations that receive social services grant funded services'.

In England the rate of people aged 65 and over per 100,000 people (aged 65 and over) who were assisted through social services was 9,900 in 2008/09. Of all English regions, Yorkshire and The Humber and the East had the highest rate of people aged 65 and over who were assisted through social services (11,300 and 11,000 per 100,000 people aged 65 and over), while the North West (8,300 per 100,000) and the South West (8,500) had the lowest rates.

Benefits and allowances

A range of allowances are available to support people who need help because they are physically or mentally disabled, and also for those who care for them. The statistics give an indication of the number of people who have certain disabilities, need help with personal care, or who care for someone who is ill or disabled.

Disability Living Allowance (Figure 1.28) is a tax free benefit paid to people aged under 65 who have care or mobility

needs as a result of a mental or physical disability. Those who are aged 65 or over may also be eligible to get Attendance Allowance. Wales (15 per cent) had the highest percentage of population aged 65 and over receiving DLA, compared with the Great Britain average of 9 per cent. The South East had the lowest take-up rate at 5 per cent, with the East and South West the next lowest at 6 per cent.

Attendance Allowance (Figure 1.29) is a tax-free benefit for people aged 65 and over who need help with personal care because they are physically or mentally disabled. They may get Attendance Allowance if they have a physical or mental disability (or both), and their disability is severe enough for them to need help caring for themselves. Again, Wales had the highest percentage of people aged 65 and over receiving this benefit (23 per cent), compared with the Great Britain average of 18 per cent. The South East had the lowest percentage of take-up of this benefit, at 15 per cent.

Figure 1.29

Percentage of people aged 65 and over receiving Attendance Allowance,[1] 2008

Percentages

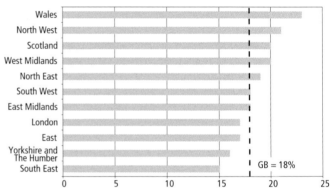

1 Statistics cover 'All entitled cases', so also incorporate those with entitlement but where the payment has been suspended, for example if they are in hospital.

Source: Department for Work and Pensions; Office for National Statistics

Figure 1.30

Percentage of people aged 60 and over receiving Carer's Allowance,[1] 2008

Percentages

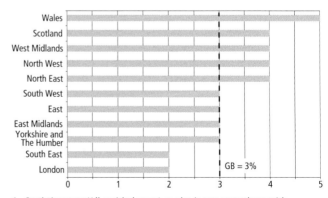

1 Statistics cover 'All entitled cases', so also incorporate those with entitlement but where the payment has been suspended, for example if they are in hospital.

Source: Department for Work and Pensions; Office for National Statistics

Older carers

Carer's Allowance (Figure 1.30) is available to those aged 16 and over who spend at least 35 hours per week caring for someone who is ill or disabled. Some of these are themselves older people. In 2008, 3 per cent of people aged 60 and over were claiming this benefit. Wales (5 per cent) had the highest percentage of claimants; the South East and London had the lowest at 2 per cent.

Older workers

Employment provides income and may provide a pension or allow personal pensions and savings to be built up for retirement. As health has improved more people wish to continue working beyond the long-established retirement ages. This has many benefits for those older people in work, and their skills and experience can be valuable to employers. The workforce generates national income which enables the

Box 4: Workforce status

Employed: The Labour Force Survey (LFS) definition of employment is consistent with the International Labour Organisation (ILO) definition, that is, anyone (aged 16 and over) who does at least one hour's paid work in the week prior to their LFS interview, or has a job that they are temporarily away from (for example on holiday). Also included are people who do unpaid work in a family business and people on government-supported employment training schemes. The employment rate is the number of people in employment as a percentage of the relevant population.

Unemployed (of the age group considered): Unemployment refers to people without a job who were available to start work in the two weeks following their LFS interview and who had either looked for work in the four weeks prior to interview or were waiting to start a job they had already obtained. The unemployment rate is calculated as the number of economically active people who are unemployed as a percentage of the economically active relevant population (employed plus unemployed).

Economically inactive: The LFS definition of inactivity refers to people who are neither in employment nor unemployed. This includes those who want a job but have not been seeking work in the last four weeks, those who want a job and are seeking work but are not available to start work, and those who do not want a job. In the LFS, economic inactivity rate is given by the number of economically inactive people as a percentage of the relevant population.

Figure 1.31

Employment, unemployment and economic inactivity rates[1] for people aged 50 to state pension age, 2008

Percentages

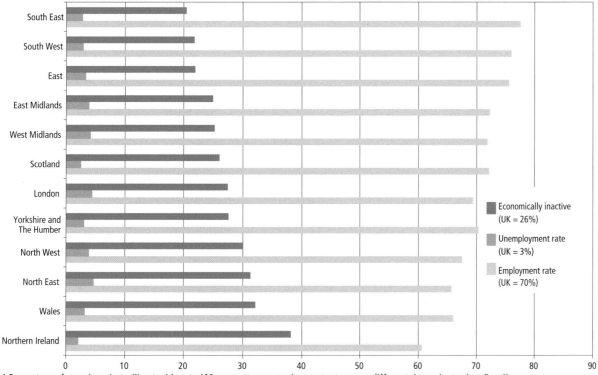

1 Percentages for each region will not add up to 100 per cent as unemployment rate uses a different denominator (see Box 4).

Source: Annual Population Survey, Office for National Statistics

of state welfare benefits. Government legislation
been passed to raise the age at which state pensions will
be payable (Box 1) and enable greater flexibility for people to
continue their careers longer.

People aged 16 and over are classed as employed,
unemployed or economically inactive, and this is a reflection
of their current status of participation in the workforce of the
UK. Those aged 50 and over and who are in employment are
usually defined as older workers.

Employment status of the workforce varies with age and sex.
The shape and size of the workforce is determined by the
inflows of younger workers balanced by older workers leaving
through retirement or as a result of personal injury, disability
or caring responsibility.

Nationally, England followed a general but expected trend
for percentages of workforce among men and women to
reduce with increasing age. Considering quinary (that is,
five-year) age groups from age 50 to just above SPA, the
percentage of men in employment (full and part-time
combined) reduced from 84 per cent for those aged
50–54 to 23 per cent for those aged 65–69. Women
showed a similar systematic withdrawal from the labour
market with age, reducing from 76 per cent for those aged
50–54 to 13 per cent for the 65–69 age group. All regions
also followed this same trend, except for men in London,
where the percentage remaining in the labour force
marginally increased between ages 50–54 and 55–59 by
about 1 per cent. Although higher than a decade ago, the
relatively small employment rates above SPA mean that
reliable regional estimates are not available.

Figure 1.31 illustrates regional variation in the percentages of
people aged 50 to SPA that are either in employment,
unemployed or economically inactive (Box 4). These data
from the Annual Population Survey (APS) (which is derived
from the Labour Force Survey) show that higher employment
rates are found in the southern regions of England, excluding
London. The South East (78 per cent), the East and the South
West (both 76 per cent) are the only regions above the UK
average of 72 per cent for the percentage of the population
aged 50 to SPA in employment. Northern Ireland has the
lowest percentage at 61 per cent, with the North East and
Wales the next lowest at 66 per cent each.

The pattern of unemployment – the percentage of the
economically active population who are out of work and
actively looking for work – shows higher proportions in the
north of England, the midlands and London. Averaged over
2008, the North East and London had the highest
unemployment rates for the 50 to SPA age group at 4.6 per
cent and 4.4 per cent respectively. The lowest rate was in
Northern Ireland (2.1 per cent).

A person is considered economically inactive if they are not
working or seeking to work: for example because they are
retired, looking after a home or family, permanently unable to
work, sick or disabled or for other reasons. Northern Ireland

Figure 1.32

Percentage of employed men and women aged 50 to state pension age that are in full- or part-time employment, 2008

Percentages

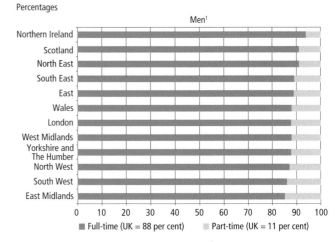

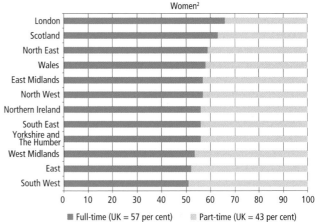

1 Denominator is all men in employment aged 50 to 64.
2 Denominator is all women in employment aged 50 to 59.

Source: Office for National Statistics

(38 per cent), Wales (32 per cent), the North East (31 per
cent) were the only countries and regions with over 30 per
cent of their 50 to SPA population economically inactive,
compared with the UK average of 26 per cent.

Figure 1.32 illustrates the percentage of men and women
aged 50 to SPA in employment who worked full-time or
part-time by English region and UK country in 2008. Different
patterns are seen depending on whether sex or employment
pattern is considered.

In all regions and countries of the UK in this age group,
higher percentages of men worked full-time (UK 88 per cent)
than women (57 per cent). Higher percentages of women
work part-time (43 per cent) than men (11 per cent).

The highest percentages of men working full-time were found in
Northern Ireland (93 per cent), Scotland (91 per cent) and the
North East (91 per cent). London (66 per cent) and Scotland (63
per cent) had the highest percentage of women in this age
group working full-time, and were the only areas having over 60
per cent of their female older workers working full-time.

In the South West, the percentage of women who worked full-time in 2008 was comparable to those working part-time (51 per cent and 49 per cent respectively); the East also showed similar percentages (52 per cent and 48 per cent respectively).

Quality of life

Health and income are important factors affecting the quality of life enjoyed by older people. The English Longitudinal Study of Ageing provides an indicative, albeit subjective, measure of the quality of life using the CASP-19 scoring system. This defines wellbeing in terms of four domains:

- Control: the ability to intervene actively in one's own environment

- Autonomy: the right of an individual to be free from unwanted interference by others

- Self-realisation: the active processes of human fulfilment

- Pleasure: the sense of fun derived from the more active (doing) aspects of life

CASP-19 scores were based on answers given by respondents aged 55–85 to a series of 19 questions in the Health Survey for England. Average scores in 2006–07 progressively decreased after age 65, indicating a reducing perception of wellbeing. This may be due to factors including poorer health in later life, loss of immediate family and friends and reduced mobility in older age. The sample size is insufficient to provide regional estimates.

The following sections show the information that is available at regional level on factors and activities that may affect the quality of life for older people.

Housing tenure

Home ownership provides a sense of security, autonomy and control over one's living arrangements, as well as being an indicator of wealth. In 2008 the majority of people aged 65 and over in the UK (71 per cent) owned their homes outright; 21 per cent rented their property; about 7 per cent owned their home with a mortgage/loan or part-rented/ part-owned; with around 1 per cent renting free or squatting.

Figure 1.33 presents housing tenure by UK country and English region with the categories of housing tenure described combined into two broad categories: home ownership (or part-ownership) and renting. In all regions and countries of the UK, at least two-thirds of people aged 65 and over owned their homes outright or with a mortgage; and for Wales, the South East and the South West regions, this proportion was over 80 per cent. The regions with the lowest levels of outright home ownership were the North East (68 per cent) and London (69 per cent).

Education and skills

One means of gaining self-realisation and pleasure is through learning and gaining qualifications. Qualifications gained

Figure 1.33

Housing tenure for people aged 65 and over, 2008

Percentages

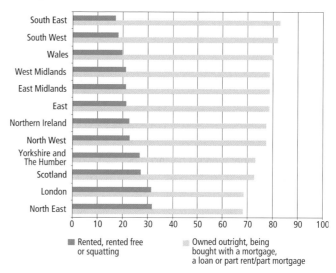

■ Rented, rented free   ☐ Owned outright, being
or squatting   bought with a mortgage,
   a loan or part rent/part mortgage

Source: Annual Population Survey, Office for National Statistics

through initial education and throughout working life are important for employment. As their children reach adulthood, people may participate in new activities outside work and others may undertake new activities after retirement. Some may undertake job-related learning to enable a career change.

Figure 1.34 shows the percentage of the UK's 50 to SPA population who had at least a National Qualification Framework (NQF) Level 4 qualification (Box 5) compared with those with no qualifications in the second quarter of 2009.

The highest percentages – those above the UK average of 29 per cent – of the population achieving a NQF Level 4 qualification were typically found in the south of England (the South East, 35 per cent; London, 34 per cent; the South West, 33 per cent). Lowest percentages were in Northern Ireland (22 per cent) and the North East (23 per cent).

Generally, those regions with the highest percentage of older people with a NQF Level 4 qualification were also those with the lowest percentages of people with no qualifications (the South East, 11 per cent, and the South West, 13 per cent).

Box 5: National Qualification Framework (NQF)

Level 4 qualifications

A Level 4 qualification in the UK is any one of the following certificates:

Teaching qualification (including PGCE); First Degree; BEC National HNC/HND; BTEC National HNC/HND; Higher Education Certificate; Higher Education Diploma; LCCI Advanced Level; NVQ Level 4; Nursing (SRN); RSA Advanced Certificate; RSA Higher Diploma.

Figure 1.34

Highest qualification level achieved for people aged 50 to state pension age, 2009 Q2

Percentages

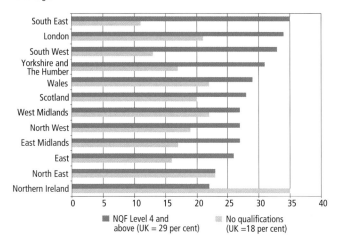

NQF Level 4 and above (UK = 29 per cent)

No qualifications (UK =18 per cent)

Source: Labour Force Survey, Office for National Statistics and Department for Business, Innovation and Skills

However, this pattern does not hold in London where a relatively high percentage had no qualifications. Similarly, areas with the lowest percentages achieving a NQF Level 4 qualification have the highest percentages with no qualifications; Northern Ireland (35 per cent) and the North East (23 per cent). However, similar levels to the North East were also found in the East Midlands (22 per cent), Wales (22 per cent) and London (21 per cent).

Qualification levels achieved have increased over time so it is interesting to compare the qualifications held by people aged 50 to SPA with those of the whole working-age population (aged 16–64 for men, 16–59 for women) (Online table 4.14). The largest difference at NQF Level 4 was only 5 percentage points in Scotland (33 per cent of working-age population; 28 per cent for those aged 50–SPA) and London (39 per cent; 34 per cent). However looking at those with no qualifications, the largest differences between these age groups in an individual UK region/country were

Figure 1.35

Percentage of people aged 50–64 undertaking adult learning in the last year, April 2008 to March 2009

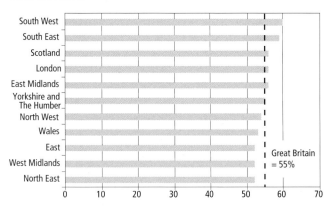

Great Britain = 55%

Source: Annual Population Survey, Office for National Statistics

13 percentage points in Northern Ireland (22 per cent of working age population; 35 per cent for those aged 50-SPA) and 9 percentage points in London (12 per cent and 21 per cent respectively). The smallest differences between these two age groups were 3 percentage points in the South East and 4 percentage points in the South West.

Figure 1.35 presents estimates for regions and countries of Great Britain of the percentage of people aged 50–64 undertaking learning in 2008/09. Learning includes attending taught courses and tuition, whether leading to a qualification, developing skills for a job or developing practical skills, or simply attending classes for any reason. It also includes studying without taking part in a taught course, keeping up with developments in the type of work a person does and supervised training at work. This is one of the indicators adopted in the Department for Work and Pension's (DWP) Opportunity Age Indicators series (2009, DWP).

The southern regions of England exhibited the highest percentages of people aged 50–64 undertaking adult learning in 2008/09 (the South West, 60 per cent, and the South East, 59 per cent). The East, the North East and the West Midlands had the lowest percentage participation in adult learning, all at 52 per cent, compared with the Great Britain average of 55 per cent.

Uptake of concessionary bus passes

Concessionary bus passes are a relatively new national initiative by the government, to encourage the older population to be more active and participate in more and new activities, although localised schemes have been run in the past in areas such as London.

Figure 1.36

Uptake of concessionary bus fare schemes[1] for people aged 60 and over, 2006 to 2008

Percentages

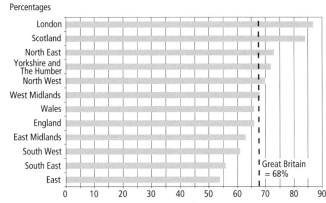

Great Britain = 68%

1 Concessionary bus pass schemes became effective as follows: Wales (national) – April 2002; England (local), Scotland (national) – April 2006; England (national) – April 2008.

Source: Department for Transport; The Scottish Government

Figure 1.36 illustrates the three-year average uptake of concessionary bus passes by people aged 60 and over by regions and countries of Great Britain in 2006–08. Highest percentages were found in London (87 per cent) and Scotland

(84 per cent). Northern regions of England (the North East, 73 per cent; Yorkshire and The Humber, 72 per cent; the North West, 70 per cent) were also above the Great Britain average of 68 per cent.

Lower percentages of bus pass uptake among people aged over 60 were found in the south of England outside London. This is likely to reflect higher levels of car ownership in these regions, as suggested by the overall levels of car ownership (Online table 11.2).

Conclusions

There is evidence of population ageing in all countries of the UK and regions of England, although it is occurring at different rates due to past fertility and mortality rates and migration into and out of each area. The highest proportions of older people in 2008 were in Wales and the South West of England and the lowest in London and Northern Ireland. However, the older population of Northern Ireland has increased more in the past five years than that of London, partly because some older people move out of London and they are replaced with younger people.

The movement of older people away from London is further demonstrated by estimates for local authority districts which show higher percentages of the population aged 50 and over living around the UK coast and in more rural areas.

The population aged 65 and over is projected to grow steadily in all regions between 2006 and 2031. The population aged 50–64 is projected to grow less rapidly or even decrease in a few regions. London's 50–64 population is projected to increase by the largest percentage of all regions, and its 65 and over population the least. For those aged 65 and over, the greatest percentage increases are projected in Northern Ireland, the East Midlands and the East of England. These areas will face the greatest challenges, in proportion to existing provision, in meeting the needs of the increasing numbers of older people, including the 'oldest old' aged over 85.

In other regions there are greater needs in terms of low incomes. Highest levels of income deprivation – illustrated in a variety of forms such as IDAOPI, pension credit take-up and household income – were generally found in the North East and London. Much of the variation between and within regions appears to reflect the level of rurality of the areas in which older people live. Fuel poverty (only available at regional level) showed a clearer north–south pattern. Life expectancy was also generally higher in the south and midlands, although there was considerable variation within regions.

The ability to work up to – or beyond – state pension age may have implications for wellbeing in older age. Northern Ireland, Wales and the North East had the highest percentages of their population aged 50 to SPA economically inactive in 2008. However, Northern Ireland and the North East (and also Scotland) had the highest percentages among those men aged 50–64 that were in employment who were working full-time.

References

General

The English Longitudinal Study of Ageing (ELSA), available at: www.ifs.org.uk/elsa/index.php

'Focus on Older People', Office for National Statistics (2005), available at: www.statistics.gov.uk/StatBase/Product. asp?vlnk=12348

'The New Performance Framework for Local Authorities and Local Authority Partnerships: Single Set of National Indicators', Communities and Local Government (2007), available at: www.communities.gov.uk/publications/ localgovernment/nationalindicator

'Public Service Agreements: The new performance management framework', HM Treasury (2007), available at: www.hm-treasury.gov.uk/pbr_csr07_psaindex.htm

'National Performance Framework', The Scottish Government (2009), available at: www.scotland.gov.uk/ About/purposestratobjs

'Ageing and Mortality in the UK – National Statistician's annual article on the population', Office for National Statistics (2008), available at: www.statistics.gov.uk/CCI/ article.asp?ID=2079

'Older People's Wellbeing Monitor for Wales' Welsh Assembly Government (2009), available at: http://wales. gov.uk/topics/olderpeople/research/ wellbeingmonitor2009/?lang=en

'Opportunity Age – First Report', Department for Work and Pensions (2008), available at: www.dwp.gov.uk/policy/ ageing-society/strategy-and-publications/opportunity-age-first-report/

'Opportunity Age Indicators: 2008 Update', available at: www.dwp.gov.uk/policy/ageing-society/evaluating-progress/opportunity-age-indicators/#OA_Indcators

'2006-based national population projections for the UK and constituent countries', Office for National Statistics (2008), available at: www.statistics.gov.uk/CCI/article.asp?ID=2085

'Estimating the changing population of the "oldest old"', Office for National Statistics (2008), available at: www. statistics.gov.uk/CCI/article.asp?ID=2089

'Subnational patterns of population ageing', Office for National Statistics (2009), available at: www.statistics.gov. uk/CCI/article.asp?ID=2244

'Employment of the older generation', Office for National Statistics (2009), available at: www.statistics.gov.uk/CCI/ article.asp?ID=2167

1

'National Statistician's Annual Article on the Population: a Demographic Review. The third in a series of annual demographic reports of the UK, providing an overview of the latest statistics on the population', Office for National Statistics (2009), available at: www.statistics.gov.uk/cci/article.asp?ID=2337

Poverty and deprivation

'Households Below Average Income: An analysis of the income distribution 1994/95 – 2007/08', Department for Work and Pensions (2008), available at: http://research.dwp.gov.uk/asd/hbai/hbai2008/contents.asp

'Income Related Benefits Estimates of Take-up in 2007–08', Department for Work and Pensions (2009), available at: http://research.dwp.gov.uk/asd/irb_2.asp

'Pensioners Incomes Series', Department for Work and Pensions (2009), available at: http://research.dwp.gov.uk/asd/pensioners_income.asp

Health and care

'Death registrations in England and Wales, 2007', Office for National Statistics (2008), Health Statistics Quarterly No. 39, pp. 89–97

'Health expectancies in the United Kingdom 2004–06', Office for National Statistics (2008), Health Statistics Quarterly No. 40, pp. 77–80

'Life expectancy at birth and at age 65 by local areas in the United Kingdom, 2005–07', Office for National Statistics (2008), Health Statistics Quarterly No. 40, pp. 81–83

Quality of life

'Transport Statistics Bulletin: National Travel Survey: 2006', Department for Transport (2006) available at: www.dft.gov.uk/pgr/statistics/datatablespublications/personal/mainresults/nts2006/

'Measuring societal wellbeing', Office for National Statistics (2007), available at: www.statistics.gov.uk/CCI/article.asp?ID=1882

'Review of the Scotland Wide Free Bus Travel Scheme for Older and Disabled People' (2009), available at: www.scotland.gov.uk/Publications/2009/05/19093131/3

'Transport Research Series: Evaluation of National Concessionary Travel in Scotland' (2009), available at: www.scotland.gov.uk/Publications/2009/05/13144419/0

Small area classifications, indices and statistics

'Urban and rural area definitions: a user guide', Communities and Local Government (2002), available at: www.communities.gov.uk/publications/planningandbuilding/urbanrural

'Rural and Urban Area Classification, 2004', Office for National Statistics (2004), available at: www.statistics.gov.uk/geography/nrudp.asp

'Northern Ireland Multiple Deprivation Measure 2005', Northern Ireland Statistics and Research Agency (2005), available at: www.nisra.gov.uk/deprivation/nimdm_2005.htm

'Report of the Inter-Departmental Urban-Rural Definition Group Statistical Classification and Delineation of Settlements February, 2005', Northern Ireland Statistics and Research Agency (2005), available at: www.nisra.gov.uk/geography/default.asp10.htm

'The English Indices of Deprivation 2007', Communities and Local Government (2008): available at: www.communities.gov.uk/documents/communities/pdf/733520.pdf

'Using the English Indices of Deprivation 2007: Guidance', Communities and Local Government (2007), available at: www.communities.gov.uk/documents/communities/doc/615986.doc

'Statistical Focus on Rural Wales, 2008', Welsh Assembly Government (2008), available at: http://wales.gov.uk/topics/statistics/publications/focusrural08/?lang=en

'Urban Rural Classification, 2007/2008', The Scottish Government (2008), available at: www.scotland.gov.uk/Publications/2008/07/29152642/0

'Rural Definition and Local Authority Classification', Department for Environment, Food and Rural Affairs, available at: www.defra.gov.uk/evidence/statistics/rural/rural-definition.htm

Neighbourhood Statistics (England and Wales), Office for National Statistics, available at: www.neighbourhood.statistics.gov.uk

Scottish Neighbourhood Statistics, The Scottish Government, available at: www.sns.gov.uk

Northern Ireland Neighbourhood Statistics, Northern Ireland Statistics and Research Agency, available at: www.ninis.nisra.gov.uk

Portrait of the North East

by Allan Worthy and Ian Gouldson, Office for National Statistics

Key points

The North East region:

- is the smallest English region outside London in terms of area

- has a high proportion of land in National Parks and Areas of Outstanding Natural Beauty and is the English region least at risk of flooding

- has the lowest population of any English region, and the slowest rate of growth over the last decade, with the lowest fertility rate

- has the highest death rates for men aged 55 and over of all English regions

- has the highest proportion of White British residents

- has the lowest average house prices and lowest rates of pay of all English regions

- has a high proportion of working-age population with no qualifications, but the highest proportion of Key Stage 4 pupils gaining 5 or more good GCSE passes

- has high rates of unemployment and of economic inactivity due to long-term sickness

- has the highest household crime rate of all English regions, but an average recorded crime rate with the highest rate of detection

- has the highest regional carbon dioxide (CO_2) emissions per resident in the UK, but concentrated in a few areas with a significant manufacturing base

Allan Worthy is Regional Statistician for the North East
Ian Gouldson is Regional Analyst
Tel: 0191 229 6435
Mobile: 07788 153723
Email: allan.worthy@ons.gsi.gov.uk

Note:
Unless otherwise stated the data used in this article were those available at the time of writing. In particular, mid-year population estimates were those released in August 2009.

Introduction

The North East covers 8,600 square kilometres (sq km) and is the second smallest region in England after London, but its population of 2.6 million in 2008 was the lowest of all regions in England (Online table 1.2). Over 80 per cent of the population live in urban areas with the two main centres of population grouped around the three main rivers in the region. In the north of the region, Newcastle upon Tyne (population 274,000) and Gateshead (population 191,000) straddle the River Tyne and Sunderland (population 280,000) lies on the Wear. In the south of the region, the River Tees flows through Middlesbrough (population 139,000) and Stockton-on-Tees (population 192,000).

The region has a long eastern coastline facing the North Sea, running from its border with Scotland in the north to North Yorkshire in the south. To the west, the Cheviot Hills and North Pennines rise towards Cumbria in the North West region (Map 2.1). The region is easily accessible via the A1 and the East Coast mainline railway as they pass through between London and Edinburgh. From east to west, the A69 connects Carlisle and Newcastle upon Tyne. There are two international airports in the region – Newcastle, which handled 5 million passengers in 2008 (Online table 11.16), and Durham Tees Valley. There is also a ferry service from Newcastle upon Tyne to Amsterdam (Ijmuiden).

Northumberland and Tyne & Wear is the largest of the sub-regions (NUTS2 areas – Map 2.2) and largely rural, with 1.4 million residents living in 5,600 sq km (Online table 1.2). The population density (people per sq km) ranges from under 30 in both Berwick-upon-Tweed and Tynedale to 2,400 in Newcastle upon Tyne (see map on page 97).

Around 60 per cent of the region's agricultural industry gross value added comes from Northumberland and Tyne & Wear. The area also contains the Northumberland National Park, the Northumberland Coast (an Area of Outstanding Natural Beauty) and Hadrian's Wall (a World Heritage Site).

Tees Valley and Durham is the smaller of the two sub-regions in terms of both population and size, with 1.2 million residents living in 3,000 sq km, although it contains the most densely populated local authority area in the region, Middlesbrough UA, with 2,600 people per sq km (Online table 1.2).

The area has a World Heritage Site in Durham Cathedral, an Area of Outstanding Natural Beauty in the North Pennines and

Map 2.1   North East: physical features

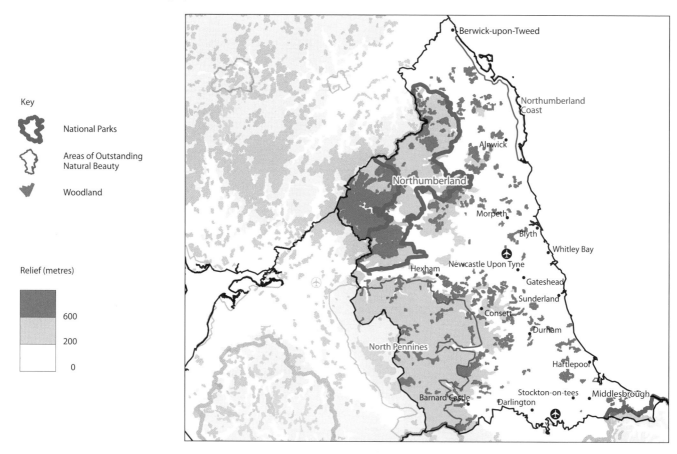

Key

National Parks

Areas of Outstanding
Natural Beauty

Woodland

Relief (metres)

600

200

0

Map 2.2   North East: local or unitary authority, NUTS 2[1] sub-regions and Rural/Urban Definition[2]

Regional boundary

NUTS 2 boundary

Local or unitary authority[3]
boundary

Rural/Urban Definition

Urban population over 10,000
– Less Sparse

Urban population over 10,000
– Sparse

Town and Fringe – Less Sparse

Town and Fringe – Sparse

Village, Hamlet and Isolated
Dwellings – Less Sparse

Village, Hamlet and Isolated
Dwellings – Sparse

1 Wansbeck
2 Blyth Valley
3 North Tyneside
4 Newcastle upon Tyne
5 South Tyneside
6 Sunderland
7 Chester-le-Street
8 Easington
9 Hartlepool
10 Stockton-on-Tees
11 Middlesbrough
12 Redcar and Cleveland

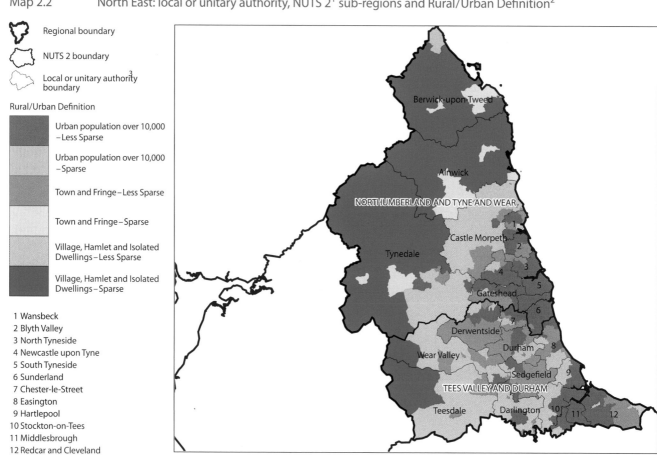

1 Nomenclature of Units for Territorial Statistics, level 2.
2 By Lower Layer Super Output Area.
3 Prior to April 2009.

also contains most of the region's main chemical industry sites (around Stockton-on-Tees, and Redcar and Cleveland). One-fifth of the sub-region's gross value added is produced by the manufacturing industry, and almost one-half of the North East's manufacturing industry gross value added is produced in this area.

The North East has been used as a location for numerous books, such as those by Catherine Cookson, and films ranging from the gritty *Get Carter* (Tyneside) to the whimsical *Billy Elliot* (Easington) and the distinctly out-of-this-world *Alien³* (Blast Beach, Seaham). Tourist attractions in the North East include, in no particular order, Alnwick Castle and its gardens, the Angel of the North, Hadrian's Wall, Lindisfarne (Holy Island), Bamburgh Castle, Beamish Open Air Museum, the Bowes Museum, the Baltic Centre for Contemporary Art, Middlesbrough's Institute of Modern Art and numerous other art galleries and museums.

The original Northumbria region designated by the National Rivers Authority (now part of the Environment Agency – see map on page 139) had a long-term average annual rainfall of 831 millimetres between 1971 and 2000, which was very similar to the England average of 819 millimetres (Online table 5.1).

Population

The North East had a population of 2.6 million in mid-2008, the least in any English region. Its population was less than that of Scotland or Wales but larger than Northern Ireland and amounted to only 4 per cent of the UK population (Online table 1.2).

The region consists of seven unitary authorities (UAs): County Durham, Darlington, Hartlepool, Middlesbrough, Northumberland, Redcar and Cleveland and Stockton-on-Tees, plus the former metropolitan county, Tyne & Wear. Tyne & Wear consists of the metropolitan districts of Gateshead, Newcastle upon Tyne, North Tyneside, South Tyneside and Sunderland. Northumberland and County Durham UAs were created in April 2009. Northumberland UA consists of the former districts of Alnwick, Berwick-upon-Tweed, Blyth Valley, Castle Morpeth, Tynedale and Wansbeck. County Durham UA consists of the former districts of Chester-le-Street, Derwentside, Durham, Easington, Sedgefield, Teesdale and Wear Valley.

Tyne & Wear had the largest population in the region in 2008 with 1.1 million residents, while the most populous unitary authority in the region was County Durham with 508,000 residents (Online table 1.2). The unitary authority with the smallest 2008 population in the region was Hartlepool with an estimated 92,000 residents. Using the more detailed Local Authority districts that existed pre-April 2009, Sunderland and Newcastle had the highest populations, and the more rural areas of Teesdale, Berwick-upon-Tweed and Alnwick had the lowest populations (Figure 2.3, Online table 1.2).

Population density in the North East in 2008 was 300 people per sq km, ranking it sixth of the nine English

Figure 2.3

Population: by local authority,[1] North East, mid-2008

Thousands

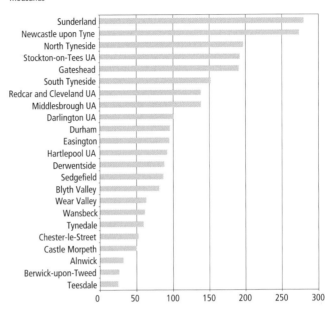

1 Unitary authorities are pre-April 2009

Source: Office for National Statistics

regions, below the England average of 395 but above the UK average of 253. Although the population of the North East was half that of its close neighbour, Scotland (population 5.2 million), the North East's population density was almost five times that of Scotland (66 people per sq km). Similarly, although the population of the North East was lower than that of Wales (population 3.0 million), the North East's population density was more than double that of Wales (population density 144 people per sq km). Population density within the North East (see Map 6.1 on page 97) ranged from over 2,600 people per sq km in Middlesbrough to under 30 in Berwick-upon-Tweed and Tynedale (Online table 1.2).

The population of the region increased by 0.4 per cent (11,000 people) between mid-2007 and mid-2008. This was a lower percentage increase than the UK population (0.7 per cent) and only the North West had a lower percentage increase than the North East (Online table 10.8).

Natural change, that is births minus deaths, accounted for 3,700 (34 per cent) of the North East increase, which means that most of the population increase was due to migration from other regions or abroad (Online table 10.8). Figure 2.4 shows that within the region, the largest increases due to migration were seen in Durham, Newcastle upon Tyne and Stockton-on-Tees, all of which have large student populations. Decreases in population as a result of natural change were seen in Berwick-upon-Tweed, Tynedale and Teesdale, all of which have relatively high proportions of the population over state pension age, resulting in unchanged or slightly lower populations. Although Castle Morpeth also saw a decrease in population as a result of natural change there was also an

1

Figure 2.4

Components of population change: by local authority,¹ mid-2007 to mid-2008

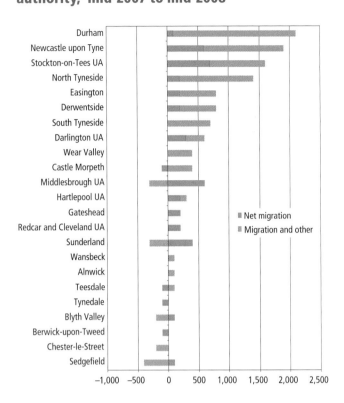

1 Unitary Authorities are pre-April 2009.

Source: Office for National Statistics

increase from migration and other changes, resulting in a small overall increase.

Figure 2.5 shows that net inter-regional migration to the region between mid-2007 and mid-2008 was small, with roughly equal numbers of people arriving from and leaving for other regions (about 40,000 in each direction). International

Figure 2.5

Net migration: by region, 2008

Rate per 10,000 residents

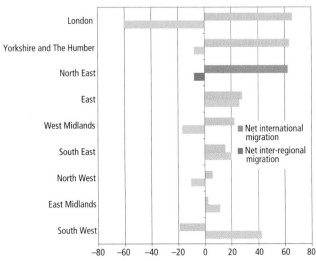

Source: National Health Service Central Register; International Passenger Survey, Office for National Statistics; Home Office

migration had a greater effect on the population; only London and Yorkshire and The Humber had higher levels of net international migration per 10,000 residents. However, international migration was at a lower level than inter-regional migration, with 23,000 people arriving and 7,000 leaving (Online table 10.6).

In the period 2001 to 2008 the population of England grew by 4.0 per cent, with the North East showing 1.4 per cent growth. This was the lowest growth of all English regions, and followed a period of decline over most of the previous two decades (Online table 10.1). Within the region, Durham showed the largest percentage increase between 2001 and 2008 at 9.8 per cent, with the population of Middlesbrough decreasing by 1.6 per cent. The 2006-based population projections estimate a 2026 population of 2.7 million for the North East, an increase of 174,000 or 7 per cent on 2006. The equivalent increase for England is 7.9 million or 16 per cent.

In mid-2008 the population structure for the North East was similar to that for the UK (Figure 2.6). The large student centres of Newcastle, Middlesbrough and Durham had a greater proportion of the population in the 20 to 24 age range than elsewhere in the region (Online table 10.2).

The projections for the North East show that by 2026 the population of the age group 0 to 19 will increase by 5,000 while the 20 to 59 age group will fall by 52,000 and the 60 and over age group will increase by 221,000. In 2006, the female population in the 20 to 59 age group exceeded the number of males by 13,000. However, projections show that the number of females in this age group will fall faster than the number of males; in 2026 the male population aged between 20 and 59 is projected to exceed females by 6,000. Falls in population of

Figure 2.6

Mid-year population estimates: by 5 year age band and sex, North East, 2008

Percentages

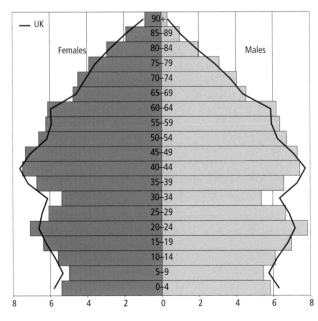

Source: Office for National Statistics

3,000 (2.0 per cent) are projected for Middlesbrough and 2,000 (0.8 per cent) for Sunderland, whereas the largest increases are in North Tyneside with 25,000 (13.0 per cent) and Newcastle with 17,000 (6.3 per cent). Durham is projected to have the highest percentage increase over that period with 14.6 per cent (14,000).

Experimental population estimates by ethnic group show that, within England, the North East had the highest proportion of the population classed as White British – 94 per cent – compared with 84 per cent for England in 2007 (Online table 10.4). Black people comprised 1 per cent, less than the England average of 3 per cent and the lowest proportion of any English region. Asian people comprised 2 per cent, less than the England average of 6 per cent and only the South West had a lower proportion. Within the North East, Newcastle and Middlesbrough had the highest proportions of those describing themselves as other than White British, with 14 and 11 per cent respectively.

In the year ending June 2009, 95 per cent of the region's residents were born in the UK. This was the largest proportion of all of the English regions. Of the 120,000 residents born outside the UK, 12 per cent were born in India, 9 per cent in Germany and 9 per cent in Poland.

There were 30,200 live births in the North East in 2008 (Online table 10.5). The Total Fertility Rate (TFR), which is the average number of children a group of women would have if they experienced the current patterns of fertility throughout their childbearing life was 1.82 in 2007, below the England average of 1.92 and the lowest of the English regions. The lowest TFR in the region was 1.50 for Durham, whilst the highest TFR in the region was 2.16 for Wear Valley (Online table 1.2).

Households and housing

There were an estimated 1.11 million households in the North East in 2006, an increase of 30,000 (2.8 per cent) on the 2001 estimate. This number is projected to increase by 170,000 (15 per cent) between 2006 and 2026, which is less than any other English region (Figure 2.7, Online table 10.15). The average household size in the region is projected to decrease from 2.26 people in 2006 to 2.09 people by 2026, in line with the average change in England.

Married couples accounted for 47 per cent of households in the North East in 2001 but by 2006 this was estimated to have decreased to 43 per cent. By 2026, the proportion of households consisting of a married couple is projected to fall further to 35 per cent and the proportion of one-person households in the region is projected to increase from 33 per cent in 2006 to 39 per cent in 2026.

There were 1.14 million dwellings in the North East in 2007, which was 44,000 more than in 1997. This represented an increase of 4 per cent, the lowest percentage increase of any English region over that period (Online table 7.1).

In 2007/08 there were around 8,000 new build completions in the North East, of which the majority (over 90 per cent) were for private enterprise. Only 5 per cent were for registered social

Figure 2.7

Household estimates[1] and projections: by household type, North East, 2001–2026

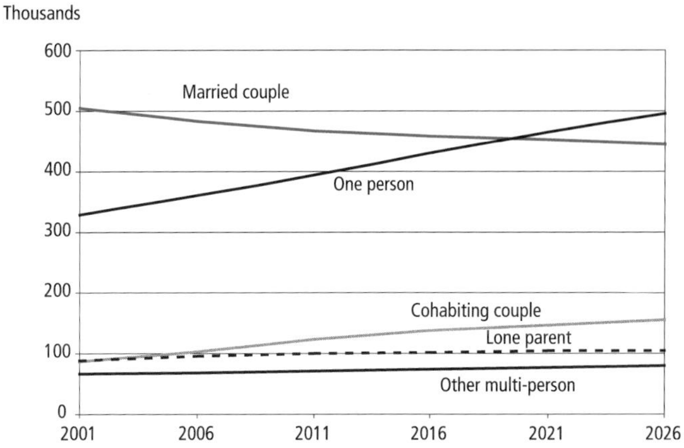

Thousands

(line chart showing Married couple, One person, Cohabiting couple, Lone parent, and Other multi-person from 2001 to 2026)

1 Estimates from 1997 to 2006 are based on ONS mid-year population estimates and projected rates of household formation from trends in census and Labour Force Survey data.

Source: Communities and Local Government

landlords, much less than the highest proportions in London (35 per cent) and the South East (17 per cent) (Online table 7.2). However, the proportion of the North East housing stock rented from local authorities or registered social landlords was 23 per cent in 2007, still among the highest of the English regions although a decline from 31 per cent in 1997 (Online table 7.3).

The median dwelling price in the North East in 2008 was £120,000, the lowest of all English regions and just under 70 per cent of the England average of £174,000. However, the median price of dwellings in the North East fell by only 1.6 per cent between 2007 and 2008, the lowest fall of any English region, compared with a fall of 2.2 per cent across the whole of England

Figure 2.8

Median dwelling prices: by local authority,[1] North East, 2008

£ (thousands)

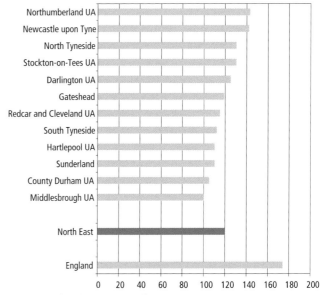

1 Unitary authorities are post April 2009.

Source: Communities and Local Government; Land Registry

Box 1: Measuring housing affordability

An important indicator of housing affordability is the ratio of lower quartile house prices to lower quartile incomes.

The lower quartile value for a particular area is determined by ranking all prices or incomes in ascending order and identifying the value below which 25 per cent fall.

The statistics used for lower quartile income are workplace-based annual full-time individual earnings from the Annual Survey of Hours and Earnings (ASHE). The ASHE is based on a 1 per cent sample of employee jobs in April of a given year. It does not cover the self-employed nor does it cover employees not paid during the reference period.

Lower quartile house prices are based on Land Registry data for the first two quarters of a given year. Each ratio is calculated by dividing the house price by income. Data for local authorities in England and Wales can be accessed on the Communities & Local Government (CLG) website:

www.communities.gov.uk/housing/housingresearch/housingstatistics/housingstatisticsby/housingmarket/livetables/

(Online table 7.4). More recent data show that the median price in the North East fell to £110,000 in the first quarter of 2009 before recovering to £120,000 in the second quarter.

Within the region (Figure 2.8), median dwelling prices in 2008 ranged from £100,000 in Middlesbrough to £143,000 in Northumberland. Changes in median dwelling prices between 2007 and 2008 ranged from a fall of 6.5 per cent in Redcar and Cleveland to an increase of 4.8 per cent in Hartlepool (Online table 7.4).

One measure of housing affordability is to compare lower quartile house prices against lower quartile earnings of workers in the area (Box 1). The higher the ratio of house prices to earnings, the less affordable are properties in the area. Using this measure, houses were more affordable in the North East than in any other English region. In 2009 the ratio of lower quartile house prices to earnings in the North East was 4.9, compared with the England average of 6.3. Within the North East, the highest ratio in North Tyneside (5.9) was still below the England average. The most affordable housing was in Hartlepool UA and County Durham UA, both with ratios of 4.2. Over the last decade, the North East's ratio increased from 2.8 in 1999 to a high of 5.5 in 2007.

Education and skills

In 2007/08, 66.4 per cent of Key Stage 4 pupils achieved five or more grades A*–C at GCSE in maintained mainstream schools in the North East. This was the largest proportion of any English region (Online table 4.8). The proportion of 16-year-olds in post-compulsory education and government-supported training in 2006/07 was 84 per cent, the third

Figure 2.9

Proportion of working age population with no qualifications: by region, 2009 Q2

Percentages

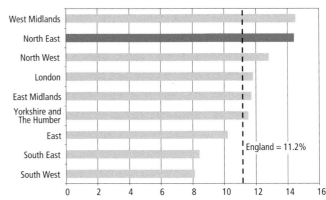

Source: Department for Business Innovation and Skills, from the Labour Force Survey, Office for National Statistics

highest English region after London and the South East, and the same as the England average (Online table 4.10).

In the second quarter of 2009 the proportion of the North East working-age population with no qualifications was 14 per cent – above the England average of 11 per cent and slightly below the West Midlands with the highest proportion, 15 per cent (Figure 2.9, Online table 4.14). However, among economically active working-age residents the proportion with no qualifications was only 9 per cent, the same as the England average.

In the second quarter of 2009 the proportion of the North East's working-age population qualified to National Qualifications Framework (NQF) level 4 and above (broadly degree level) was 24 per cent, the lowest proportion of any English region and below the UK average of 30 per cent (Online table 4.14). However, the proportion of economically active North East working-age residents with degree level qualifications in 2008 was 19 per cent, slightly closer to the UK average of 24 per cent, although still the lowest of the English regions and half that of the region with the largest proportion (38 per cent for London residents).

For those economically active and aged 20 to 24, the proportion qualified to degree level or equivalent or above in the North East in 2008 was 15 per cent, 4 percentage points below the England average of 19 per cent. There were similar gaps between the North East and England proportions at ages 25 to 29, 30 to 39, 40 to 49 and 50 to retirement age (currently 59 for women and 64 for men).

Labour market

In the North East, 69.0 per cent of working-age people were employed in the fourth quarter of 2009. This was the lowest rate of all English regions except London's 68.7 per cent, lower than Scotland but higher than Wales and Northern Ireland (Online table 1.1b). The UK average was 72.4 per cent in this quarter. Since the early 1990s, the UK average has been higher

Figure 2.10

Employment rate:[1] North East, 1992 Q4 to 2009 Q4[2]

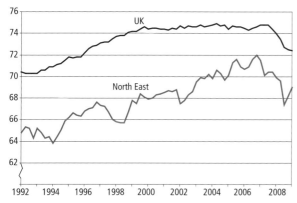

Percentages

1 Working age.
2 Seasonally adjusted, three monthly data.

Source: Labour Force Survey, Office for National Statistics

Figure 2.11

Claimant count: by sex, North East, January 2006 to January 2010

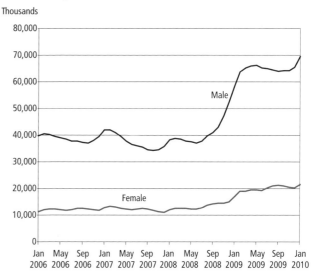

Thousands

Source: Office for National Statistics

than the North East by a margin that ranged from 8 percentage points in 1999 to 4 percentage points in 2009 (Figure 2.10).

Working-age employment rates within the region ranged from 62 per cent in Durham to 85 per cent in Chester-le-Street for the year ending June 2009. The regional average in this period was 70 per cent.

The unemployment rate for residents aged 16 and over in the North East was 9.3 per cent in the fourth quarter of 2009, similar to the West Midlands with 9.4 per cent – one of the highest among the regions of England and countries of the UK (Online table 1.1b). The UK rate was 7.8 per cent. Modelled unemployment rates for local authority districts in the region for the year ending June 2009 (when the unemployment rate for the North East was 8.8 per cent) ranged from 4.8 per cent in Alnwick to 11.0 per cent in Newcastle upon Tyne.

The Jobseeker's Allowance claimant count rate for residents aged 18 and over as a percentage of the estimated workforce in the region (seasonally adjusted) in April 2008 was 4.0 per cent, 1.5 percentage points higher than the UK average of 2.5 per cent. By October 2008 it was 5.0 per cent, 1.9 percentage points higher than the UK average of 3.1 per cent. The claimant count for males increased sharply from October 2008, with month-on-month percentage increases reaching over 10 per cent in November 2008 to January 2009, before starting to level off in March 2009. The claimant count for females showed lower increases until January and February 2009, when month-on-month increases exceeded 10 per cent, before levelling off (Figure 2.11).

In the fourth quarter of 2009, 23.7 per cent of working-age residents were economically inactive, more than the UK average of 21.3 per cent (Online table 1.1b). The North East had a higher proportion of working-age residents who were economically inactive than Scotland and any other English region except London. It was, however, below that of Northern Ireland.

The three main reasons for being economically inactive in the year ending June 2009 were long-term sick at 33 per cent, looking after their family or home at 26 per cent and students at 24 per cent (Figure 2.12). The proportion of working-age people who were economically inactive because of long-term sickness was higher than the UK average of 25 per cent and was the highest of all English regions. Inactivity rates by age in the North East were similar to that of the UK except for the 50 to 59/64 and 60/65 plus age groups, which were the highest of all English regions. Between 2004 and the fourth quarter of 2009, working-age economic inactivity rates in the North East dropped from 26 per cent to 24 per cent.

Median weekly gross earnings, including overtime, of full-time employees resident in the North East in April 2009 were £439, with £478 for men and £385 for women. UK median earnings

Figure 2.12

Reasons for economic inactivity:[1] North East, 2004 to 2009

Percentages

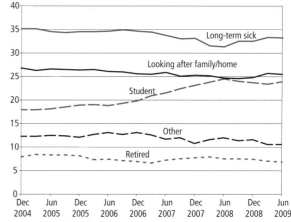

1 As a percentage of all working age economically inactive.

Source: Annual Population Survey, Office for National Statistics

were £489, with £531 for men and £426 for women (Online table 9.19). Men in the North East had the lowest weekly pay and full-time hourly earnings of any English region. Only Northern Ireland had lower weekly and hourly earnings for men. Women in the North East had the lowest median weekly gross earnings of any English region. Only Wales had lower median weekly gross earnings and women in the North East had the lowest full-time hourly earnings in the UK.

Economy and industry

The North East's economy generated £40.9 billion gross value added (GVA) in 2008, 3.2 per cent of UK total GVA (excluding extra-regio and statistical discrepancy) (Online table 3.1).

GVA per hour worked is the Office for National Statistics' preferred measure of productivity and takes into account factors such as commuting patterns and variations in hours worked. Figure 2.13 shows that GVA per hour worked in the North East was 90 per cent of the UK average in 2008, higher than Northern Ireland, Wales, North West, Yorkshire and The Humber and the West Midlands (Online table 3.2).

GVA per head in the North East was £15,900 per resident, 77 per cent of the UK average, in 2008. This was the lowest of all the English regions, and in the UK only Wales had a lower GVA per head in 2008 (Online table 3.3). Although both sub-regions (Map 2.2) produced GVA per head below the UK average in 2007, there was a marked difference between the two: Tees Valley and Durham with 69 per cent of the UK average and Northumberland and Tyne & Wear with 85 per cent (Online table 3.5). At a more local level (NUTS3 – see Reference Map on page 134), Hartlepool and Stockton-on-Tees' GVA per head relative to the UK fell from 92 per cent in 1997 to 74 per cent in 2007. Tyneside, which produced the largest GVA in the region with £14.9 billion in 2007, increased

Figure 2.13

Labour productivity: gross value added per hour worked, by region, 2008

UK = 100

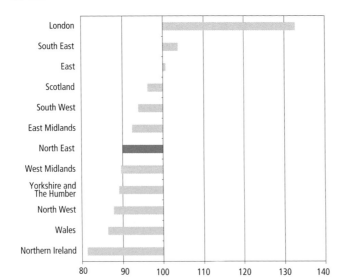

Source: Office for National Statistics

its GVA per head relative to the UK from 86 per cent in 1997 to 92 per cent in 2007.

In 2007, 17 per cent of the region's GVA was from manufacturing, more than the UK average of 13 per cent. The chemicals, chemical products and man-made fibres industry produced 22 per cent of the region's manufacturing GVA. Only 19 per cent of GVA was from real estate, renting and business activities, less than the UK average of 24 per cent (Online table 3.7).

Short-Term Employment Survey data show that in June 2009 the employment pattern in the North East was similar to that for GVA but the proportion of employee jobs in manufacturing was lower, at 12 per cent, and closer to the UK average of 10 per cent. The proportion of employee jobs in the public administration and defence industry group (8.0 per cent) was the highest of any English region and only Northern Ireland had a higher proportion (Online table 9.4).

Smaller geographies can be compared using the Annual Business Inquiry 2008. The data are for local authority districts that existed prior to April 2009. Figure 2.14 shows that Sedgefield and Derwentside had high proportions of manufacturing employment (28 and 25 per cent respectively). The proportion of manufacturing employment exceeded 20 per cent in three other authorities (Teesdale, Easington and Blyth Valley). Manufacturing employment within the region tends to be relatively specialised. For example, in Sunderland almost half of the 17,700 employees in manufacturing were in the motor vehicles, trailers and semi-trailers industry. Although the

Figure 2.14

Percentage employed in manufacturing:[1] by local authority,[2] North East, 2007

Percentages

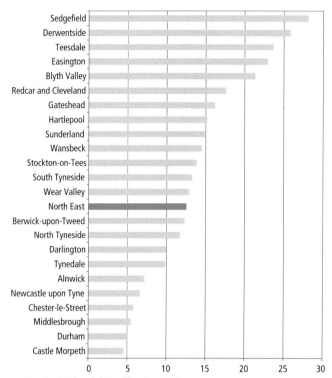

1 Standard Industrial Classification 2003.
2 Unitary authorities are pre-April 2009.

Source: Annual Business Inquiry, Office for National Statistics

proportion of manufacturing GVA produced by the chemicals industry in the North East in 2007 was over 20 per cent, only 10 per cent of employment was in that industry, concentrated around Stockton-on-Tees, and Redcar and Cleveland. A number of districts have large proportions of employees in public administration and defence, including Castle Morpeth, Durham and Newcastle upon Tyne, which all had in excess of

Figure 2.15

Business enterprise research and development expenditure as a proportion of gross value added: by region, 2007

Percentages

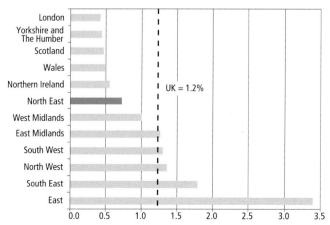

Source: Office for National Statistics

10 per cent employment in that sector. Wansbeck and Middlesbrough both had over 20 per cent of employment in the human health and social work industry.

Employment in the banking, insurance and business services industry in the North East was 15 per cent of the total. Just under one-quarter of total employment in that industry in the region was based in Newcastle upon Tyne. Within the region, the district with the lowest proportion of employment in the banking, insurance and business services industry was Castle Morpeth, with 6 per cent.

Although at a low level compared with other regions, the value of exports of goods by North East businesses (Online table 3.21) expressed as a percentage of GVA, 28 per cent, was the highest of all English regions in 2008. In comparison, the UK average was 19 per cent. Just under half of the North East's total exports of goods were of machinery and transport equipment and around one-third were of chemicals and chemical products.

Business enterprises in the North East spent £310 million on research and development (R&D) in 2007. Figure 2.15 shows that as a proportion of GVA (0.8 per cent) this was less than the UK average of 1.3 per cent but greater than that of London, Yorkshire and The Humber, Wales, Scotland and Northern Ireland (Online table 3.22).

In the North East, gross disposable household income (GDHI) per head of resident population was £12,200 in 2007, 85 per cent of the UK average and the lowest of any English region. It was also lower than Wales, Scotland and Northern Ireland (Online table 3.4). Within the North East, GDHI ranged from 80 per cent of the UK average in Sunderland to 99 per cent in Northumberland.

Disadvantage

According to the 2007 Index of Multiple Deprivation (IMD2007), 34 per cent of Lower Layer Super Output Areas (LSOAs) in the North East were in the most deprived quintile (20 per cent – Box 3) in England, the highest proportion of any English region (Figure 2.16). The North East also had the largest percentage of its population (34 per cent) living in LSOAs in the most deprived quintile in England. The North East had 10 per cent of its LSOAs in the least deprived quintile of England. Only London had a smaller proportion with 9 per cent.

Within the North East, the highest proportions of LSOAs in the most deprived quintile were in Easington with 65 per cent and Middlesbrough with 57 per cent (Figure 2.17). The highest proportions of LSOAs in the least deprived quintile were in Castle Morpeth with 33 per cent and Durham City with 31 per cent. Alnwick, Berwick-upon-Tweed and Tynedale had no LSOAs in the most deprived quintile.

More recently, estimates from the Labour Force Survey show that in the second quarter of 2009, 23 per cent of households in the North East were workless, higher than the other regions of England and higher than Scotland, Wales and Northern Ireland. The England and Great Britain averages were both 17 per cent.

Figure 2.16

Distribution of LSOA[1] rankings on the 2007 Index of Multiple Deprivation: by region

Percentages

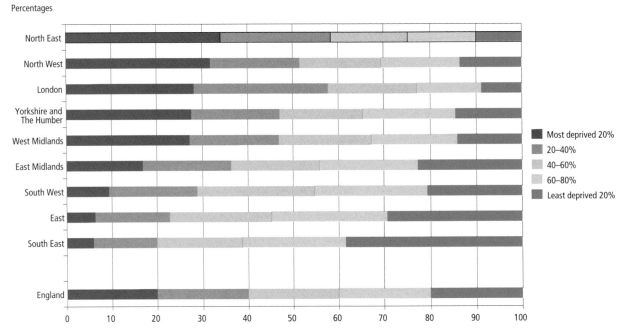

1 Local Layer Super Output Areas

Source: Communities and Local Government

Box 3: Index of Multiple Deprivation 2007

The Index of Multiple Deprivation (IMD) provides a summary measure of relative deprivation at Lower Layer Super Output Area (LSOA) level in England. The IMD aims to provide a nationally consistent measure of how deprived an area is by identifying the degree to which people are disadvantaged by factors such as low income, unemployment, lack of education, poor health, and crime. Particular points to note:

- not all deprived people live in deprived areas and conversely, not everyone living in a deprived area is deprived; the indicators identify areas with characteristics associated with deprivation – not deprived people

- the indices should not be used as a measure of affluence. A lack of income deprivation does not necessarily equate to affluence

The indices provide a relative measure of deprivation and therefore cannot be used to determine *how much* more deprived one LSOA is than another.

This article uses the rankings of all LSOAs in England, which have been divided into five equal-sized groups, or quintiles. In England, 20 per cent of LSOAs are in the most deprived quintile and 20 per cent in the least deprived quintile and so on. If an area (region or local authority) had the average distribution of deprivation they would have 20 per cent of LSOAs in each quintile.

For more information on the IMD see the article in **Regional Trends 41,** pages 93 to 114, and the Communities and Local Government website: www.communities.gov.uk/indices

Male life expectancy at birth in the North East was also among the lowest in England, similar to the North West and Northern Ireland but above Scotland. Male life expectancy at birth was 76.5 years in the North East compared with 77.5 years in the UK (Online table 6.8).

However, in the period between 1991–1993 and 2006–2008, life expectancy in the North East increased by 4.5 years for males and 3.2 years for females, more than Wales, Scotland, Northern Ireland and any other English region except London. The gap between female and male life expectancy at birth in the North East narrowed from 5.4 years in 1991–1993 to 4.1 years in 2006–2008, in line with the UK average.

Within the region, the highest life expectancy at birth for males was in Tynedale, with 79.6 years, while for females, it was in Berwick-upon-Tweed with 84.3, both in Northumberland. The lowest life expectancy at birth was in Hartlepool with 75.3 years for males and 79.0 years for females.

Age standardised mortality rates for the region show 657 deaths per 100,000 residents in 2008, compared with 592 for the UK. The North East's mortality rate was the highest of the English regions and higher than those of Wales and Northern Ireland but lower than that of Scotland. The North East in 2008 had the highest mortality rate for bronchitis and cancer of all English regions and countries of the UK (Online table 6.4). In the North East in 2008, death rates for ages up to 54 were similar to the UK average, but for both men and women aged 55 and over death rates exceeded the UK average. For males, the death rates for ages 65 and over were the highest of all English regions (Online table 10.10).

In 2007 the North East had the lowest proportions of men and women drinking alcohol on five or more days in the previous

Figure 2.17

Distribution of LSOA[1] rankings on the 2007 Index of Multiple Deprivation, for local authorities[2] in the North East

Percentages

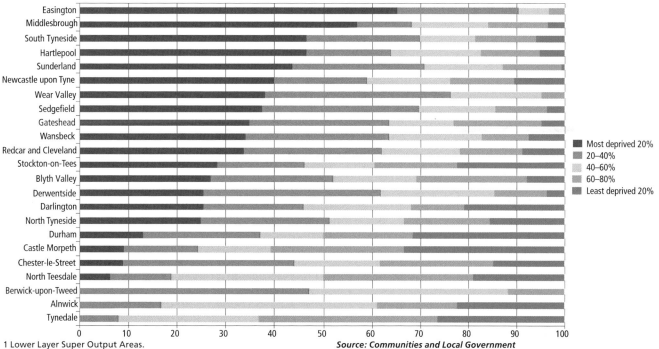

Legend:
- Most deprived 20%
- 20–40%
- 40–60%
- 60–80%
- Least deprived 20%

1 Lower Layer Super Output Areas.
2 Unitary authorities are pre-April 2009.

Source: Communities and Local Government

week of all English regions, at 18 and 9 per cent respectively, compared with the Great Britain averages of 22 and 12 per cent. Only Scotland had lower proportions. The proportion of men in the North East who drank more than four units on at least one day in the week was above the GB average but the proportion drinking more than eight units was below the average. The proportion of women in the North East drinking more than three units on at least one day in the week and the proportion of women drinking more than six units were both below the GB averages (Online table 6.15, Figure 2.19).

Figure 2.18

Difference in life expectancy at birth between the regions and the UK average, 2006 to 2008

Years

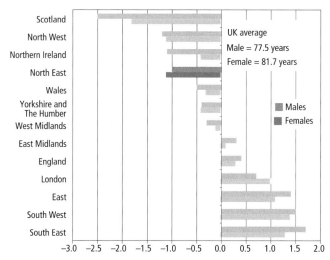

UK average
Male = 77.5 years
Female = 81.7 years

Legend:
- Males
- Females

Source: Office for National Statistics

Over one-fifth of North East men smoked cigarettes in 2007, just below the Great Britain average of 22 per cent. Among women, 22 per cent smoked cigarettes, just over the Great Britain average of 20 per cent. The North East had the highest proportion of any English region of men smoking 20 or more cigarettes per day, 9 per cent, and only Northern Ireland had a higher proportion, at 11 per cent. The proportion of women smoking 20 or more cigarettes per day was the highest of any English region or UK country (Online table 6.14).

In common with the North West and Yorkshire and The Humber, in 2008/09 around 10 per cent of 16 to 24-year-olds had used class A drugs, compared with the England average of 8 per cent and the Wales average of 9 per cent (Online table 6.16).

There were 2,400 conceptions in 2008 to women aged under 18 in the region. The under-18 conception rate was 49 per 1,000 women aged 15 to 17, the highest rate amongst the English regions, compared with the England average of 40. The proportion of under-18 conceptions that led to a legal abortion was 42 per cent, the lowest of all English regions and well below the England average of 50 per cent (Online table 10.12).

The North East had an infant mortality (deaths under one year of age) rate of 4.2 per 1,000 in 2008 (Online table 6.3), below the UK average of 4.7. The North East region's proportion of live births weighing under 2.5 kg in 2008 was 7.6 per cent, slightly above the England average, 7.2 per cent, similar to that of Wales (birth weights are not collected at registration by Scotland and Northern Ireland) and below the English region with the highest rate, West Midlands, 8.5 per cent (Online table 6.2).

Figure 2.19

Alcohol drunk on 5 or more days in week, men and women aged 16 or over: by region, 2007

Units of alcohol

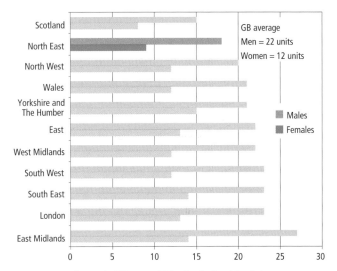

GB average
Men = 22 units
Women = 12 units

Source: General Household Survey, Office for National Statistics

Transport

The average distance travelled per person per year in the North East by all modes of transport during 2007 to 2008 was relatively low at 6,400 miles. This was the same as the North West and, within Great Britain, higher than only London, which had the lowest distance travelled, 5,300 miles per person per year. Average mileage in cars and other private road vehicles was 5,250 miles per person per year, or 82 per cent of travel by all modes. Around 14 per cent of the average distance travelled

per person in the North East was by public transport, close to the Great Britain average of 15 per cent (Online table 11.4). Only the South West, Wales and Scotland had lower average daily motor vehicle flows on major roads than the North East's 17,100 vehicles per day in 2008 (Online table 11.11).

The usual method of travelling to work for 76 per cent of residents in the fourth quarter of 2008 was a car, van or minibus (Figure 2.20). An estimated 10 per cent of North East residents walked to work (Online table 11.7). Both figures are similar to other English regions, with the exception of London where only 35 per cent of residents used a car, van or minibus.

The proportion of 5 to 16-year-olds resident in the region that walked to school in 2007 to 2008 was 59 per cent, higher than the Great Britain average of 45 per cent. The average journey length to school was 1.0 miles for 5 to 10-year-olds (lower than the Great Britain average of 1.6 miles) and 2.2 miles for 11 to 16-year-olds (lower than the Great Britain average of 3.2 miles) (Online table 11.8).

Environment

National Park land in the North East amounts to 1,110 sq km. This represents 13 per cent of the region's land area, compared with a UK figure of 8 per cent. A further 17 per cent of the region's land is designated as an Area of Outstanding Natural Beauty (AONB), compared with only 13 per cent for the UK (Online table 5.8).

The original Northumbria region designated by the National Rivers Authority (now part of the Environment Agency (EA)) had a long-term average annual rainfall of 831 millimetres

Figure 2.20

Usual method of travel to work: by region of residence, 2008 Q4

Percentages

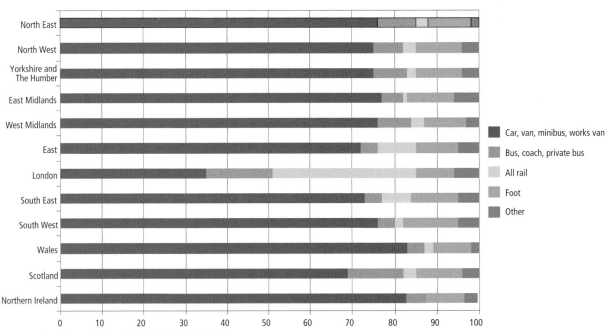

- Car, van, minibus, works van
- Bus, coach, private bus
- All rail
- Foot
- Other

Source: Labour Force Survey, Office for National Statistics

Figure 2.21

CO$_2$ emissions per resident: by region, 2007

Tonnes per resident

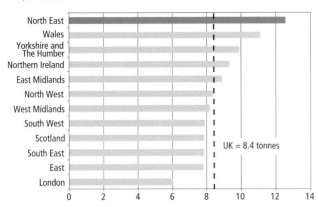

Source: Department of Energy and Climate Change

between 1971 and 2000. This was lower than the UK average of 1,084 millimetres but very similar to the England average (819mm) and less than the North West, South West, Wales, Scotland and Northern Ireland, which each had over 1,000 mm. In 2008, annual rainfall in the North East was 34 per cent higher than the 1971 to 2000 average, a larger differential than any other NRA region, Wales, Scotland or Northern Ireland (Online table 5.1).

Although floods in Chester-le-Street, North Tyneside, Darlington, Morpeth, and Rothbury in 2007 and 2008 caused severe damage, a National Assessment of Flood Risk by the EA found that, in terms of the number of properties at risk and the number of people living in floodplains, the North East was the English region least at risk from flooding.

In 2007 the biological quality of 49 per cent of rivers and canals in the North East EA Region (see map on page 139) was classified as good (based on the River Invertebrate Prediction and Classification System (RIVPACS)), compared with an England average of 40 per cent. Also, the chemical quality of 68 per cent of rivers and canals in the North East EA Region were classified as good (based on the General Quality Assessment (GQA) Scheme), compared with the England average of 52 per cent (Online table 5.5).

The North East produced 12.6 tonnes of carbon dioxide per resident in 2007 compared with the UK average of 8.4 tonnes, the highest of all the English regions and above Wales (11.1 tonnes per resident), Scotland (7.9 tonnes per resident) and Northern Ireland (9.3 tonnes per resident) (Figure 2.21, Online table 5.15). The industrial and commercial sector was responsible for 21,100 kilotonnes (66 per cent) of the North East region's 32,200 kilotonnes total CO$_2$ emissions. The highest levels for this sector were in the local authorities of Redcar and Cleveland with 8,200 kilotonnes and in Stockton-on-Tees and Wansbeck, both with 3,200 kilotonnes. These areas have a significant manufacturing base, including the production and recycling of base metals.

In 2007/08 the North East recycled 28 per cent of household waste. This was the second lowest English region after London

(26 per cent), lower than the England average of 35 per cent. However, in 2007/08, the North East recycled more than double the percentage recycled in 2003/04 (Online table 5.11).

Crime and justice

British Crime Survey (BCS) data show that the North East household crime rate of 3,300 per 10,000 households in 2007/08 was the highest of all English regions, above the England average of 2,700 per 10,000 (Figure 2.22). The proportion of the North East population victimised at least once by violent crime was 4.7 per cent, the highest of all English regions, above the England average of 3.2 per cent (Online tables 2.1 and 2.2).

Recorded crime figures for 2008/09 show a rate of 8,000 recorded crimes per 100,000 population for the North East, well below the highest English region, London, with 11,200 per 100,000 population, and lower than the England average of 8,600 per 100,000 population. With 2,100 recorded instances of criminal damage per 100,000 population in 2008/09, the North East had the highest rate of all English regions, more than the England average of 1,700. On the other hand, the North East had the lowest rate of recorded instances of robbery in England, with 50 per 100,000 population, compared with the England average of 150. The region also had the lowest rate of fraud and forgery, with 180 instances per 100,000 population, compared with the England average of 300 (Online table 2.3).

The BCS does not provide results at local authority level but the recorded crime figures include a set of BCS comparator offences for 2008/09 which covers about 60 per cent of all recorded crimes and allows differences at a local level to be highlighted. Within the North East, Middlesbrough had the highest rates of BCS comparator offences across all categories and in total with 85 per 1,000 population, whereas Teesdale had the lowest rate of recorded crime, with 15 BCS comparator offences per 1,000 population (Online table 2.4).

Figure 2.22

Crimes committed against households: by region, 2007/08

Rate per 10,000 households

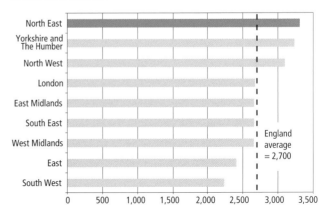

Source: British Crime Survey, Home Office

1

Detection rates in the North East in 2008/09 were the highest among the English regions across all categories, with 37 per cent in total (the ratio of offences cleared up in the year to offences recorded in the year) compared with the England average of 28 per cent (Online table 2.5).

Rates of conviction in the North East were among the highest of all English regions, with 1,700 per 100,000 population in the 10 to 17 age group, compared with an England average of 1,200. Furthermore, for the 18 and over age group, the rate of conviction in the North East was 900 per 100,000 population, compared with the England average of 700 (Online table 2.8).

Immediate custodial sentences in 2007 comprised 6 per cent of outcomes for men and 2 per cent for women, both below the England averages of 8 per cent and 3 per cent respectively. Of those immediate custodial sentences, 67 per cent for men and

76 per cent for women were for a year or less, both less than for England at 71 and 81 per cent respectively (Online tables 2.9 and 2.10).

The number of Anti-Social Behaviour Orders issued by courts in the North East has dropped from 268 in 2005 to 122 in 2007. In common with other areas of England there has been a move away from ASBOs to using other tools and judicial powers. However, at 54 per cent, this was the largest percentage fall of any English region (Online table 2.6).

The March 2009 police service strength of 7,500 officers on ordinary duty corresponded to one officer to 350 people in the region. This was fewer residents per police officer than the England average of 380. The North East also had a smaller ratio of special constables than the England average, 58 per 1,000 police officers compared with 99 per 1,000 across England (Online table 2.13).

Portrait of the South West

by Eddie Smith, Office for National Statistics

Key points

The South West region:

- is the largest English region in terms of area

- has more people living in villages, hamlets and isolated dwellings than in any other English region – almost one in five of the region's total population

- includes more than a quarter of the land within National Parks or Areas of Outstanding Natural Beauty in England

- has the highest proportion of people of state pension age and above

- includes more second homes than any other English region

- has a smaller proportion of working-age people without qualifications than any other region

- has among the highest proportions of self-employed workers, part-time workers and people with more than one job

- has the largest hotels and restaurants sector in the UK, in terms of percentage of both employment and GVA and receives more domestic tourists than any other UK region or country

- has highest regional life expectancy at birth for females and second highest for males

- receives the highest average annual rainfall in England and the largest proportion of rain falling in winter months

Eddie Smith is Regional Analyst for the South West
Tel: 01392 229186
Email: eddie.smith@ons.gsi.gov.uk

Introduction

The South West region is the largest in England, with 18 per cent of the total area (Online table 1.2), and is also bigger in area than both Wales and Northern Ireland. It includes the most southerly and westerly points in England and is bordered by Wales, the West Midlands and the South East. It has the longest coastline of any English region, 638 km of which is defined as heritage coast (Online table 5.8).

The largest conurbations in the region are Bristol, Bournemouth/Poole and Plymouth which have estimated populations, respectively, of over 600,000, 350,000 and 250,000.[1] Administratively, the region includes four counties (Devon, Dorset, Gloucestershire and Somerset) that contain 25 districts, most of which are rural. Two new unitary authorities (UAs – Cornwall and Wiltshire) were created in 2009 from former counties. There are 10 further UAs that centre on many of the region's largest towns and cities but also include the smallest local authority in the UK – the Isles of Scilly.

Over five million people live in the region (Online table 1.2). Although not the largest region on this basis, it has a population slightly above that of Scotland, more than that of Wales and Northern Ireland combined, and just over a tenth of the total for England. About a third of the region's population (1.7 million) live in settlements of less than 10,000 people, the largest proportion in England. Almost a million of these live in villages, hamlets and isolated dwellings, more than in any other English region. The region's population grew faster than that of the whole UK between 2003 and 2008, with nearly all of the growth due to in-migration rather than natural change.

More than 22 per cent of the South West population (almost 1.2 million people) is of state pension age and above (as defined in 2008), the largest proportion of any UK region (Online table 10.3). Between 2003 and 2008 the number of people in this age group in the South West grew at more than twice the rate of overall population growth. The region has the lowest percentage of working-age people in England but this disguises a relatively large population of those aged 50 to state pension age, only the North East has a higher proportion.

Note:
Unless otherwise stated the data used in this article were those available at the time of writing. In particular, mid-year population estimates were those released in August 2009.

---

1 Urban Area population data from mid-2008 Lower Layer Super Output Area population estimates aggregated to best fit 2001 Census Urban Area boundaries

Map 3.1 **South West: physical features**

Key

National Parks

Areas of Outstanding Natural Beauty

Woodland

Relief (metres)

600

200

0

1 The Cotswolds
2 Mendip Hills
3 North Wessex Downs
4 Quantock Hills
5 Blackdown Hills
6 Cranborne Chase & West Wiltshire Downs
7 Dorset
8 East Devon
9 South Devon
10 Bodmin Moor
11 Tamar
12 North Devon
13 Cornwall
14 Isles of Scilly

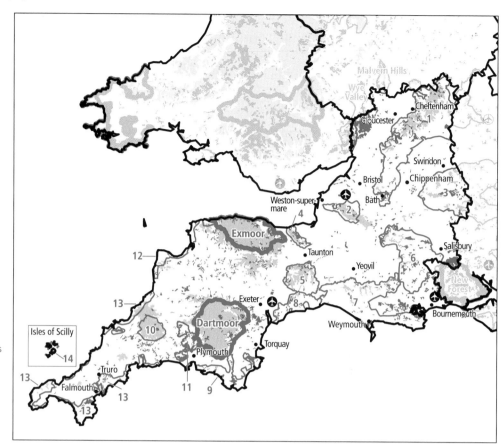

Map 3.2 **South West: local or unitary authority, NUTS 2[1] sub-regions and Rural/Urban Definition[2]**

Regional boundary

NUTS 2 boundary

Local or unitary authority[3] boundary

Rural/Urban Definition

Urban population over 10,000 −Less Sparse

Urban population over 10,000 −Sparse

Town and Fringe−Less Sparse

Town and Fringe−Sparse

Village, Hamlet and Isolated Dwellings−Less Sparse

Village, Hamlet and Isolated Dwellings−Sparse

1 Forest of Dean
2 Tewkesbury
3 Gloucester
4 Cheltenham
5 South Gloucestershire UA
6 Swindon UA
7 City of Bristol UA
8 North Somerset UA
9 Bath and North East Somerset UA
10 West Wiltshire
11 Poole UA
12 Bournemouth UA
13 Christchurch
14 Restormel

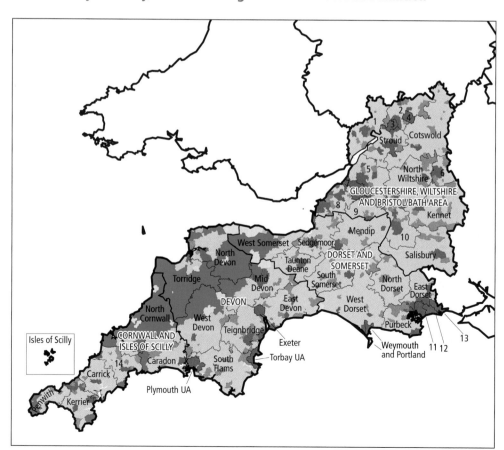

1 Nomenclature of Units for Territorial Statistics, level 2.
2 By Lower Layer Super Output Area.
3 Prior to April 2009.

The South West contains two national parks, Dartmoor and Exmoor. It also includes 35 per cent of the land that lies within Areas of Outstanding Natural Beauty in England and 60 per cent of the Heritage Coast. There are almost a thousand Sites of Special Scientific Interest and four World Heritage Sites. According to the latest long-term climate data, the region had the highest average annual rainfall in England between 1971 and 2000 and the largest proportion of rainfall in winter months (Online tables 5.1 and 5.2). The Environment Agency estimates that more than 86,000 South West properties are at significant risk of flooding from rivers or the sea, 18 per cent of the total in England.

Service industries are responsible for about four out of every five employee jobs in the South West and three-quarters of gross value added. The hotels and restaurants sector makes a relatively larger contribution to the region's economy than in any other region or country of the UK.

The South West receives more domestic tourists than any other UK region or country, with more than a fifth of the UK total number of tourist nights being spent there. The region also has the fourth highest number of nights spent by overseas tourists. Tourists spent £4,600 million in the South West in 2007 and nearly one in ten of the region's jobs were tourism related. In 2008 the most popular paid attractions in the region were the Eden Project in Cornwall, Stonehenge in Wiltshire and the Roman Baths in Bath. Among UK towns and cities, Bristol had the seventh highest number of visits from overseas residents while Bath, Bournemouth and Plymouth were ranked 14th, 25th and 28th respectively.

Among UK regions, the South West has higher than average rates of employment and economic activity and one of the lowest unemployment rates. The patterns of working also differ from elsewhere. No other region has a higher proportion of part-time workers or of workers with a second job and only London has a higher percentage of self-employed workers.

The north and east of the region is intersected by two major motorways, the M4 and M5, which meet to the north of Bristol, with the latter ending at Exeter. However, large parts of the South West are not served by motorways, including two of the three most populous urban areas (Bournemouth/Poole and Plymouth) and the largest unitary authority (Cornwall). Despite being in the south of England, the region includes places that are as distant from London and the South East as many in the north of England: The third largest settlement, Plymouth, is further from London by road than York, while Penzance in Cornwall is the same distance away as Carlisle.

Population

In 2008 the estimated population of the South West was 5.2 million, about 8.5 per cent of the population of the UK. This was the seventh largest among the 12 UK regions, with marginally more than Scotland and almost half a million more than Wales and Northern Ireland combined (Online table 1.2).

Figure 3.3 shows the mid-2008 population of all 16 South West counties and unitary authorities as defined from April 2009. Among these, the counties of Devon (755,000) and Gloucestershire (583,000) had the largest populations. The Isles of Scilly (2,100) had the smallest population of any local authority in the UK. The two new UAs created in the region in 2009 (Cornwall and Wiltshire) were among the 10 most populous UAs in England, together with Bristol.

The mid-2008 populations of the region's districts ranged from 36,000 in West Somerset to 159,000 in South Somerset. West Somerset, Christchurch (45,800) and Purbeck (46,000) have the lowest populations of the 201 post-April 2009 English lower tier authorities. South Somerset, on the other hand, has the 12th largest population, with more people than Poole and Torbay UAs.

The South West's population density in 2008 was 219 people per sq km, compared with the UK and England densities of 253 and 395, respectively. The figure is the lowest among English regions, but above that of Scotland, Northern Ireland and Wales. Among South West counties and unitary authorities, the population density ranges from 115 per sq km in Devon to 3,830 in Bristol. The former has the seventh lowest population density in England but there are 34 English unitary authorities that are more densely populated than Bristol.

In mid-2008, 33 per cent of the South West population (1.7 million) lived in rural settlements according to the Rural/Urban Definition defined at LSOA level, the largest proportion among the nine English regions. This includes almost 20 per cent who lived in villages, hamlets or isolated dwellings, again the highest percentage in England.

Five of the 45 pre-2009 districts and UAs in the South West are classified according to the LA Classification, as Large Urban

Figure 3.3

Population: by county and unitary authority, South West, mid-2008

Mid-2008 population (thousands)

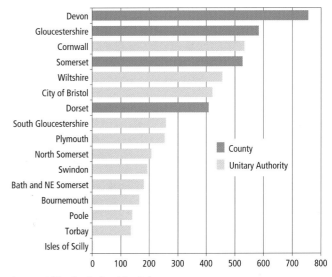

Source: Office for National Statistics

(Bristol, South Gloucestershire, Bournemouth, Poole and Christchurch). In 2008 these contained about 20 per cent of the region's population while a further 19 per cent lived within the seven authorities classified as Other Urban (Cheltenham, Exeter, Gloucester, Plymouth, Swindon, Torbay, and Weymouth and Portland). The remaining 61 per cent of people in the South West lived in Rural or Significant Rural authorities; the largest proportion of any English region.

ONS used 2001 Census data to classify each LSOA by its characteristics into one of seven 'supergroups'.[2] In mid-2008, 28 per cent of the South West population lived in an area classified as 'countryside', the highest percentage among the English regions. A further 24 per cent and 23 per cent respectively lived in 'White Collar Urban' and 'Miscellaneous Built Up' areas. The 20 subdivisions of these classifications ('groups') suggest that, in 2008, the South West had the highest proportions among English regions of people living in areas defined as 'Rural Economies', 'Small Town Communities' and 'Resorts and Retirement' and the second highest percentage in 'Educational Centres'.

---

2   Information about the National Statistics 2001 Area Classification is available via: www.statistics.gov.uk/about/methodology_by_theme/ area_classification/default.asp

In the five years to mid-2008, the region's population grew by 4.1 per cent, the fourth largest growth rate of the 12 UK regions (Online table 1.2). Among the 45 pre-2009 South West districts and UAs, percentage growth was highest in Exeter (9.8 per cent), Mid Devon (7.4 per cent), North Somerset (7.2 per cent) and Bristol (7.1 per cent). The Isles of Scilly was the only one of the 45 where population did not grow in this period (it remained unchanged). In the other South West districts and UAs, percentage growth was lowest in West Somerset, Salisbury (both 0.3 per cent) and Bournemouth (0.9 per cent).

Map 3.4 classifies South West districts and UAs relative to all such areas in England. (See also Map 7.1 on page 113).

Between mid-2007 and mid-2008 the South West population grew by 31,300 or 0.6 per cent (Online table 10.8). This was a similar percentage change to the UK average. Most of this population growth (24,900 or 0.5 per cent) was due to net migration and other changes. This was the third highest percentage change among UK regions. The population change of 0.1 per cent due to natural change (births minus deaths) was one of the lowest.

Figure 3.5 shows the components of population change (in percentage terms) in the year to mid-2008 for South West county and unitary authorities. Swindon, Bath & North East

Map 3.4   Percentage change in population by local or unitary authority,[1] 2003 to 2008

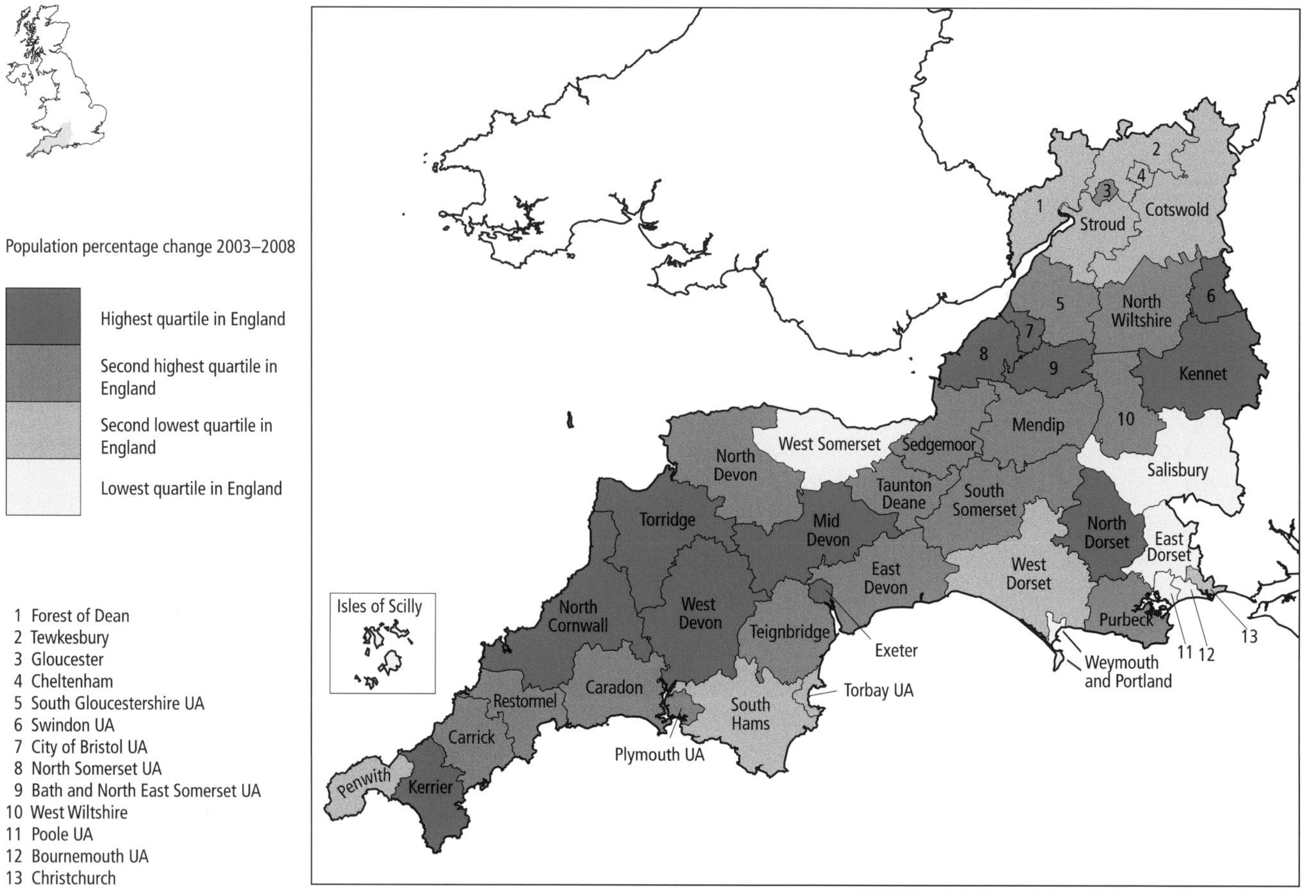

Population percentage change 2003–2008

- Highest quartile in England
- Second highest quartile in England
- Second lowest quartile in England
- Lowest quartile in England

1 Forest of Dean
2 Tewkesbury
3 Gloucester
4 Cheltenham
5 South Gloucestershire UA
6 Swindon UA
7 City of Bristol UA
8 North Somerset UA
9 Bath and North East Somerset UA
10 West Wiltshire
11 Poole UA
12 Bournemouth UA
13 Christchurch

1 Unitary authorities in 2008

Source: Office for National Statistics

Figure 3.5

Components of population change: by county and unitary authority, South West, mid-2007 to mid-2008

Percentages

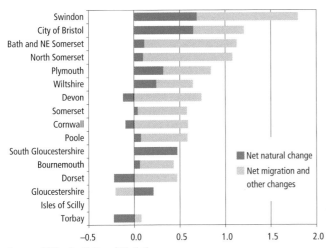

Source: Office for National Statistics

Somerset and North Somerset were 3 of the 10 English upper tier authorities with the highest increases in population due to migration and other changes, while Torbay, Dorset, Devon and Cornwall were 4 of the 10 with the biggest decreases due to natural population change.

Recent population increase in the South West due to migration has largely been a result of internal migration (from elsewhere in the UK) rather than international migration. In fact, in the year to mid-2008, estimates suggest slightly more international migration out of the South West than into it. Figure 3.6 shows net migration into the South West by UK region between mid-2007 and mid-2008 and illustrates the impact of people moving from the South East.

The 2006-based population projections provide an estimation of future population growth if recent trends continue. These

Figure 3.6

Net internal migration into the South West: by region of origin, mid-2007 to mid-2008

Thousands

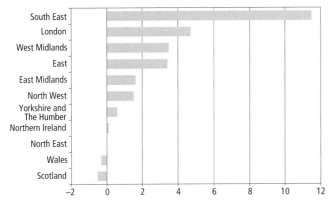

Source: National Health Service Central Register; General Register Office for Scotland; Northern Ireland Statistics and Research Agency

project that by 2026 the South West will have over 6.1 million residents, an increase of 20 per cent on the 2006 population, the third highest percentage change among the English regions. Within the region, the Isles of Scilly, Exeter, Torridge and North Somerset are projected to have the largest percentage changes in population, over 32 per cent.

The population of the South West has an older age structure than that of the UK average, as the mid-2008 population pyramid in Figure 3.7 indicates. The differences are most noticeable in the 25 to 34-year-old age groups where the national proportions are almost one percentage point higher than those of the South West and among 60 to 69-year-olds where the reverse is true.

The South West had the highest proportion (over 22 per cent) of people of state pension age and above (as defined in 2008 – see Glossary) among the nine English regions. Almost 1.2 million people were in this age group in 2008, the third highest regional total. The proportions of children and working-age people (18 and 60 per cent respectively) were the lowest of any English region, but the latter figure hides the fact that the South West had the second highest proportion of people aged 50 to retirement age (after the North East) in 2008.

Figure 3.7

Mid-year population estimates: by five-year age band and sex, South West, 2008

Percentages

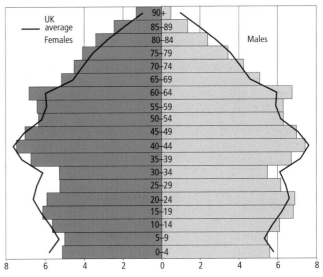

Source: Office for National Statistics

Within the region, the South West includes 7 of the 11 English counties and UAs with the highest proportions of people of retirement age and above in 2008. Dorset and the Isles of Scilly (almost 29 and over 27 per cent) had the highest proportions in England. Torbay (27 per cent) had the largest percentage of any urban UA. At district level, Christchurch and West Somerset were the only authorities in England where more than a third of the population were in this age group. Among South West counties and UAs, Bristol and Plymouth had the largest proportion of their population of working-age, while Swindon and Wiltshire had the largest percentage of children.

Population projections suggest that, based on trends and incorporating planned changes to the state pension age, the working-age population in the region in 2026 will have grown by almost 610,000 or 20 per cent. The number of children will be 130,000 or 14 per cent higher and there will be 280,000 more people of pension age and above, a rise of 25 per cent.

According to mid-2007 experimental estimates by ethnicity, people from non-White ethnic groups made up 5 per cent of the region's population. This was the second lowest of all the English regions; only the North East had a similar proportion. Asian or Asian British people were the largest non-White ethnic group in the region with almost 2 per cent of the total population but this is a smaller proportion than the 3 per cent of South West people describing themselves as 'White – other' (that is, White, non-British and non-Irish). More than one-fifth of the non-White population of the South West lived in the City of Bristol UA, despite the fact that it had only 8 per cent of the region's total population. Bristol contained a quarter of the people in the region who considered themselves Black or Black British and almost a quarter of those who were Asian or Asian British. However, almost half of England's other UAs have higher percentages of people of a non-White ethnicity than Bristol.

According to the Annual Population Survey, in the year to June 2009, around 94 per cent of the population of the South West were born in the UK, the second highest proportion among the English regions behind the North East. The survey suggests that more South West residents were born in Germany and Poland than in any other foreign country, the former mainly due to the large number of families of armed forces personnel in the region.

Households and housing

There were an estimated 2.2 million households in the South West in 2006 (Online table 10.15), approximately 10 per cent of the total in England. The average household size was 2.26 people, the joint lowest (with the North East) among the nine English regions.

Approximately 46 per cent of South West households contained a married couple, while 31 per cent were one-person households. Both of these proportions were the fourth highest among the nine English regions and close to the England average (44 per cent and 32 per cent).

About 10 per cent of South West households consisted of a cohabiting couple and 6 per cent were lone parent households.

The total number of households in the South West is expected to reach almost 2.9 million in 2026, according to projections based on mid-2006 data. This is equivalent to a 29 per cent increase over the preceding 20 years, the second largest change among English regions in percentage terms. The increase reflects the projected 20 per cent growth in the region's population during this period combined with the expected fall in the average South West household size to 2.10.

Figure 3.8 illustrates actual and projected changes in the number of households in the region between 2001 and 2026

broken down by type. It particularly highlights the fact that the number of one-person households is projected to overtake the number of married couple households towards the end of this period.

In 2007 there were 2.3 million dwellings in the South West (Online table 7.1). This stock of dwellings grew by 5.2 per cent between 2002 and 2007, the highest rise of any English region. Almost three-quarters of this stock was owner-occupied; one of the highest proportions of any region, while 14 per cent were privately rented or with a job or business, the highest percentage outside London. The remaining 13 per cent were rented from registered social landlords or local authorities, the smallest proportion in England (Online table 7.3).

Although the proportion of houses or bungalows was fairly typical, the South West had a larger proportion of detached houses and bungalows (29 per cent of total housing stock) than the England average (22 per cent). The region had the second lowest percentage of purpose-built flats or maisonettes (8 per cent) but the second largest proportion of flats created by conversions (5 per cent).

In 2008/09, 16,800 dwellings were completed in the South West, the lowest number since 2003/04 and 11 per cent less than in 2007/08, although all but one of the other English regions had even larger percentage decreases. The number of completions for the private sector in the region (13,700) was at its lowest level since 2000/01 but completions for registered social landlords (3,100) had increased in each of the most recent five years, with the largest increases coming in the latest two.

The median house price in the South West in 2008 was £185,000, compared with the England average of £174,000. The regional median in 2008 was 3 per cent less than in 2007 (Online table 7.4) and more up-to-date data indicate that in the third quarter of 2009, it was £180,000, 4 per cent below that of the same period a year earlier. In 2008, 38 of the 45 pre-2009

Figure 3.8

Household estimates¹ and projections: by household type, South West, 2001–2026

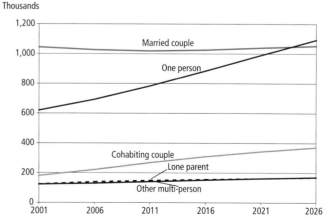

1 Estimates from 2001 to 2006 are based on ONS mid-year population estimates and projected rates of household formation from trends in Census and Labour Force Survey data. Projections are 2006-based.

Source: Communities and Local Government

districts and UAs in the region had a median house price above the English equivalent. None were within the lowest quarter of English local authorities for median house prices.

A common indicator of housing affordability compares house prices towards the lower end of the range (lower quartile) with lower quartile earnings of workers in the area (Box 1). On this measure, in 2009 lower quartile houses and flats in the South West, like those in the South East, were slightly more affordable to local workers than London houses and flats were to workers in London on lower quartile earnings. Lower quartile house prices in the South West and the South East were 7.6 and 7.7 times the lower quartile for earnings, respectively, compared with a ratio of 8.0 in London. This contrasted with ratios of 5.8 or below in the five northern and midland regions of England.

As Map 3.9 illustrates, the South West has more than its share of local authority districts with high house prices relative to earnings. In 15 of the South West's 37 post-2009 districts and UAs the lower quartile house price ratio was among the highest 25 per cent of ratios found in English local authorities. Two of these, East Dorset (11.2) and Cotswold (10.9), were among the 10 authorities in England with the highest ratios.

Box 1: Measuring housing affordability

An important indicator of housing affordability is the ratio of lower quartile house prices to lower quartile incomes.

The lower quartile value for a particular area is determined by ranking all prices or incomes in ascending order and identifying the value below which 25 per cent fall.

The statistics used for lower quartile income are workplace-based annual full-time individual earnings from the Annual Survey of Hours and Earnings (ASHE). The ASHE is based on a 1 per cent sample of employee jobs in April of a given year. It does not cover the self-employed, nor does it cover employees not paid during the reference period.

Lower quartile house prices are based on Land Registry data for the first two quarters of a given year. Each ratio is calculated by dividing the house price by income. Data for local authorities in England and Wales can be accessed on the Communities and Local Government (CLG) website:

www.communities.gov.uk/housing/housingresearch/ housingstatistics/housingstatisticsby/housingmarket/livetables/

Map 3.9 **Ratio[1] of lower quartile house price to lower quartile earnings by local or unitary authority,[2] 2009**

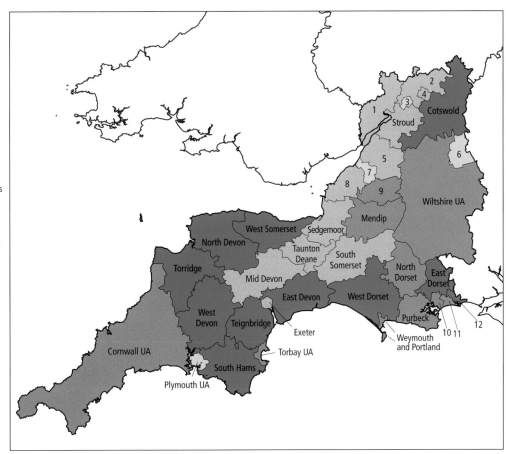

Lower quartile house price ratio[3]

- Highest 20% of ratios in England
- Second highest 20% of ratios in England
- Middle 20% of ratios in England
- Second lowest 20% of ratios in England
- Lowest 20% of ratios in England

1 Forest of Dean
2 Tewkesbury
3 Gloucester
4 Cheltenham
5 South Gloucestershire UA
6 Swindon UA
7 City of Bristol UA
8 North Somerset UA
9 Bath and North East Somerset UA
10 Poole UA
11 Bournemouth UA
12 Christchurch

1 See Box 1. A higher ratio means less affordable house prices.
2 Unitary authorities in 2009. No data available for Isles of Scilly.
3 There were no local authorities in the South West in 2009 with a lower quartile house price ratio in the lowest 20 per cent of these ratios across England.

Source: Annual Survey of Hours and Earnings (Office for National Statistics); Communities and Local Government; HM Land Registry

1

Figure 3.10

Second homes: by region,¹ average 2005/06 to 2007/08
Thousands

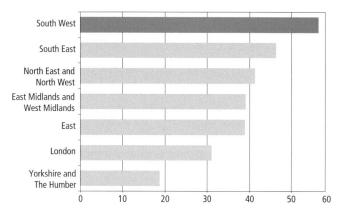

1 Not all regions can be shown separately due to small sample sizes.

Source: Survey of English Housing, Communities and Local Government

Figure 3.10 shows the number of second homes in England in 2005/06 to 2007/08 by location. This is based on data from the Survey of English Housing and includes information for seven areas, with some regions combined. The South West, with an estimated 57,000 second homes, had the highest of any of the seven areas. In total, some 21 per cent of all second homes in England were in the region, despite the fact that it had only 11 per cent of the total number of dwellings.

Information produced from local authority (LA) council tax systems gives an indication of the proportion of dwellings in an area that are second homes, although totals are not available for all councils. These statistics suggest that 2 per cent of

dwellings in the South West were second homes in 2008, the highest proportion of any English region. Within the region, of the 36 district and UAs for which data are available, South Hams (10 per cent) and North Cornwall (9 per cent) had the highest proportions of second homes.

Education and Skills

The proportion of Key Stage 4 pupils who achieved five or more GCSEs at grades A* to C or equivalent in 2008/09 was lower in the South West maintained schools sector than in any other English region, 67.9 per cent compared with the England average of 70.0 per cent. However, the differences between English regions were small. The region also had the joint lowest percentage of pupils not getting any GCSE passes (1.1 per cent). Within the South West, excluding the Isles of Scilly (with only 15 pupils), the proportion of pupils achieving 5 or more GCSEs at grades A* to C ranged from 76 per cent in Bath and North East Somerset to 62 per cent in Swindon and Bristol.

The proportions of 16 and 17-year-olds participating in post-compulsory full-time education and government-supported training in the South West (83 per cent and 71 per cent respectively in 2006/07) were similar to the England average of 84 and 72 per cent (Online table 4.10).

In 2009 the proportion of the South West's working-age population that had no qualifications was lower than in any other English region; just over 8 per cent compared with the England average of 11 per cent (Figure 3.11 and Online table 4.14). The region had the third highest proportion of working-age people with qualifications at National Qualifications Framework (NQF) Level 3 (see Glossary) and above, 51 per cent

Figure 3.11

Population of working age:¹ by level of highest qualification,² 2009 Q2
Percentages

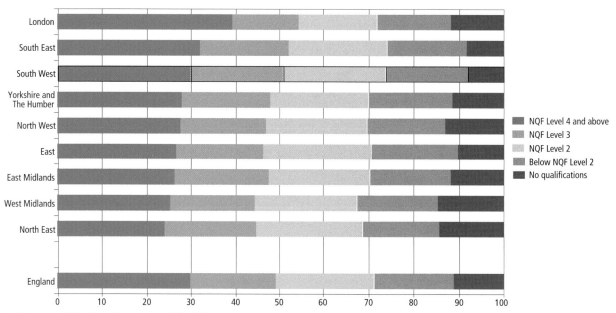

1 Males aged 16 to 64 and females aged 16 to 59.
2 For information on the National Qualifications Framework (NQF) equivalent level qualifications see Glossary.

Source: Department for Business Innovation and Skills, from the Labour Force Survey, Office for National Statistics

compared with 49 per cent in the England average and a similar proportion educated to NQF Level 4, (30 per cent). Among the English regions, only London and the South East had higher proportions educated to this level.

Labour market

The South West has rates of employment that are among the highest in the UK. In the fourth quarter of 2009, the employment rate for residents of working-age was 75.5 per cent compared with 72.4 for the UK average (Online table 1.1b). This was the third highest rate among UK regions but was 2.5 percentage points lower than in the same quarter of 2008, the second highest percentage point decrease. Figure 3.12 illustrates that the long-term trend has been broadly in line with the UK average.

The South West labour force contains high proportions of self-employed workers, part-time workers and people with more than one job. In 2008, 14.5 per cent of employees and self-employed workers in the region were self-employed in their main job, compared with 12.6 per cent in the UK as a whole – only London had a greater proportion. Almost half of women in employment in the South West were part-time workers and the same was true of one in eight men. Both proportions were the highest among UK regions. The South West also had the highest percentage of people in employment with second jobs, 5.1 per cent compared with 3.9 per cent for the UK average (Online tables 9.3 and 9.8).

In the fourth quarter of 2009 the South West unemployment rate was the third lowest among the 12 UK regions at 6.4 per cent of the economically active population, compared with the national rate of 7.8 per cent (Online table 1.1b). The South West rate was 1.6 percentage points higher than a year earlier, the UK rate had risen by 1.4 percentage points in the same period.

At a local level, unemployment rates are modelled (see Glossary). The latest available are for the year to June 2009, with equivalent regional and UK rates of 5.4 and 6.8 per cent, respectively. Within the South West, the highest UA/district unemployment rates were in Torbay (7.4 per cent), Gloucester (7.3) and Swindon (7.0) and the lowest were in Purbeck (3.3 per cent) and West Devon (3.5).

The Jobseeker's Allowance claimant count rate, a timelier but more narrowly defined indicator of unemployment, also tends to be lower in the South West than across the UK average. In January 2010, 3.1 per cent of the region's working-age population were claiming Jobseeker's Allowance, compared with 4.3 per cent nationally. At a local level, this rate was highest in Torbay (4.9 per cent), and Gloucester and Swindon (both 4.6). It was lowest in the Isles of Scilly (0.6), North Dorset (1.8), West Devon and West Dorset (both 1.9).

In 2009, 18 per cent of working-age people in the region were economically inactive, compared with 21 per cent for the UK average (Online table 1.1b). Only the East and South East had lower rates. About 15 per cent of South West working-age men and 21 per cent of women were economically inactive; the latter was the lowest proportion of any region. The breakdown of reasons for inactivity in the region in 2008 differed slightly from nationally, with a smaller proportion looking after family and home in the South West (26 per cent compared with 28 per cent). The South West had a relatively high proportion of working-age people who were economically inactive because of retirement (10 per cent compared with less than 8 per cent for the UK average). Figure 3.13 illustrates reasons for inactivity in English regions (Online table 9.16).

In April 2009 median gross weekly earnings for full-time employees working in the South West were £454, compared with £489 for the UK average (Online table 9.20). The figure

Figure 3.12

Employment rate,[1] South West, 1992 Q4 to 2009 Q4[2]

Percentages

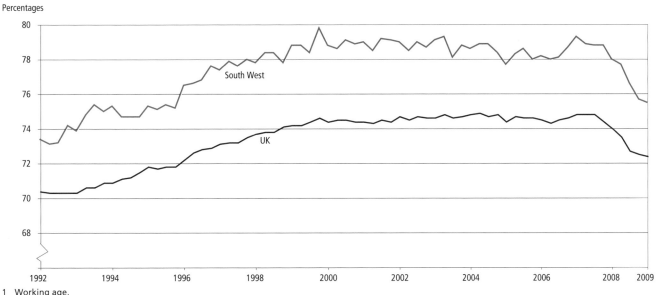

1 Working age.
2 Seasonally adjusted, three monthly data.

Source: Labour Force Survey, Office for National Statistics

Figure 3.13

Economic inactivity by reason: by region, 2008

Percentage of working age economically inactive

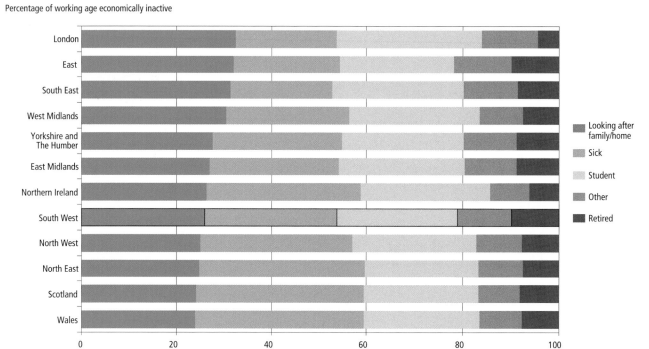

Source: Annual Population Survey, Office for National Statistics

was the third lowest of the nine English regions but very similar to that in regions in the north and midlands, as Figure 3.14 illustrates. It was 1.6 per cent higher than in 2008, the lowest percentage change of any region. Median hourly earnings of full-time employees on adult rates of pay in the region were lower than national equivalents (£11.33 compared with £12.34) but among part-time employees they were higher (£7.96 compared with £7.83).

In the fourth quarter of 2009, 19.1 per cent of working-age people in the region were economically inactive, compared with the UK average of 21.3 per cent. Only the East and South

East had lower rates. 17.1 per cent of South West males of working-age and 21.2 per cent of females were economically inactive, the latter was the lowest proportion of any region. The breakdown of reasons for inactivity in the region in 2008

Box 2: Measuring regional economic performance

When measuring the economic performance of regions or sub-regions, the following should be considered:

Gross Value Added (GVA) is a good measure of the economic output of a region.

GVA per head which divides output of those working in a region by everybody living in the region, should not be used as an indicator of either regional productivity or income of residents.

GVA per hour worked and **GVA per filled job** are the preferred measures of productivity of an area.

Gross Disposable Household Income (GDHI) per head is a good indicator of the welfare of residents living in a region.

Productivity, Income and Labour Market indicators should be used together to provide a more complete picture of regional and sub-regional economic performance.

For further information, see the National Statistician's article 'Measuring regional economic performance' which can be found at

www.statistics.gov.uk/cci/article.asp?ID=2103

Figure 3.14

Median gross weekly pay for full-time employee jobs, workplace based: by region, April 2009

£ per week

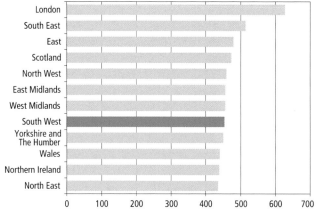

Source: Annual Survey of Hours and Earnings, Office for National Statistics

Figure 3.15

Labour productivity: gross value added per hour worked: by region, 2008

UK = 100

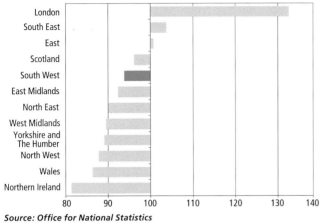

Source: Office for National Statistics

Figure 3.16

Employee jobs: by industry,[1] South West, September 2009

Percentages

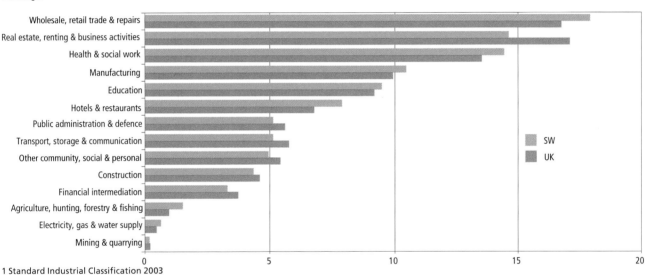

1 Standard Industrial Classification 2003

Source: Short-Term Employment Surveys, Office for National Statistics

Figure 3.17

Expenditure on research and development: by sector and region, 2007

£ million

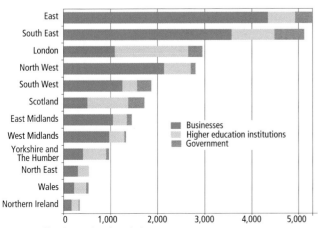

Source: Office for National Statistics

differed slightly from nationally, with a smaller proportion looking after family and home in the South West (26 per cent compared with 28 per cent in the UK). The South West had a relatively high proportion of working-age people who were economically inactive because of retirement (10 per cent compared with less than 8 per cent for the UK as a whole). Figure 3.13 illustrates reasons for inactivity in English regions.

Economy and industry

In 2008 the South West generated £98 billion of gross value added (GVA), almost 8 per cent of the UK total (Online table 3.1). The total GVA was 3.6 per cent higher than in 2007, a similar increase to that of the UK average (3.5 per cent). In 2007 more than half (53 per cent) of the region's total GVA was produced in the Gloucestershire, Wiltshire and North Somerset sub-region, which includes Bristol and Swindon (Online table 3.5).

Productivity, as measured by GVA per hour worked, was 94 per cent of the UK rate in 2008, the fifth highest of the 12 UK regions, as shown in Figure 3.15. GVA per filled job in the South West in 2008 was 91 per cent of the UK rate, the sixth highest of the UK regions

The industry groups that most contributed to total GVA in 2007 were broadly similar in the South West to the UK average (Online table 3.7). In both cases, three industry groups were responsible for almost half: real estate, renting and business activities (23 per cent of South West GVA, 24 per cent of the UK's), manufacturing (13 per cent in both cases) and the wholesale and retail trade (12 per cent in both cases). The South West had higher proportions of its GVA produced by hotels and restaurants and by electricity, gas and water supply than any other region (3.3 and 2.7 per cent compared with 2.9 and 1.7 per cent across the UK), the only industry groups for which this was the case.

Industry groups where the South West was a particularly important contributor to UK GVA in 2007 include mineral mining and quarrying (19 per cent of the UK's GVA from this industry); agriculture (13 per cent); fishing; electricity, gas and water supply (both 12 per cent); and public administration and defence (10 per cent). Specific types of manufacturing where this was the case include transport equipment (13 per cent of UK GVA from this industry); electrical and optical equipment; and leather and leather products (both 11 per cent).

In terms of employment, service industries (see Glossary) provide the majority of jobs, although a slightly smaller proportion than across the UK average. Short-term Employment Survey data show that in September 2009, 83 per cent of employee jobs were in service industries (compared with 84 per cent nationally) while just over 10 per cent were in manufacturing (just under 10 per cent in the UK average). As Figure 3.16 illustrates, the three largest service industry groups were the same in the South West as nationally. However, of these, the region had higher than average proportions of employee jobs in wholesale, retail trade and repairs, and in health and social work. It had a below average percentage of employee jobs in real estate, renting and business activities. Hotels and restaurants was the only industry group where the South West had a higher proportion of jobs (8 per cent) than in any other region, although it was only 1 percentage point above the UK average.

Among the region's 16 counties and UAs, Bournemouth (93 per cent), Torbay and Bristol (both 90 per cent) had the highest proportions of employee jobs in service industries,

according to the 2008 Annual Business Inquiry. Poole (16 per cent) and Gloucestershire (15 per cent) had the highest proportions in manufacturing.

In 2008 UK residents visiting the South West spent 72 million nights and £3,600 million in the region, the largest numbers of any UK country or region, representing 19 per cent and 17 per cent of the UK totals respectively (Online table 3.17). Overseas visitors spent 20 million nights and £980 million, the third highest among UK regions. According to the Annual Business Inquiry, an estimated 200,000 jobs in the South West were tourism-related in 2008; this was 9 per cent of total jobs, the highest proportion of any UK country or region. In the Isles of Scilly (31 per cent), Torbay (17 per cent) and Cornwall (14 per cent) more than one in eight jobs were tourism-related.

In 2007 almost £1.9 billion was spent on research and development in the South West, the fifth highest figure among UK regions (Figure 3.17). Some 68 per cent of this was spent by businesses, a higher proportion than nationally (63 per cent), and 16 per cent each from government and higher education institutions (compared with 9 per cent and 26 per cent, nationally).

In the South West, gross disposable household income (GDHI) per head was £14,200 in 2007, the fourth highest among UK regions (Online table 3.4). This was just below the UK equivalent (£14,300 per head). Within the region, GDHI per head ranged from 16 per cent below the UK figure in Plymouth to 8 per cent above in Wiltshire (Online table 3.6).[3]

Box 3: Index of Multiple Deprivation 2007

The Index of Multiple Deprivation (IMD) provides a summary measure of relative deprivation at Lower Layer Super Output Area (LSOA) level in England. The IMD aims to provide a nationally consistent measure of how deprived an area is by identifying the degree to which people are disadvantaged by factors such as low income, unemployment, lack of education, poor health and crime.

The IMD brings together 37 different indicators which cover specific 'domains' of deprivation. These are weighted as follows and combined to create the overall IMD 2007:

- Income; employment (both with a weight of 22.5 per cent)

- Health and disability; education, skills and training (both 13.5 per cent)

- Barriers to housing and services; living environment; and crime (with a combined weight of 28 per cent)

Particular points to note about the IMD are:

- Not all deprived people live in deprived areas and conversely, not everyone living in a deprived area is

deprived; the indicators identify areas with characteristics associated with deprivation – not deprived people

- The indices should not be used as a measure of affluence. A lack of income deprivation does not necessarily equate to affluence

- The indices provide a relative measure of deprivation and therefore cannot be used to determine how much more deprived one LSOA is than another

This article uses the rankings of all LSOAs in England, which have been divided into five equal sized groups, or quintiles.

In England, 20 per cent of LSOAs are in the most deprived quintile and 20 per cent in the least deprived quintile and so on. If an area (region or local authority) had the average distribution of deprivation they would have 20 per cent of LSOAs in each quintile.

For more information on the IMD see the article in *Regional Trends 41*, pages 93 to 114, and the Communities and Local Government website: www.communities.gov.uk/indices

---

3 These were the latest data available at the time of writing. Data for 2008 are available in Online tables 3.4 and 3.6.

Figure 3.18

Distribution of LSOA[1] rankings in the 2007 Index of Multiple Deprivation: by South West county and unitary authority[2]

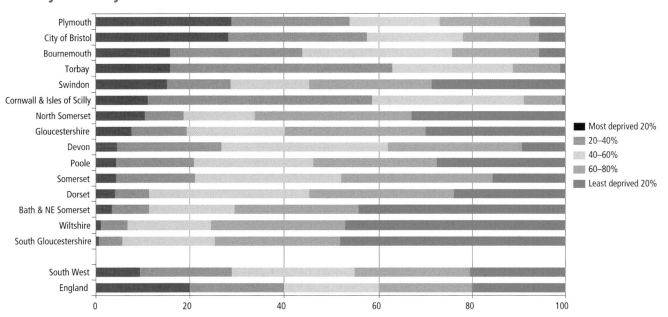

1 Lower Layer Super Output Areas.
2 Unitary authorities are pre-April 2009.

Source: Communities and Local Government

Disadvantage

According to the 2007 Index of Multiple Deprivation (IMD, 2007), just over 9 per cent of South West Lower Layer Super Output Areas (LSOAs) were within the most deprived quintile (20 per cent – Box 3) in England. This was the third lowest proportion among the nine English regions, behind the South East and East of England. As Figure 3.18 indicates, Plymouth and Bristol had by far the largest proportions of LSOAs in the most deprived quintile and, in fact, included almost 40 per cent

Figure 3.19

Indices of deprivation 2007: South West population living in LSOAs in the 10 per cent most deprived in England, by domain of deprivation

Population (thousands)

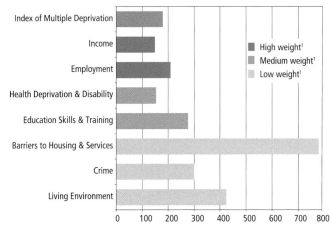

1 The domains are weighted so that some contribute more to the overall IMD and some less (See Box 3).

Source: Communities and Local Government

Figure 3.20

Workless households: by county and unitary authority, South West, 2008

Percentage of working age households with no adult working

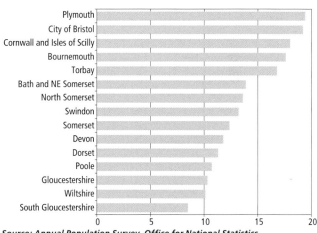

Source: Annual Population Survey, Office for National Statistics

of all such LSOAs in the South West. However, both cities also had a greater percentage of their population within the least deprived quintile than either Cornwall or Torbay.

An indication of the number of people in the region that lived in the areas most affected by deprivation can be estimated by aggregating LSOA population estimates and focusing on the most deprived decile (10 per cent) of LSOAs. Using the domains of IMD (Box 3) can also highlight the most prevalent types of deprivation in the region. As Figure 3.19 illustrates, more people in the South West lived in areas affected by deprivation relating to barriers to housing and services than in those affected by other types. The Indices also suggested that deprivation relating to the three topics of the living environment – crime and education, skills and training were more common in the region than income, health and employment deprivation.

In the second quarter of 2009 there were 217,000 working-age households in the South West where no adult worked (Online table 8.6). This number of workless households was 15 per cent of the total number of households in the South West, more than 1 percentage point higher than a year earlier but still the joint third lowest proportion among UK regions. About 14 per cent of children in the region lived in a workless household, also more than 1 percentage point higher than in 2008 but the third lowest regional proportion. The latest data for local areas in 2008 indicated that, within the South West, the proportion of workless households ranged from more than 19 per cent in Plymouth and Bristol to less than 9 per cent in South Gloucestershire (Figure 3.20).

Health

Life expectancy at birth for females in the South West in 2006–08 was the highest of any UK region (83.1 years). For males it was the second highest (79.0 years). In both cases, South West life expectancy was approximately 1.5 years above the UK equivalent and was almost a year higher than in 2003–05 (Online table 6.8).

Among South West counties and UAs, life expectancy at birth in 2006 to 2008 ranged from 76.9 years to 80.2 years for males and from 81.7 years to 84.1 years for females. For both genders the highest values were for Dorset and the lowest for

Figure 3.21

Difference in life expectancy at birth between counties and unitary authorities[1] and the UK average, South West, 2006 to 2008

Years

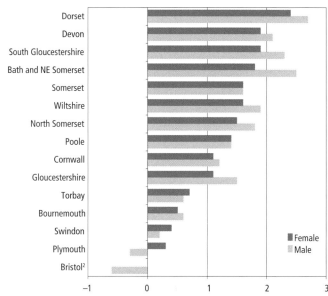

UK average: males = 77.5 years; females = 81.7 years.
1 No data for the Isles of Scilly.
2 Female life expectancy in Bristol is the same as for the UK as a whole.

Source: Office for National Statistics

Bristol. As Figure 3.21 shows, none of these South West areas had a female life expectancy at birth below the UK equivalent and, for males, only two had a life expectancy below the national level (Online table 6.8).

Figure 3.22

Age-standardised mortality rates:[1] by cause and region, 2008

Rate per 100,000 population

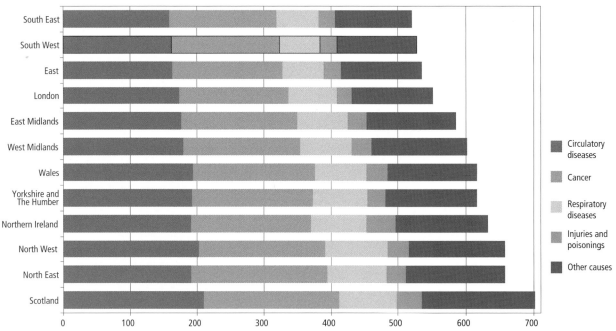

1   Based on deaths registered in 2008. Rates standardised to the European population.

Source: Office for National Statistics; General Register Office for Scotland; Northern Ireland Statistics and Research Agency

In 2008 the South West had the second lowest age-standardised mortality rate for all causes among UK regions, behind the South East (Figure 3.22 and Online table 6.4). The rate of 526 per 100,000 people was 11 per cent below the UK equivalent (592). Mortality rates in the South West for all main groups of causes were below the UK equivalent and the region had the lowest mortality rate for respiratory diseases and the second lowest for both cancer and circulatory diseases.

The South West consistently has an infant mortality rate below the UK equivalent. In 2008 the rate was 4.0 per 1,000 live births compared with 4.7 nationally. In the same year, 4.5 per 1,000 births were stillbirths, also below the UK rate of 5.1 (Online table 6.3).

In 2008 the proportion of adults who smoked in the South West was the same as the Great Britain average (21 per cent). About 30 per cent of adults in the region were non-smokers who were former regular smokers, with no other region having a higher proportion. Alcohol consumption among adults in the South West was slightly above that of the Great Britain average in 2008, with 66 per cent drinking at least once in the previous week compared with 62 per cent nationally and 18 per cent drinking on five or more days in the previous week, compared with the Great Britain average of 15 per cent. The average weekly alcohol consumption in the South West in 2008 was 12.5 units compared with 12.2 nationally.

According to the 2008/09 British Crime Survey, about 10 per cent of 16 to 59-year-olds in the South West reported that they had used drugs in the previous year, similar to the equivalent for England and Wales. The region had the second highest proportion of people who stated that they had used a Class A drug (4.4 per cent compared with 3.7 per cent across England and Wales) and a higher proportion of people using a stimulant drug than nationally (4.8 per cent compared with 4.4) (Online table 6.16).

Conception rates for women aged under 18 were lower in the South West than across England in 2008 (35 per 1,000 women aged 15 to 17 compared with 40 nationally). The region had the second lowest overall conception rate in England, 73 per 1,000 women aged 15 to 44 compared with 80 nationally.

Transport

According to the National Travel Survey, in the two years of 2007 and 2008 the average South West resident made about 1,100 journeys within Great Britain each year. Apart from in London, where the number of journeys was smaller, totals for all regions were similar. About 33 per cent of the South West journeys were for leisure purposes, just under 20 per cent were for shopping and 15 per cent were commuting journeys, all similar proportions to the national equivalents (Online table 11.5).

In distance terms, these journeys totalled 7,700 miles, one of the highest regional mileages, along with the South East and East of England (Online table 11.4). About 6,700 or 87 per cent of these miles were undertaken as a car driver or passenger or by other private road vehicle, compared with the Great Britain average of 81 per cent. The proportion by public transport (10 per cent) was lower than nationally (15 per cent).

In the last quarter of 2008, 76 per cent of journeys to work (excluding those working at home) were by car or van, a larger percentage than the England average (69 per cent) (Figure 3.23). The proportion of such journeys made on foot or bicycle (17 per cent) was similar to the average – 14 per cent – (Online table 11.7) but a much lower proportion was made by public transport (6 per cent rather than 15 per cent). Data from 2007 indicate that 65 per cent of journeys to work in the South West were of 20 minutes or less, higher than the average percentage for England (56 per cent) (Online table 11.6).

Figure 3.23

Usual method of travel to work: by region of residence, 2008 Q4

Percentages

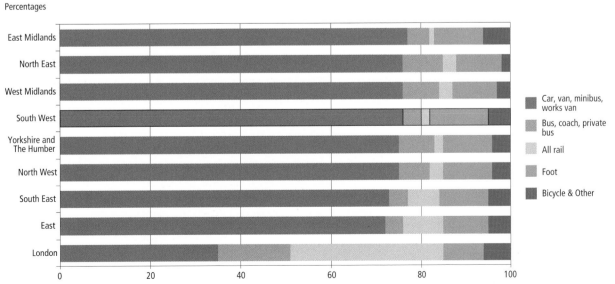

Source: Labour Force Survey, Office for National Statistics

In the ten years to 2008 the overall volume of traffic on the region's major roads increased by 14 per cent, the highest percentage change among the English regions and well above the 9 per cent increase in the average for England (Online table 11.12). The average weekly household expenditure on transport in the South West in 2006–08 was £66, the third highest regional average and above the UK equivalent (£62). Over half of the South West expenditure (£34) was spent on operation of personal transport, compared with the UK average of £30. Around £24 was spent on purchase of vehicles and £8 on transport services, compared with £22 and £10 nationally.

Environment

A key feature of the South West is the high proportion of land in the region that falls within national and international statutory designations protecting the natural environment. Almost 900 hectares (36 per cent of the region) are within a National Park or Area of Outstanding Natural Beauty (AONB). This is more than a quarter of the total land in such areas in England (Online table 5.8). The South West also includes 60 per cent of England's Heritage Coast, 24 per cent of its Sites of Special Scientific Interest (SSSIs) and 22 per cent of its National Nature Reserves. The only natural World Heritage Site in England is also in the region, the Dorset and East Devon Coast.

The South West had a high proportion of good quality rivers in 2008. Almost 88 per cent were of good biological quality while over 89 per cent were of good chemical quality. Both proportions were the second highest in England (Online table 5.5). The region has almost half of the identified coastal bathing waters in England and, in the 2008 bathing season, 95 per cent of these complied with European bathing water standards. This proportion was slightly below the national equivalent of 96 per cent and 3 percentage points less than in 2007 (Online table 5.6).

The latest long-term climate averages indicate that the South West region as originally designated by the National Rivers Authority, which covers most of the region, had the third highest rainfall in the UK in the 30 years to 2000 (behind Scotland and Wales) (Online table 5.1). The region also had the joint biggest seasonal variation with 62 per cent of rain in winter (October to March) (Online table 5.2). The latest available annual rainfall for the South West (2008) was 9 per cent higher than this 30-year average but single year totals for the region vary considerably; from 22 per cent below, to 21 per cent above the 30-year average in the years since 2000.

In 2008 the Environment Agency estimated that more than 86,000 South West properties were at significant risk of flooding from rivers or the sea, 18 per cent of the total in England and the second highest regional total. Almost a quarter of these properties (20,400) are in the North Somerset unitary authority area, with a further 9 per cent (8,100) in the Somerset district of Sedgemoor.

Carbon dioxide emissions in the South West totalled 40,800 kilotonnes in 2007, around 7.9 per cent of the UK total. This

Figure 3.24

Household recycling rates: by region, 2003/04 and 2008/09

Percentage of household waste recycled

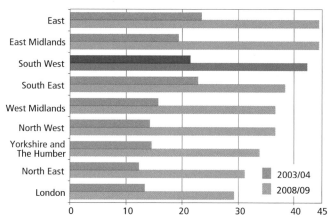

Source: Department for Environment, Food and Rural Affairs

was 600 kilotonnes less than in 2006, a 1.4 per cent fall that was slightly below the 1.7 per cent decrease for the UK average. Industrial and commercial users were responsible for 38 per cent of these emissions, a smaller proportion than nationally (45 per cent). The South West total equates to 7.9 tonnes per person of CO_2 in 2007, below the UK equivalent of 8.4 tonnes (Online table 5.15).

South West residents had the third lowest levels of residual household waste (see Glossary) among the nine English regions in 2008/09, 626 kg per household. In the previous five years this figure had fallen by 31 per cent. Over the same period, the household recycling rate for the South West rose from 21 per cent to 42 per cent with the 2008/09 rate being the third highest in England (Figure 3.24).

Crime

The South West has a comparatively low number of crimes committed against households, as estimated by the British Crime Survey (BCS). In 2008/09 there were 2,500 household offences per 10,000 households. As Figure 3.25 illustrates, this was the lowest rate among the nine English regions (the estimated rate for the England average was 2,900). According to the survey, households within the South West had a lower risk of being victims of crime than those in all other regions, with 16 per cent being a victim at least once compared with 18 per cent nationally. The rate of vehicle related theft was below the England average; 500 offences per 10,000 households compared with 640 nationally.

The BCS also suggests that the rate of crimes against the person in the region is similar to the England equivalent, around 890 per 10,000 adults in 2008/09 compared with 910 per 10,000 adults in England. The risk of being a victim of this type of crime at least once in the South West was 6 per cent, the same as nationally.

According to responses to the BCS, anti-social behaviour, drugs and drunk or rowdy behaviour in the local area are all perceived

Figure 3.25

Crimes committed against households: by type and region, 2008/09

Crimes per 10,000 households

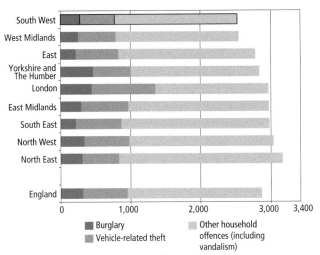

Legend:
- Burglary
- Vehicle-related theft
- Other household offences (including vandalism)

Source: British Crime Survey, Home Office

by the public in the region as less of a problem than the average perception nationally. In the South West in 2008/09, 13 per cent of respondents perceived a high level of anti-social behaviour in their area (compared with 16 per cent in the England average), 23 per cent thought that there was a problem with drug use or dealing (27 per cent) and 23 per cent identified a problem with drunk or rowdy behaviour (26 per cent).

The rate of recorded crime in the South West is also among the lowest of the English regions. In 2008/09 there were 73 recorded crimes per 1,000 people, compared with 86 across England. Only the East of England had a lower rate. The number of recorded crimes was 5 per cent lower than in 2007/08, the same percentage decrease as for the England average (Online table 2.3).

The BCS does not provide results at local authority level but the recorded crime figures include a set of BCS comparator offences[4] which covers about 60 per cent of all recorded crimes and allows differences at a local level to be highlighted. Within the South West, Bristol had a BCS comparator offence rate of 83 per 1,000 people, 25 per cent higher than that of the local authority with the second highest rate (Bournemouth, 66 per 1.000 people) (Online table 2.4). The combined rate in the region's 12 unitary authorities and districts classified by the Department for Environment, Food and Rural Affairs (DEFRA) as 'Large Urban' and 'Other Urban' was almost twice the rate of more rural authorities (59 and 31 per 1,000 people respectively).

Annex: Rural and urban totals

The Rural/Urban Definition and Local Authority (LA) Classification were developed to produce a rural/urban view from government statistics. Depending on the geographic level for which data are available, the Definition or Classification must be used to produce rural and urban totals.

The Rural/Urban Definition for small geographies was introduced in 2004 and is based on the settlement type that an area is within. Each Lower Layer Super Output Area (LSOA) is defined as one of three settlement types:

- Urban (population over 10,000)

- Rural – Town and Fringe

- Rural – Village, Hamlet and Isolated Dwellings

These three types are assigned to either a 'sparse' or 'less sparse' regional setting to give six classes of LSOAs. The Definition also applies to Middle Layer Super Output Areas (MSOAs), wards and output areas, but with four settlement types in the latter.

The LA Classification was introduced in 2005 in order to differentiate between rural and urban for those statistics which are only available at LA level. It provides six classifications:

- **Major Urban:** LAs with either 100,000 people or 50 per cent of their population in urban areas with a population of more than 750,000

- **Large Urban:** LAs with either 50,000 people or 50 per cent of their population in one of 17 urban areas with a population between 250,000 and 750,000

- **Other Urban:** LAs with fewer than 37,000 people or less than 26 per cent of their population in rural settlements and larger market towns

- **Significant Rural:** LAs with more than 37,000 people or more than 26 per cent of their population in rural settlements and larger market towns

- **Rural-50:** LAs with at least 50 per cent but less than 80 per cent of their population in rural settlements and larger market towns

- **Rural-80:** LAs with at least 80 per cent of their population in rural settlements and larger market towns

---

4   The crimes included in the recorded crime BCS comparator measure are theft of and from a vehicle, vehicle interference and tampering, domestic burglary, theft of a pedal cycle, theft from a person, criminal damage, common assault, wounding and robbery (of personal, not business property).

Regional health inequalities in England

By Amy Ellis and Robert Fry, Office for National Statistics

Abstract

This article aims to provide an up-to-date picture of regional health inequalities in England. Health inequalities can start early in life and persist not only into old age, but subsequent generations. To address these health inequalities, a better understanding is needed of how health compares across the country.

This article brings together a range of health indicators for each of the nine government office regions, making comparisons across regions and against England as a whole. Indicators include life expectancy, alcohol consumption, smoking, drug usage, child obesity and mortality rates by cause. Bringing these indicators together in this manner provides a fuller picture of health differences between regions, instead of looking at each indicator in isolation.

The article confirms other studies showing that the north-south divide between regions persists, as the overall picture of health is better in the south than it is in the north. However, the article also reveals exceptions where some health indicators do not fit in with this trend.

Introduction

Which English region has the highest level of alcohol consumption? In which region are cancer incidence rates high? How does life expectancy at birth vary between the regions?

Over the last 50 years, there have been impressive social, economic and health improvements in this country. People from every class and region are healthier and live longer than ever before. Unfortunately, not everyone shares the benefits of these improvements.

Health inequalities can start early in life and persist not only into old age but subsequent generations. To reduce these health inequalities, the health gap needs to be narrowed between disadvantaged groups or communities and the rest of the country. This is an aim of Public Service Agreement (PSA) 18, to promote better health and wellbeing for all.

This article looks at inequalities among 18 health indicators by region. The aim is to provide an up-to-date picture of regional health inequalities and determine how the indicators compare against England as a whole. Bringing these indicators together in this manner provides a fuller picture of health differences between regions, instead of looking at each indicator in isolation.

The indicators analysed in this article are:

- male and female life expectancy at birth in 2006–08

- age-standardised mortality rates in 2008 – all causes of death, cancer, diseases of the respiratory and circulatory systems

- age-standardised cancer incidence rates in 2005–07 – breast cancer (females) and lung cancer (males and females)

- infant mortality rates in 2007

- drug use among 16 to 24-year-olds – British Crime Survey 2008/09

- average weekly alcohol consumption (males and females) – General Lifestyle Survey (GLF) 2008

- current smokers (males and females) – GLF 2008

- self-reported limiting longstanding illness – GLF 2008

- childhood obesity in 2008/09, (reception and Year 6) – National Child Measurement Programme (NCMP)

Notes

The authors would like to thank colleagues in contributing departments and other organisations for their generous support and helpful comments without which this article would not have been possible.

Unless otherwise stated the data used in this article were those available at the time of writing.

Further information on the sources and context for these indicators is available in the Annex: Data sources.

The values for each indicator have been standardised (Box 1) and compared against the national figure for England, creating the spine charts shown in this article. The patterns emerging from the spine charts are discussed in detail in the section Regional Comparisons.

The robustness of the data (the width of the confidence intervals – Box 2) can affect whether significant differences are identifiable (Box 3). Caution needs to be exercised when analysing regional health data, largely because a lot of the indicators are based on sample surveys with small regional samples.

Regional comparisons

Figure 4.2 provides a set of spine charts showing the chosen health indicators for each region, whereas Figure 4.3 compares the regions for each indicator.

The England values for each indicator are represented by the centre line at zero, the actual non-standardised values of each indicator are shown in Table 4.4. If the indicator's bar is to the right-hand side of this, it suggests that region or indicator performed 'well' in comparison to England, whereas if it is on the left-hand side, it appears the region or indicator performed 'badly'. A regional example using London shows that the levels of childhood obesity are 'worse' than England, and the drug use prevalence is 'better'. Where no bar is

Box 1: Spine charts range standardisation methodology

The method used to create the spine charts, using the regional values for each indicator, is explained here.

The indicators featured are all different, some being proportions, some rates and some years. To ensure each region's set of health indicators are comparable on one chart, the data are standardised. The specific technique, known as range standardisation, compares each value to the minimum value for that indicator if a high value is 'good' (such as life expectancy) or the maximum value if a high value is 'bad' (such as alcohol consumption). This is then standardised in relation to the England value. These figures are then altered so that England falls on zero, and any values below zero are worse, and any values above are better. These standardised figures are then plotted to create the spine charts.

An example of this calculation is shown in Table 4.1 for childhood obesity in reception year in the North East.

The proportion of children in reception year who were obese was 10.2 per cent in the North East in 2008/09. As higher proportions of obesity are bad, this figure must be standardised using the maximum value of the full set of regional figures (11.2 per cent in London), using the following calculation:

$$= \left(\frac{\text{regional value} - \text{maximum value}}{(\text{England value} - \text{maximum value}) \times 0.5} \right) - 0.5$$

$$= ((10.2 - 11.2) / (9.6 - 11.2) \times 0.5) - 0.5$$

$$= 0.3155 - 0.5$$

$$= \mathbf{-0.1845}$$

The value -0.1845 has been plotted on the spine chart for the North East (Figure 4.5), revealing that it had higher reception obesity levels than England.

This calculation is repeated for each indicator in turn.

Table 4.1

An example – Prevalence of childhood obesity in reception years

Percentages

Region	Prevalence of obese children in reception 2008/09
North East	10.2
North West	9.6
Yorkshire and The Humber	9.6
East Midlands	9.1
West Midlands	10.1
East of England	8.7
London	11.2
South East	8.7
South West	8.9
England	9.6
Minimum	8.7
Maximum	11.2

Source: Department of Health

Box 2: Confidence intervals

The GLF and NCMP provide a selection of the indicators analysed in this article. These are sample surveys which interview a sample of the population of interest. The estimated rates or proportions resulting from these surveys will rarely be identical to the true population value, and an indication of the accuracy of these estimates is provided using confidence intervals.

In addition, rates or figures based on a small number of events (such as deaths) or within a small population can also be subject to variability. Examples in this article include the age-standardised mortality rates, infant mortality rates, and cancer incidence rates. The estimates of these can be subject to fluctuation due to chance alone. For this reason, confidence intervals are also calculated around these figures.

Confidence intervals give a range in which the true value for the population is likely to fall. Upper and lower 95 per cent confidence intervals mean there is a 95 per cent chance that the range contains the 'true' rate.

For further information about calculating confidence intervals, please see the *General Lifestyle Survey (GLF) 2008 Appendix C: Sampling Errors*.

Box 3: Statistically significant differences

This article focuses solely on regional differences which are statistically significant, as opposed to differences that could have occurred by chance. The differences are assumed to be significant if the confidence intervals of the two comparator figures do not overlap. If there is an overlap, the values could fall within the same range, and no significant difference can be inferred. For example, the 95 per cent confidence intervals for the prevalence of childhood obesity in reception class children for the North East and London are 9.8–10.6 and 11.0–11.5 respectively. Given that these intervals do not overlap, there is a statistical significant difference between the two regions.

In this article, the same method (overlapping confidence intervals) has been used to compare regional values with England to see if significant differences exist, even though it is acknowledged that a value for a region is not independent from the England value that includes data from the region.

shown against a region, this represents a value equal to that of England.

These spine charts show the indicators' standardised values for each region (Box 1) compared against England, but each of these comparisons may not actually be a statistically significant difference (Box 3). Please refer to the section for each region to see whether the differences are significant.

The following section compares how the selected 18 health indicators performed in each region, and compared with England as a whole, referring to statistically significant differences only (Box 3). Background information for each indicator can be found in the Data Annex.

In summary, this article shows that the northern regions generally do less well than the midlands and London, and the best performing regions are the East of England and southern regions. This regional pattern corroborates findings from previous health inequality publications such as the *Association of Public Health Observatories (APHO) Health Profiles 2009*.

Table 4.4

England indicators

Indicator	Rate per 100,000	Indicator	Percentages
Deaths – Circulatory (2007)	177	Drug use 16–24 – Age (2008/09)	23
Deaths – Respiratory (2007)	73	Alcohol consumption – Male (2008)	22
Deaths – Cancer (2007)	172	Alcohol consumption – Female (2008)	15
Deaths – All causes (2007)	575	Smoking – Male (2008)	21
Breast cancer – Female (2008)	123	Smoking – Female (2008)	20
Lung cancer – Male (2008)	59	Limiting illness (2008)	17
Lung cancer – Female (2008)	36	Childhood obesity – Reception (2008/09)	10
		Childhood obesity – Year 6 (2008/09)	18

Indicator	Years at birth	Indicator	Rate per 1,000 live births
Life expectancy at birth – Males (2006–08)	78	Infant mortality (2007)	4.8
Life expectancy at birth – Females (2006–08)	82		

Source: Office for National Statistics; Department of Health; Home Office

Figure 4.2

Health indicator spine charts by region – standardised values, 2006 to 2008

Relative to England average

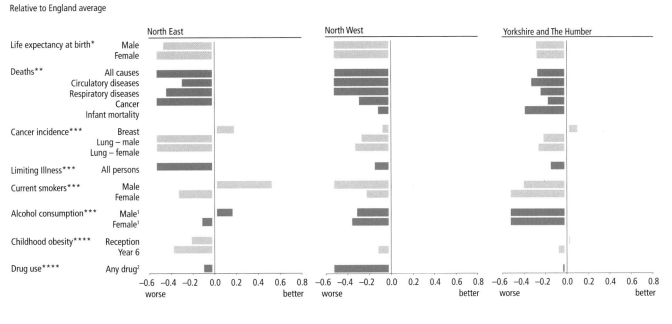

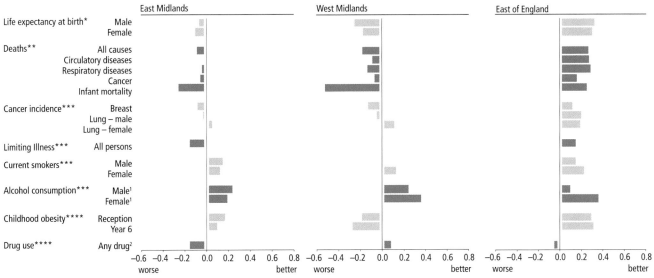

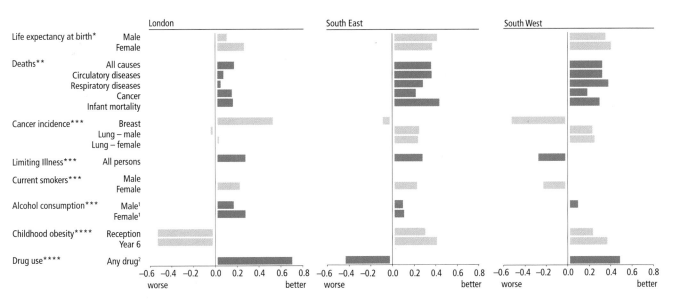

1 Males 8+ units; females 6+ units at least once a week.
2 16–24 year olds.

* 2006–08   ** 2007   *** 2008   **** 2008/09

Source: Office for National Statistics; Department of Health; Home Office

Figure 4.3

Health indicator spine charts by indicator – standardised values, 2006 to 2008

Relative to England average

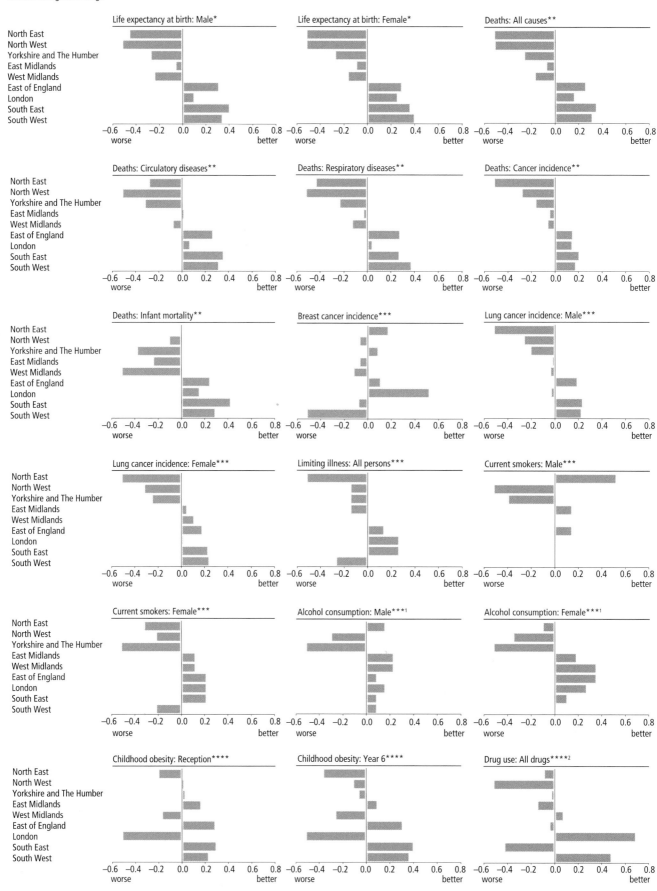

1 Males 8+ units; females 6+ units at least once a week.
2 16–24 year olds.

* 2006–08   ** 2007   *** 2008   **** 2008/09

Source: Office for National Statistics; Department of Health; Home Office

Figure 4.5

Spine chart for North East

Relative to England average

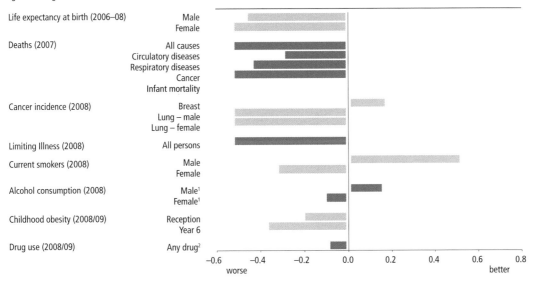

1 Males 8+ units; females 6+ units at least once a week.
2 16–24 year olds.

Source: Office for National Statistics; Department of Health; Home Office

North East

The spine chart for the North East (Figure 4.5) shows a picture of poor health when compared with England. The North East, along with the North West and Yorkshire and The Humber, all show a similar number of indicators that were worse than England. The life expectancy for both males and females was lower than the England average and significantly lower than all other regions except for the North West.

Poor life expectancy is linked to the other indicators that were lower than the England figure. Age-standardised mortality rates from all cancer, respiratory, circulatory and 'all causes' were worse than England and the majority of regions.

Incidence rates of lung cancer for both men and women (82 and 53 newly diagnosed cases in 2005–7 per 100,000 population respectively – Table 4.6) were greater than the rates for England (59 and 36 cases respectively) and all other regions.

However, some indicators such as incidence of breast cancer, childhood obesity in reception years, alcohol consumption and drug use were not significantly worse than the England average.

Surprisingly, the proportion of males smoking was much lower than the England average. Because of a large confidence interval around this figure, it was only significantly different from the region with the highest proportion of male smokers, the North West (Figure 4.7).

Table 4.6

North East indicators

Indicator	Rate per 100,000	Indicator	Percentages
Deaths – Circulatory (2007)	191	Drug use 16–24 (2008/09)	23
Deaths – Respiratory (2007)	88	Alcohol consumption – Male (2008)	20
Deaths – Cancer (2007)	204	Alcohol consumption – Female (2008)	16
Deaths – All causes (2007)	657	Smoking – Male (2008)	17
Breast cancer – Female (2008)	119	Smoking – Female (2008)	23
Lung cancer – Male (2008)	82	Limiting illness (2008)	21
Lung cancer – Female (2008)	53	Childhood obesity – Reception (2008/09)	10
		Childhood obesity – Year 6 (2008/09)	20

Indicator	Years at birth	Indicator	Rate per 1,000 live births
Life expectancy at birth – Males (2006–08)	77	Infant mortality (2007)	4.8
Life expectancy at birth – Females (2006–08)	81		

Source: Office for National Statistics; Department of Health; Home Office

Figure 4.7

Spine chart for North West

Relative to England average

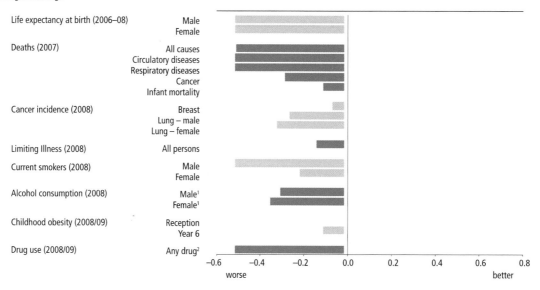

1 Males 8+ units; females 6+ units at least once a week.
2 16–24 year olds.

Source: Office for National Statistics; Department of Health; Home Office

North West

In common with the North East, the spine chart for the North West shows a picture of poor health when compared with England. Along with the North East and Yorkshire and the Humber, the region shows a similar number of indicators that are worse than those of England. The life expectancy for both males and females was lower than the England average and lower than all other regions except for the North East.

Poor life expectancy is linked to other indicators that were also different to England. The age-standardised mortality rates from all cancer, respiratory, circulatory and 'all causes' were significantly worse than England and the majority of regions.

The proportions of male smokers and drug use amongst 16 to 24-year-olds (25 and 27 per cent respectively) appear much higher than the England averages (21 and 23 per cent) and are the highest across all regions. However, these differences were not significantly different compared with England as the confidence intervals for these statistics are wide.

Lung cancer rates for both males and females (70 and 46 people per 100,000 respectively) were higher than the England averages and only lower than one region, the North East.

In contrast, the levels of some indicators were more moderate and close to the England average. For example, breast cancer, childhood obesity (reception), long-term limiting illness and infant mortality indicators were not significantly different compared with England.

Table 4.8

North West indicators

Indicator	Rate per 100,000	Indicator	Percentages
Deaths – Circulatory (2007)	203	Drug use 16–24 (2008/09)	27
Deaths – Respiratory (2007)	92	Alcohol consumption – Male (2008)	26
Deaths – Cancer (2007)	189	Alcohol consumption – Female (2008)	19
Deaths – All causes (2007)	656	Smoking – Male (2008)	25
Breast cancer – Female (2008)	124	Smoking – Female (2008)	22
Lung cancer – Male (2008)	70	Limiting illness (2008)	18
Lung cancer – Female (2008)	46	Childhood obesity – Reception (2008/09)	10
		Childhood obesity – Year 6 (2008/09)	19

Indicator	Years at birth	Indicator	Rate per 1,000 live births
Life expectancy at birth – Males (2006–08)	76	Infant mortality (2007)	5.0
Life expectancy at birth – Females (2006–08)	81		

Source: Office for National Statistics; Department of Health; Home Office

Figure 4.9

Spine chart for Yorkshire and The Humber

Relative to England average

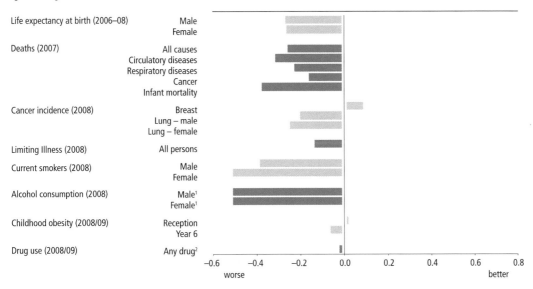

1 Males 8+ units; females 6+ units at least once a week.
2 16–24 year olds.

Source: Office for National Statistics; Department of Health; Home Office

Yorkshire and The Humber

The Yorkshire and The Humber spine chart also illustrates poor health generally, although more moderate for some indicators when compared with the North East and the North West. For example, life expectancy for males was higher than the North East and North West, although it was lower than England.

The region shows the highest level of alcohol consumption (29 and 21 per cent respectively), measured as the percentage of males/females drinking more than 8/6 units of alcohol at least once in the survey week. The level was higher than the England average and the majority of regions.

Table 4.10

Yorkshire and The Humber indicators

Indicator	Rate per 100,000	Indicator	Percentages
Deaths – Circulatory (2007)	193	Drug use 16–24 (2008/09)	23
Deaths – Respiratory (2007)	81	Alcohol consumption – Male (2008)	29
Deaths – Cancer (2007)	181	Alcohol consumption – Female (2008)	21
Deaths – All causes (2007)	616	Smoking – Male (2008)	24
Breast cancer – Female (2008)	121	Smoking – Female (2008)	25
Lung cancer – Male (2008)	68	Limiting illness (2008)	18
Lung cancer – Female (2008)	44	Childhood obesity – Reception (2008/09)	10
		Childhood obesity – Year 6 (2008/09)	19

Indicator	Years at birth	Indicator	Rate per 1,000 live births
Life expectancy at birth – Males (2006–08)	77	Infant mortality (2007)	5.6
Life expectancy at birth – Females (2006–08)	81		

Source: Office for National Statistics; Department of Health; Home Office

1

Figure 4.11

Spine chart for East Midlands

Relative to England average

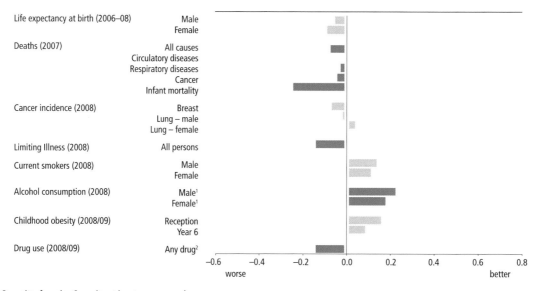

1 Males 8+ units; females 6+ units at least once a week.
2 16–24 year olds.

Source: Office for National Statistics; Department of Health; Home Office

East Midlands

The spine chart for the East Midlands shows that the health in this area was similar to the England average for many of the indicators. It clearly shows that the health in this area was better than that demonstrated in North East, North West and Yorkshire and The Humber regions.

Life expectancy in this area for both males and females was close to the England average. It is the only region where the life expectancy for males was not significantly different to the England average.

There are some indicators that appear to be better than the England average – such as alcohol consumption and smoking

– but these were not significantly different to the England average. The level of child obesity was low in this region and this was better than the England average.

To add to the mixed picture of health in this region, there are some indicators that were worse than the England average – such as breast cancer, long-term limiting illness, drug use and infant mortality. However, only one indicator was significantly worse compared with England – deaths from all causes.

The infant mortality rate in 2007 appeared to be higher than the England average according to the spine chart, but was only significantly higher than the South East. Comparisons with England and the other regions were not significantly different.

Table 4.12

East Midlands indicators

Indicator	Rate per 100,000	Indicator	Percentages
Deaths – Circulatory (2007)	177	Drug use 16–24 (2008/09)	24
Deaths – Respiratory (2007)	74	Alcohol consumption – Male (2008)	19
Deaths – Cancer (2007)	174	Alcohol consumption – Female (2008)	13
Deaths – All causes (2007)	584	Smoking – Male (2008)	20
Breast cancer – Female (2008)	124	Smoking – Female (2008)	19
Lung cancer – Male (2008)	59	Limiting illness (2008)	18
Lung cancer – Female (2008)	35	Childhood obesity – Reception (2008/09)	9
		Childhood obesity – Year 6 (2008/09)	18

Indicator	Years at birth	Indicator	Rate per 1,000 live births
Life expectancy at birth – Males (2006–08)	78	Infant mortality (2007)	5.3
Life expectancy at birth – Females (2006–08)	82		

Source: Office for National Statistics; Department of Health; Home Office

Figure 4.13

Spine chart for West Midlands

Relative to England average

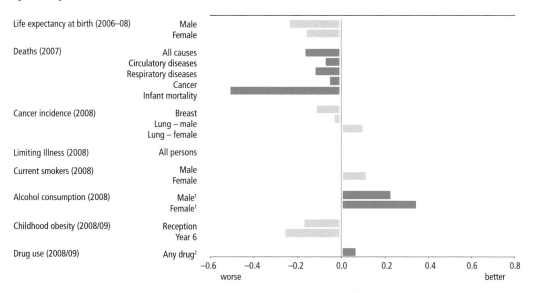

1 Males 8+ units; females 6+ units at least once a week.
2 16–24 year olds.

Source: Office for National Statistics; Department of Health; Home Office

West Midlands

The West Midlands' spine chart shows a mixed picture of health across the range of indicators. Life expectancy for males and females was lower than the East Midlands and the England average.

The low life expectancy relates to several indicators that performed worse than the England average. Childhood obesity (reception and Year 6), deaths by all causes, deaths by respiratory causes, and infant mortality were all higher than the figures for England.

Most of these indicators had moderate values compared with the northern regions but the rate of infant mortality was the highest across all regions and was significantly higher than four of the regions.

By contrast, some indicators were better than the England average. The level of alcohol consumption by females (measured as the percentage of females drinking more then 6 units of alcohol at least once in the survey week) was lower than the England average (11 per cent versus 15 per cent). The incidence of female lung cancer was also lower than the England average.

Table 4.14

West Midlands indicators

Indicator	Rate per 100,000	Indicator	Percentages
Deaths – Circulatory (2007)	180	Drug use 16–24 (2008/09)	22
Deaths – Respiratory (2007)	77	Alcohol consumption – Male (2008)	19
Deaths – Cancer (2007)	175	Alcohol consumption – Female (2008)	11
Deaths – All causes (2007)	600	Smoking – Male (2008)	21
Breast cancer – Female (2008)	125	Smoking – Female (2008)	19
Lung cancer – Male (2008)	60	Limiting illness (2008)	17
Lung cancer – Female (2008)	33	Childhood obesity – Reception (2008/09)	10
		Childhood obesity – Year 6 (2008/09)	20

Indicator	Years at birth	Indicator	Rate per 1,000 live births
Life expectancy at birth – Males (2006–08)	77	Infant mortality (2007)	5.9
Life expectancy at birth – Females (2006–08)	82		

Source: Office for National Statistics; Department of Health; Home Office

1

Figure 4.15

Spine chart for East of England

Relative to England average

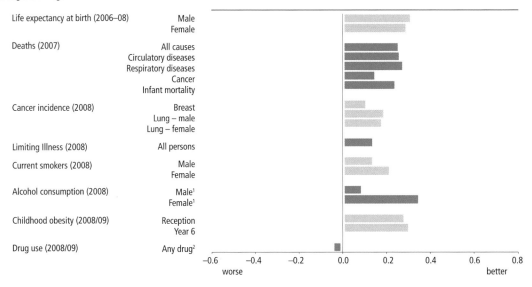

1 Males 8+ units; females 6+ units at least once a week.
2 16–24 year olds.

Source: Office for National Statistics; Department of Health; Home Office

East of England

The spine chart for the East of England shows one of the best depictions of health across all regions, with almost every indicator better than the England average.

Of the 18 indicators, 11 performed significantly better than the England average. This included child obesity (reception and Year 6), deaths from all causes and deaths from cancer, respiratory and circulatory conditions. It was the region with the lowest percentage of females who consumed more than 6 units of alcohol on one or more occasions in a survey week. This was lower than the England figure and the North West and Yorkshire and The Humber.

The indicators which were better than average related to the high life expectancy in this region. Only the South East and the South West had a significantly higher life expectancy.

Table 4.16

East of England indicators

Indicator	Rate per 100,000	Indicator	Percentages
Deaths – Circulatory (2007)	164	Drug use 16–24 (2008/09)	23
Deaths – Respiratory (2007)	63	Alcohol consumption – Male (2008)	21
Deaths – Cancer (2007)	164	Alcohol consumption – Female (2008)	11
Deaths – All causes (2007)	535	Smoking – Male (2008)	20
Breast cancer – Female (2008)	120	Smoking – Female (2008)	18
Lung cancer – Male (2008)	51	Limiting illness (2008)	16
Lung cancer – Female (2008)	30	Childhood obesity – Reception (2008/09)	9
		Childhood obesity – Year 6 (2008/09)	17

Indicator	Years at birth	Indicator	Deaths per 1,000 live births
Life expectancy at birth – Males (2006–08)	79	Infant mortality (2007)	4.3
Life expectancy at birth – Females (2006–08)	83		

Source: Office for National Statistics; Department of Health; Home Office

Figure 4.17

Spine chart for London

Relative to England average

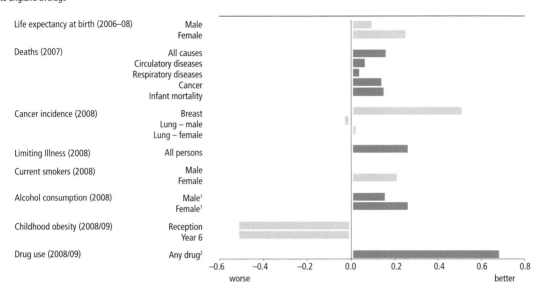

1 Males 8+ units; females 6+ units at least once a week.
2 16–24 year olds.

Source: Office for National Statistics; Department of Health; Home Office

London

The London spine chart shows that health in this region was broadly better than, or closer to the England average.

Infant mortality, long term limiting illness, alcohol consumption, smoking percentages, respiratory deaths, circulatory deaths and incidence of lung cancer were all indicators that were not significantly different to the England average.

There are several indicators that stand out as performing much better than the England average. The incidence of breast cancer was lower than England and all the regions. The

percentage of 16 to 24-year-olds using drugs was lower than the North East, North West, East Midlands, East of England and the South East.

In contrast, the level of child obesity (11 per cent for reception years and 21 per cent for Year 6) in London was significantly higher than the England average (10 and 18 per cent respectively) and every other region.

Life expectancy seems to be in line with the picture of good health in London. Only the South East, South West and the East of England had significantly higher life expectancy.

Table 4.18

London indicators

Indicator	Rate per 100,000	Indicator	Percentages
Deaths – Circulatory (2007)	174	Drug use 16–24 (2008/09)	17
Deaths – Respiratory (2007)	72	Alcohol consumption – Male (2008)	20
Deaths – Cancer (2007)	164	Alcohol consumption – Female (2008)	12
Deaths – All causes (2007)	551	Smoking – Male (2008)	21
Breast cancer – Female (2008)	111	Smoking – Female (2008)	18
Lung cancer – Male (2008)	60	Limiting illness (2008)	15
Lung cancer – Female (2008)	36	Childhood obesity – Reception (2008/09)	11
		Childhood obesity – Year 6 (2008/09)	21

Indicator	Years at birth	Indicator	Rate per 1,000 live births
Life expectancy at birth – Males (2006–08)	78	Infant mortality (2007)	4.5
Life expectancy at birth – Females (2006–08)	83		

Source: Office for National Statistics; Department of Health; Home Office

Figure 4.19

Spine chart for South East

Relative to England average

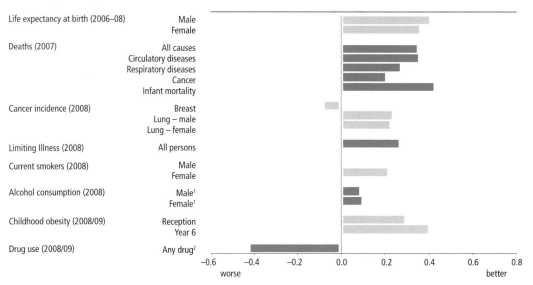

1 Males 8+ units; females 6+ units at least once a week.
2 16–24 year olds.

Source: Office for National Statistics; Department of Health; Home Office

South East

The South East spine chart depicts a very positive picture of health, with almost every indicator better than the England average. The region had similar rates and percentages to the East of England and South West regions. This is reflected in the high life expectancy, which was higher than the England average and all other regions.

This high level of life expectancy is linked to the better than average values for the majority of the indicators. In particular, the mortality rates for cancer, respiratory, circulatory and all

causes were lower than the England average and most of the regions.

Other indicators also performed strongly with 12 out of the 18 indicators significantly better than the England average. Levels of childhood obesity and infant mortality were both lower than the England average and many of the regions.

The only indicator that dramatically differs from the rest was the percentage of drug use amongst 16 to 24-year-olds (26 per cent). It was higher than the other southern regions; London (17 per cent), and the South West (19 per cent).

Table 4.20

South East indicators

Indicator	Rate per 100,000	Indicator	Percentages
Deaths – Circulatory (2007)	159	Drug use 16–24 (2008/09)	26
Deaths – Respiratory (2007)	64	Alcohol consumption – Male (2008)	21
Deaths – Cancer (2007)	160	Alcohol consumption – Female (2008)	14
Deaths – All causes (2007)	520	Smoking – Male (2008)	21
Breast cancer – Female (2008)	124	Smoking – Female (2008)	18
Lung cancer – Male (2008)	49	Limiting illness (2008)	15
Lung cancer – Female (2008)	28	Childhood obesity – Reception (2008/09)	9
		Childhood obesity – Year 6 (2008/09)	16

Indicator	Years at birth	Indicator	Rate per 1,000 live births
Life expectancy at birth – Males (2006–08)	79	Infant mortality (2007)	3.9
Life expectancy at birth – Females (2006–08)	83		

Source: Office for National Statistics; Department of Health; Home Office

Figure 4.21

Spine chart for South West

Relative to England average

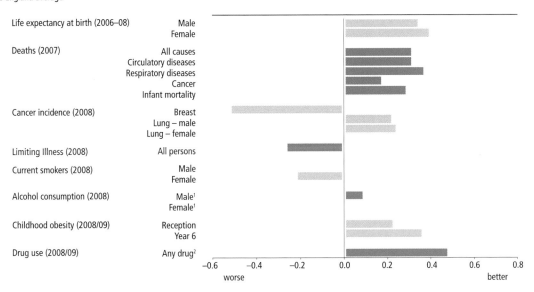

1 Males 8+ units; females 6+ units at least once a week.
2 16–24 year olds.

Source: Office for National Statistics; Department of Health; Home Office

South West

The South West spine chart shows an indication of relatively good health, similar to that seen in the South East and the East of England. Life expectancy was very similar to the South East, East of England and London and was better than the England average.

Like the South East, the high life expectancy appears to be linked to the low mortality rates for cancer, respiratory and circulatory causes, all of which were lower than the England average.

There were also low levels of lung cancer and child obesity, both lower than the England average and most of the northern and midland regions. The region also had one of the lowest levels of drug use amongst 16 to 24-year-olds, lower than the North West and the South East, but not compared with the other regions due to the relatively wide confidence intervals.

There were three indicators that performed worse than the England average, but only one of these indicators was significantly lower than the England average. The South West had the highest level of breast cancer across all regions (135 cases per 100,000 population) and was higher than the England average (123 per 100,000 population) and all other regions.

Table 4.22

South West indicators

Indicator	Rate per 100,000	Indicator	Percentages
Deaths – Circulatory (2007)	162	Drug use 16–24 (2008/09)	19
Deaths – Respiratory (2007)	60	Alcohol consumption – Male (2008)	21
Deaths – Cancer (2007)	162	Alcohol consumption – Female (2008)	15
Deaths – All causes (2007)	526	Smoking – Male (2008)	21
Breast cancer – Female (2008)	135	Smoking – Female (2008)	22
Lung cancer – Male (2008)	49	Limiting illness (2008)	19
Lung cancer – Female (2008)	28	Childhood obesity – Reception (2008/09)	9
		Childhood obesity – Year 6 (2008/09)	16

Indicator	Years at birth	Indicator	Rate per 1,000 live births
Life expectancy at birth – Males (2006–08)	79	Infant mortality (2007)	4.2
Life expectancy at birth – Females (2006–08)	83		

Source: Office for National Statistics; Department of Health; Home Office

Conclusions

This article has shown that there are many regional variations, leading to inevitable health inequalities. Overall, there was a north–south divide in health experiences. The northern regions (North East, North West and Yorkshire and The Humber) were at one end of the scale where health experiences were generally poorer than average, but in the south (South East, South West, East of England and London) the health experiences were largely better than average. The East Midlands and the West Midlands appeared to be around the England average.

This regional trend is consistent with findings from previous health inequality publications such as the Association of Public Health Observatories (APHO) Health Profiles 2009. See the References section for more north–south divide publications.

This article has highlighted that some indicators do not follow this north–south divide for health experiences. Some indicators which oppose the general trend are:

- High levels of childhood obesity in London – this contrasts the majority of indicators doing better than England in this region. This finding is backed up by the APHO Profiles

- High proportion of drug use in the South East – goes against the trend of good health in this region

- High levels of breast cancer incidence in the South West – opposing the picture of good health in this region

Annex: Data sources

Life expectancy

Life expectancy is a widely used summary indicator of the state of the nation's health, but it does not take into account quality of life and whether it is lived in good health, with disability or dependency.

Life expectancy is defined as the average amount of time people can expect to live. This can be time from birth, or remaining time from any particular age. More precisely, period life expectancy – used in this article – is an estimate of the average number of years a person would live if he or she experienced the particular age-specific mortality rates of that region, for that time period, throughout the rest of their lives.

All figures are three-year averages, produced by aggregating the number of deaths and mid-year population estimates across each three-year period to provide large enough numbers to ensure that the figures presented are sufficiently robust.

This article focuses on the life expectancy at birth by region and England for 2006–08 only, but it is also possible to view this over a longer time period.

Over the period 1991–93 to 2006–08, life expectancy at birth has improved in all English regions. Figure 4.23 shows the life expectancy in the North East, as this region experienced a consistently low life expectancy compared with the other regions, and the life expectancy for England. The life expectancy in the North East increased by 4.5 years for males and 3.2 years for females over this time period. The trend for England increased by a similar magnitude, with female life expectancy being consistently higher than male life expectancy in both cases.

Infant mortality

The infant mortality rate (IMR) is defined as the number of deaths under the age of one year per 1,000 live births.

Figure 4.24 shows how the IMR has changed over time in the West Midlands (with a consistently high rate) and the South East (with a consistently low rate), in comparison to England.

The West Midlands had a consistently higher IMR than the South East over this period, and the gap did not obviously narrow. In 1996, the IMR in the West Midlands was 6.8 deaths per 1,000 live births, and this reduced slightly to 6.5 in 2008. In contrast, the South East's rate decreased from 5.3 to 4.0 deaths per 1,000 live births. There is greater variability in the regions' data because of the relatively small number of such events that occur in each region compared with England as a whole.

Age-standardised mortality rates

Age-standardised mortality rates allow comparisons to be made between populations which may contain different age structures, for example, between the regions. They are standardised to the European Standard Population and measured per 100,000 population. The European Standard Population is a hypothetical population that is useful for comparisons between different countries, over time and between sexes. The analysis in this article focuses on the mortality rate from all causes, diseases of the respiratory and circulatory systems, and cancer. These were the underlying causes of death, as defined by the International Classification of Diseases (ICD). Data are for deaths registered in 2008.

Cardiovascular disease (CVD) is a form of circulatory disease, a generic term covering diseases of the heart or blood vessels. The major types of CVD are angina, heart attack, and stroke. CVD is associated with risk factors such as smoking, sedentary lifestyles, heavy alcohol consumption and poor diets.

Respiratory diseases refer to causes of death such as influenza, pneumonia and lung diseases (see ICD).

To provide an indication of the magnitude of the data, Table 4.25 compares the age-standardised mortality rates per

Figure 4.23

Life expectancy at birth in the North East and England, 1991–93 to 2006–08

Life expectancy at birth

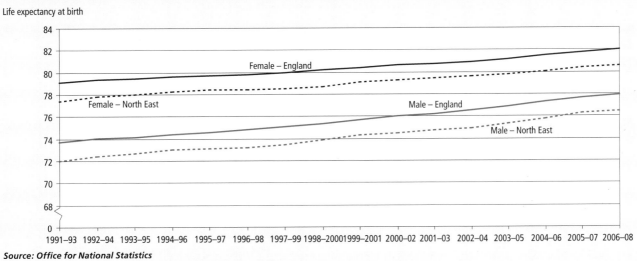

Source: Office for National Statistics

1

Figure 4.24

Infant mortality rate, England, West Midlands and South East, 1996 to 2008
Rate per 1,000 live births

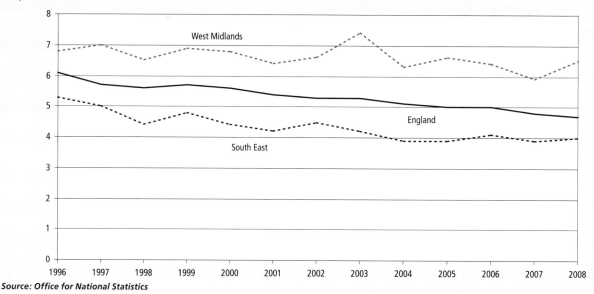

Source: Office for National Statistics

100,000 population for all causes and each of the three other causes considered in this article, for England only.

Drug use among 16 to 24-year-olds

The British Crime Survey (BCS), carried out by the Home Office, is an important source of information about levels of crime and public attitudes to crime as well as other criminal justice issues. The results play an important role in informing Government policy.

The BCS measures the amount of crime in England by asking people aged 16 and over about crimes they have experienced in the last year. It includes crimes which are not reported to the police, or recorded by them, so it is an important alternative to police records. The survey collects information about:

- the victims of crime

- the circumstances in which incidents occur

- the behaviour of offenders in committing crimes

A self completion module on the BCS is used to provide data on drug use among young people, focusing on 16 to 24-year-olds. This article focuses on 'all' drug use among 16 to 24-year-olds, without breaking this down by type of drug.

Table 4.25

Age-standardised mortality rates, selected causes, 2008

England	Rate per 100,000 population
All causes	575.3
Diseases of the circulatory system	176.6
Cancer	172.2
Diseases of the respiratory system	73.2

To add further context to this indicator, the most common drug taken by this age category in 2008/09 was cannabis. In England, 18.8 per cent of 16 to 24-year-olds had taken cannabis. The equivalent proportion in London was 13.6 per cent, contrasted against the South East at 22.6 per cent. These are the lowest and highest proportions across England respectively.

General Lifestyle Survey

In 2008 the Office for National Statistics launched the Integrated Household Survey (IHS). In the IHS, a questionnaire is comprised of two sections: a suite of core IHS questions, followed by individual survey modules, one of which is the General Lifestyle Survey (GLF). The GLF is the new name for the General Household Survey now that it is part of the IHS. The GLF is a multi-purpose survey carried out by ONS, and the results used in this article are for the 2008 calendar year.

The GLF can provide information and statistics for certain health indicators, including alcohol consumption, cigarette smoking and limiting longstanding illness as reported by the respondent.

Prevalence of cigarette smoking: by sex

This article solely focuses on 2008 smoking trends, but the GLF also provides regional time series data for the proportion of males and females aged 16 and over who are current smokers. Figure 4.26 shows the prevalence of cigarette smoking for men, women and all people in England from 2000 to 2008.

When using time series data from the GHS/GLF, it is important to remember that in 2005, a new sample design was adopted in line with European requirements, changing from a cross-sectional to a longitudinal format. As a consequence, datasets from 2006 are not independent from one another as the

Figure 4.26

Prevalence of adult[1] cigarette smoking by sex and for all people, England, 1998 to 2008

Percentages

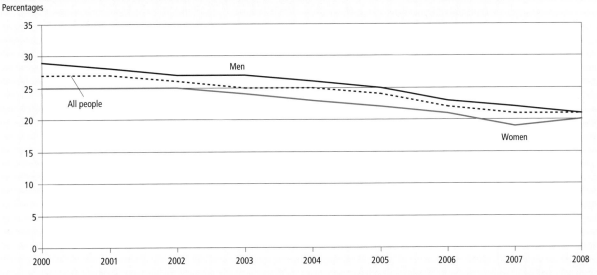

1   People aged 16 and over.
2   2005 data include last quarter of 2004/05 data due to survey change
    from financial to calendar year

Source: General Lifestyle Survey 2008, Office for National Statistics

sample of respondents overlaps. This new format is more efficient at detecting statistically significant estimates of change over time.

Other measures of smoking prevalence are recorded by the GLF, such as mean number of cigarettes people smoke per day.

It is likely that the survey underestimates cigarette consumption. Please see the report Smoking and drinking among adults, 2008 published alongside the GLF data.

Alcohol consumption: by sex

The measure used in the article is the maximum amount consumed on any one day in the previous seven days, as recorded by the GLF. For men, this is benchmarked at eight units or more, and for women six units or more. This indicator gives an estimate of the level of binge drinking in a region as the benchmark is twice the recommended safe maximum amount to drink in a day.

Other measures of alcohol consumption are available from the GLF such as the number of respondents drinking over four or three units in a day, for males and females respectively, as well as respondents drinking over 21 or 16 units over a week, for males and females respectively.

Obtaining reliable information about drinking behaviour is difficult, and social surveys consistently record lower levels of consumption than would be expected from data on alcohol sales. This is partly because people may consciously or unconsciously underestimate how much alcohol they consume.

Limiting longstanding illness

The GLF provides information about the self-reported health of adults and children, and about their use of health services.

This includes statistics of people aged 16 and over with a self-reported limiting longstanding illness, used as an indicator in this article. The question asked to the respondent is whether they have a long-standing illness, disability or infirmity. The question wording clarifies that longstanding means anything that has troubled the respondent over a period of time.

Childhood obesity

Obesity is a major public health concern due to its association with serious chronic diseases such as type 2 diabetes and hypertension, which are major risk factors for cardiovascular disease and cardiovascular related mortality. Obesity is also associated with cancer, disability and reduced quality of life, and can lead to premature death. It is therefore important to measure levels of childhood obesity as this could be a predictor of obesity prevalence in adult life.

Established in 2005, the National Child Measurement Programme (NCMP) for England weighs and measures children in reception year (typically aged 4–5 years) and Year 6 (aged 10–11 years). It is operated jointly by the Department of Health (DH) and the Department for Children, Schools and Families (DCSF). The findings are used to inform local planning and delivery of services for children and gather population-level surveillance data to allow analysis of trends in weight. The programme also engages with parents about the importance of healthy weight in children.

Prevalence rates were calculated by deriving every child's Body Mass Index (BMI) (an indicator of body fat based on height and weight) and referencing the age and sex-specific UK National BMI percentiles classification to count the number of children defined as underweight, healthy weight, overweight or obese. Obesity is defined as a BMI greater than or equal to the 95th percentile, that is the top 5 per cent of the assessed group in a specific year.

Pupils eligible for inclusion in the NCMP were all children in reception and Year 6 attending non-specialist, maintained schools in England. Geographical analyses are based on the location of the child's school rather than their home address. Parents and pupils are able to opt out of the measurement programme. Participation rates have increased over time, from 80 per cent in 2006/07 to 90 per cent in 2008/09. Participation rates were slightly higher in reception (91 per cent) than Year 6 (89 per cent). There is evidence that obese children in Year 6 were slightly more likely to opt out of being measured than other Year 6 children and so the figures for Year 6 are likely to be slightly underestimated. However, participation rate was shown to have little or no effect on prevalence estimates for reception children.

For charts, trends and geographical maps for national data,

please refer to the NHS Information Centre for health and social care report entitled 'National Child Measurement Programme: England 2008/09 school year'.

Cancer incidence

Age-standardised cancer incidence rates per 100,000 population are available with confidence intervals from the Office for National Statistics. This article selects lung cancer for both males and females and breast cancer. These rates are standardised to the European Standard Population as this allows comparisons between populations which may contain different proportions of people of different ages.

The incidence is defined as the number of newly diagnosed cases registered in each calendar year, and the data have been combined for the years 2005–07. Breast and lung cancer are defined by the International Classification of Diseases (ICD-10), Tenth Revision.

References

Regional Trends online data tables, March 2010, Office for National Statistics, available at: www.statistics.gov.uk/statbase/Product.asp?vlnk=14161

Health inequalities, Department of Health, available at: www.dh.gov.uk/en/Publichealth/Healthinequalities/index.htm

PSA target, Department of Health, 2008, available at: www.dh.gov.uk/en/Publichealth/Healthinequalities/ Healthinequalitiesguidancepublications/DH_064183

PSA Delivery Agreement 18: Promote better health and wellbeing for all, June 2009, HM Government, available at: www.hm-treasury.gov.uk/d/pbr_csr07_psa18.pdf

Methods for Area classification for statistical wards, Neighbourhood Statistics, available at: www.statistics.gov.uk/about/methodology_by_theme/area_ classification/wards/methodology.asp

North–south divide

Association of Public Health Observatories (APHO) Health Profiles 2009, available at: www.apho.org.uk/default.aspx?QN=HP_REGIONS_2009

People and places: A 2001 Census atlas of the UK, University of Sheffield, 2004, available at: www.sasi.group.shef.ac.uk/ publications/peopleandplaces.htm and North–south split 'getting wider', BBC News, 30 June 2004, available at: http://news.bbc.co.uk/1/hi/uk/3852227.stm

Health Profile of England 2008, Department of Health, January 2009, available at: www.dh.gov.uk/en/Publicationsandstatistics/Publications/ PublicationsStatistics/DH_093465 and

North–south divide widens in health map of England, *The Guardian*, 23 October 2007, available at: www.guardian.co.uk/society/2007/oct/23/health. northsouthdivide

Life expectancy

Life expectancy at birth and at age 65 by local areas in the United Kingdom, 2006–08, Online data tables, Office for National Statistics, available at: www.statistics.gov.uk/StatBase/Product.asp?vlnk=8841

Life expectancy at birth and at age 65 by local areas in the United Kingdom, 2006–08, *Statistical Bulletin*, October 2009, Office for National Statistics, available at: www.statistics.gov.uk/pdfdir/liex1009.pdf

Social Trends 39, Office for National Statistics, available at: www.statistics.gov.uk/downloads/theme_social/Social_ Trends39/Social_Trends_39.pdf

Life expectancy at birth 2006–08, General Details, Neighbourhood Statistics, available at: http://neighbourhood.statistics.gov.uk/dissemination/ MetadataDownloadPDF.do?downloadId=25602

Regional Trends online data tables, March 2010, Office for National Statistics, available at: www.statistics.gov.uk/statbase/Product.asp?vlnk=14161

Infant mortality rate

Regional Trends online data tables, March 2010, Office for National Statistics, available at: www.statistics.gov.uk/statbase/Product.asp?vlnk=14161

Health Statistics Quarterly 44, Winter 2009, Office for National Statistics, available at: www.statistics.gov.uk/downloads/theme_health/HSQ44.pdf

Infant mortality rate 2003–05, General Details, Neighbourhood Statistics, available at: http://neighbourhood.statistics.gov.uk/dissemination/ MetadataDownloadPDF.do?downloadId=20396

Age-standardised mortality rates

Regional Trends online data tables, March 2010, Office for National Statistics, available at: www.statistics.gov.uk/statbase/Product.asp?vlnk=14161

Mortality statistics: Deaths registered in England and Wales by area of usual residence, Online 2007 data tables, Office for National Statistics, available at: www.statistics.gov.uk/statbase/product.asp?vlnk=15229

Social Trends 39, Office for National Statistics, available at: www.statistics.gov.uk/downloads/theme_social/Social_ Trends39/Social_Trends_39.pdf

Health Statistics – Technical Assistance, Tools of the Trade, Confidence Intervals for a Crude Rate, Pennsylvania Department of Health, available at: www.health.state.pa.us/hpa/stats/techassist/cicruderate.htm

International Classification of Diseases (ICD), World Health Organisation, 2010, available at: www.who.int/classifications/icd/en/

Drug use

Regional Trends online data tables, March 2010, Office for National Statistics, available at: www.statistics.gov.uk/statbase/Product.asp?vlnk=14161

British Crime Survey and other surveys, Home Office, available at: www.homeoffice.gov.uk/rds/bcs1.html

Table 4.4 in the *Drug Misuse Declared* 2008/09 publication provides data on all drug use estimates, available at: www.homeoffice.gov.uk/rds/pdfs09/hosb1209.pdf

General Lifestyle Survey

Results from the General Lifestyle Survey (GLF) 2008, Office for National Statistics

www.statistics.gov.uk/downloads/theme_compendia/GLF08/ GeneraLifestyleSurvey2008.pdf

Smoking and drinking among adults 2008, General Lifestyle Survey, Office for National Statistics, available at: www.statistics.gov.uk/downloads/theme_compendia/GLF08/ GLFSmoking&DrinkingAmongAdults2008.pdf

Appendix B: Sample Design and Response, *General Lifestyle Survey,* Office for National Statistics, available at: www.statistics.gov.uk/StatBase/Product.asp?vlnk=5756&Pos =2&ColRank=1&Rank=272

Appendix C: Sampling error, *General Lifestyle Survey,* Office for National Statistics, available at: www.statistics.gov.uk/StatBase/Product.asp?vlnk=5756&Pos =2&ColRank=1&Rank=272

Overview Report, *General Lifestyle Survey 2007,* Office for National Statistics, available at: www.statistics.gov.uk/downloads/theme_compendia/GLF08/ GLFoverview2008.pdf

Regional Trends online data tables, March 2010, Office for National Statistics, available at: www.statistics.gov.uk/statbase/Product.asp?vlnk=14161

Childhood obesity

National Child Measurement Programme: England, 2008/09 school year, Tables, December 2009, NHS The Information Centre for Health and Social Care, available at: www.ic.nhs.uk/statistics-and-data-collections/health-and-lifestyles/obesity/national-child-measurement-programme-england-2008-09-school-year

National Child Measurement Programme: England, 2008/09 school year, December 2009, NHS The Information Centre for Health and Social Care, available at: www.ic.nhs.uk/webfiles/publications/ncmp/ncmp0809/ NCMP_England_2008_09_school_year_report_2.pdf

Cancer incidence

Regional Trends online data tables, March 2010, Office for National Statistics, available at: www.statistics.gov.uk/statbase/Product.asp?vlnk=14161

International Classification of Diseases (ICD), World Health Organisation, 2010, available at: www.who.int/classifications/icd/en/

Understanding income at small area level

By Stephen Bond and Cecilia Campos, Office for National Statistics

Abstract

The Office for National Statistics has produced experimental estimates of average household income for Middle Layer Super Output Areas (MSOAs) in England and Wales. These are based on the Family Resources Surveys of 2004/05 and 2007/08, using a model which draws on administrative data to produce estimates for small areas.

This article looks at spatial disparities in average income, in particular how it was distributed within regions and local authorities.

The article found wide variation in patterns of average household income, in particular London had the widest spread whilst Wales had the narrowest spread, based on net income before housing costs (BHC) in 2007/08.

Wales had the largest increase in average household income BHC since 2004/05, with the North West and South West having the smallest.

West Midlands and the North East had seen the gap between the richest and poorest areas decrease the most, with only the East Midlands having a large increase in gap.

Summary guidance is provided on issues associated with using model-based estimates.

The article should be of interest to planners and regeneration specialists, and those who want to understand local economies.

Introduction

This article focuses on the model-based estimates of average household income[1] for Middle Layer Super Output Areas (MSOA) – see Glossary – produced by the Office for National Statistics. It aims to explore how income was spread within regions and whether there had been any major changes over a three-year time period.

The article consists of the following sections:

- An introduction to the model-based estimates and how they should be used

- A study of how income was distributed across and within Wales and the nine regions of England

- An assessment of how income in each region has changed between 2004/05 and 2007/08. Also, whether the variation in income within-region has changed, including whether the gap between the areas with highest incomes and those with lowest incomes has changed.

Small area income estimates, 2007/08

The new model-based income estimates for England and Wales have been produced to fulfill a requirement for more up to date income information at the local level. They are estimates of average weekly household income for MSOAs based on data from the Family Resources Surveys (FRS) of 2004/05 and 2007/08. They are currently classed as experimental statistics.

Four estimates of average weekly household income were produced:

- Gross income

- Net income

- Net income before housing costs (equivalised) (BHC)

- Net income after housing costs (equivalised) (AHC).

This article focuses mainly on the equivalised BHC data, but also shows the impact of housing costs particularly in London and the South East using AHC income.

---

1 For brevity, this article uses the term 'income' to refer to 'average household income'.

Equivalisation adjusts the income estimates to take account of household size and composition, so that more meaningful comparisons can be made between households with different numbers of occupants.[2]

Gross income includes earnings, self-employment, investments, various benefits and other sources of income. Net income is gross income less income tax and national insurance payments, council tax, pension contributions, maintenance and child support payments and parental contribution to students living away from home.

Because the estimates were averages of household incomes within each MSOA, households with very high levels of income were combined with those of low levels. This resulted in distributions of average income that were much less extreme than the distributions of individual household income. Therefore caution needs to be exercised when comparing this analysis with other analyses of spread of income that use household level data.[3]

Box 1: Model-based estimates

The model-based approach to producing the estimates was based on determining a relationship between household income measured in the FRS, and administrative data for the MSOAs. Having established this relationship, the administrative data are used to estimate household income for each MSOA. Both sources of data borrow strength from each other to arrive at an unbiased and consistent set of small area estimates that could not be produced from either source in isolation.

The main limitation of estimates for small areas is that they are subject to uncertainty due to survey sampling and the modelling process. ONS have produced confidence intervals associated with the estimates to make the accuracy of the estimates clear. The model-based confidence intervals provide a range of income for each MSOA within which one would expect the true value to fall 95 per cent of the time.

Box 2: Guidance on using the income estimates

There are five main considerations when using the income estimates.

1. **Other geographical areas**. MSOA estimates can be aggregated to provide average income for higher geographical levels, for example, local authorities. No accuracy estimates are available for such aggregations.

2. **Ranking**. Care needs to be taken when using ranks based on MSOA estimates due to their uncertainty.

3. **Extreme areas.** The modelling process tends to shrink estimates towards the average level, so the true distribution of MSOA average incomes will have more extreme high and low values than the estimated values.

4. **Consistency between the four estimates**. Due to the modelling approach, some inconsistencies may arise when comparing the different estimates.

5. **Comparison over time**. Consistent estimates have been produced using 2004/05 data and 2007/08 data. If the confidence intervals of estimates at the two time points for a particular MSOA do not overlap, then there is evidence of change over time. However, the difference between the estimates should not be interpreted as an accurate measure of change.

Regional patterns of income

The first stage in this analysis looks at regional patterns in average household net income, firstly using estimates from the FRS, and then the model-based MSOA estimates which were constrained to add up to the regional estimates from the FRS.

Income distribution across the English regions and Wales

Table 5.1 shows a wide range of net average household income when looking across England and Wales.[4] The highest income levels before housing costs were in London, followed by the South East and East of England. The lowest occurred in the North East, closely followed by the North West, and the West Midlands. London's average income BHC was 55 per cent greater than the North East average, a difference of £220 per week.

For net income after housing costs (AHC), Table 5.2 shows the same regional distribution of income, with all income levels lowered by the amount spent on housing costs. After the cost of housing had been taken into consideration, London's income was 46 per cent greater than the North East, a difference of £160, illustrating the impact of housing

2 In the 2007/08 estimates, the OECD method of equivalisation has been used. Previously the McClements method was used, the differences between the two are minor, marginally changing the estimates of the MSOAs with highest levels of income. For more information, see: *Economic and Labour Market Review*, Vol 14, No 1, January 2010, Grace Anyaegbu.

3 For example, see *Economic and Labour Market Review*, Vol 3, No 8, August 2009, Andrew Barnard or Department of Work and Pensions data series on Households Below Average Income http://research.dwp.gov.uk/asd/hbai/hbai2008/contents.asp

4 All data rounded to the nearest £10 as additional precision is beyond the accuracy of the estimates.

Table 5.1

Average weekly household net income (equivalised BEFORE housing costs)

April 2007 to March 2008	£ per week
North East	400
North West	420
West Midlands	420
Wales	430
Yorkshire and The Humber	430
East Midlands	440
South West	460
East of England	510
South East	570
London	620

Source: Family Resources Survey.

Table 5.2

Average weekly household net income (equivalised AFTER housing costs)

April 2007 to March 2008	£ per week
North East	350
North West	370
West Midlands	370
Wales	380
Yorkshire and The Humber	380
East Midlands	390
South West	400
East of England	440
South East	490
London	510

Source: Family Resources Survey.

Box 3: Spread of income

Four percentiles are used to help determine the spread of income within each region.

- P10 (lower decile): the income level below which 10 per cent of MSOAs lie.

- P25 (first quartile): the income level below which 25 per cent of MSOAs lie.

- P75 (third quartile): the income level below which 75 per cent of MSOAs lie.

- P90 (upper decile): the income level below which 90 per cent of MSOAs lie.

Percentiles are defined in three different ways in this article:

- Nationally, using all MSOAs in England and Wales

- Regionally, using all MSOAs in a selected region

- Locally, using all MSOAs in a selected local authority.

The spread of income is defined by the ratios of these percentiles.

- P90/P10 is the spread of the extremes of income levels.

- P75/25 is the spread of the central part of the distribution.

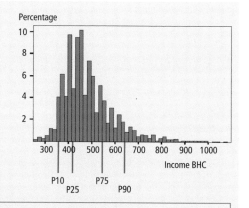

Example calculation of P90/P10 ratio:

P90 - £630

P10 = £370

P90/P10 = 630/370 = 1.7

Or P90 is 70% bigger than P10.

So the lowest average income of the upper 10% group of MSOAs is 70% higher than the highest average income of the bottom 10% of MSOAs.

costs in London (the difference between London and the North East has reduced from £220 to £160 per week).

Income distributions within the English regions and Wales

Patterns of income for each region show relative levels across England and Wales. They do not mean that all households within each region had the same level of income. To look at how income was distributed within each region, MSOA estimates are useful.

Figure 5.3 shows distributions of net average income before housing costs for MSOAs within each English region and Wales in 2007/08. The two regions which had the broadest distributions of

MSOA income were London and the South East. These were the two regions which also had the highest average income levels (Table 5.1). The average MSOA income for the remaining regions was much more tightly distributed, with Wales seeming to have a particularly small spread of income.

The spread of income was explored numerically in Table 5.4 using P10, P25, P75 and P90 thresholds, and the two ratios P90/P10 and P75/25 (see box for a full explanation of the P values) where the percentiles were calculated from MSOAs within each region.

Looking at all MSOAs in England and Wales, Table 5.4 shows that 10 per cent of MSOAs had an average net income BHC

Figure 5.3

Distribution of MSOA average household net income BHC, model-based estimates, 2007/08

Percentages

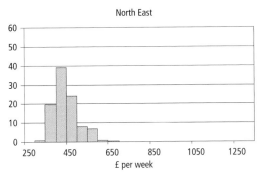

North East

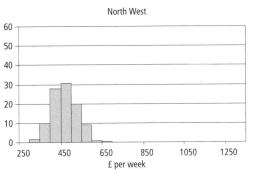

North West

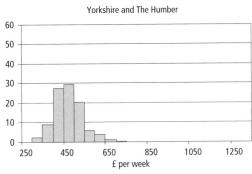

Yorkshire and The Humber

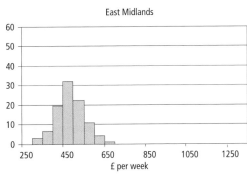

East Midlands

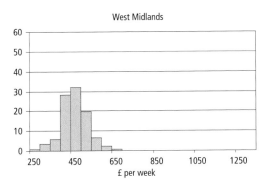

West Midlands

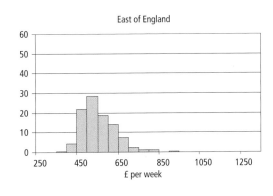

East of England

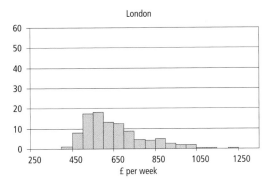

London

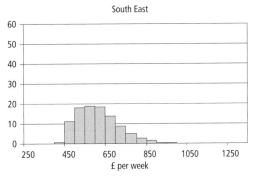

South East

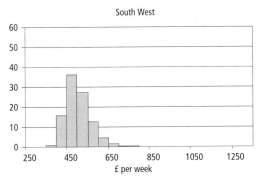

South West

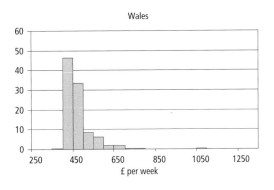

Wales

less than the P10 threshold of £370 per week, and 25 per cent less than the P25 threshold of £410 per week. At the upper end of the distribution, 25 per cent of all MSOAs had BHC income greater than £540 per week and 10 per cent greater than £630 per week. A P90/P10 ratio for all MSOAs of 1.7 means that the lowest average income of the upper 10 per cent of MSOAs was 70 per cent higher than the highest average income of the bottom 10 per cent of MSOAs. The P75/P25 ratio of 1.3 means that the upper end of the centre of the distribution was 30 per cent higher than the lower end of the centre.

The region with the smallest ratios (for both the P75/P25 and P90/P10) was Wales, confirming what Figure.5.3 is showing. For MSOAs in Wales, the upper end of the distribution (P90) was 34 per cent higher than the lower end (P10). For the centre of the income range, the top was 13 per cent higher than the bottom.

Although Wales had the narrowest spread of income, it did not have the lowest percentage of extreme incomes. The P10 value for MSOAs in Wales of £380 per week was higher than the P10 values for North East, North West, Yorkshire and The Humber, West Midlands and East Midlands. At the higher end of the distribution, only the North East and West Midlands had a lower P90 value.

In contrast, London was the region with the highest P10 value (£460 per week), the highest P90 value (£820 per week) and the highest percentage difference between the two (78 per cent). This high P90/P10 ratio arose mainly from the very high P90 value. Comparing the P90 value for London (£820 per week) with the South East (£710 per week) we found a difference of £110 per week, whereas the P10 values for these two regions differed only by £10 per week.

The South West was interesting in that it was the region with

the fourth highest average income, and yet had the third smallest spread as measured by P90/P10.

Similar patterns emerge when looking at the central part of the spread of regional income, the P75/P25 measure. London still has the highest spread, but was a lot closer to the South East which, in turn, was close to spreads in the North West, Yorkshire and The Humber, and the East of England. The English region with the smallest central spread was the South West.

In summary, this section showed that regions with the highest average income levels also had the highest spread of income. However, the regions with the smallest spread of income were not necessarily the regions with the lowest average levels of income.

Spatial patterns of income

Map 5.5 shows the pattern of MSOAs which had the highest and lowest average income estimates within England and Wales. When looking at spatial patterns of income distribution using the small area model estimates, it is important that model uncertainty is taken into consideration. MSOAs were included in the map if their entire 95 per cent confidence interval lay within the thresholds which define the top and bottom deciles (10 per cent) of MSOAs in England and Wales, or if their confidence interval fell within the top and bottom quartile (25 per cent). These were areas that we were very confident had high or low levels of income.

The patterns shown in Map 5.5 reveal how London and the South East were very different to the midlands and north of England. The majority of MSOAs with high levels of income in England and Wales (green stars) were to be found in London and the South East. Equally, none of the MSOAs with very low levels of income (grey circles) were to be found in these regions.

Table 5.4

Thresholds and ratios for MSOA BHC net income estimates, model-based estimates 2007/08
£ per week/ratios

	P10	P25	P75	P90	P75/P25	P90/P10
Wales	380	390	440	510	1.13	1.34
North East	350	360	430	480	1.19	1.37
South West	390	420	490	540	1.17	1.38
West Midlands	354	380	460	500	1.21	1.41
East of England	420	450	560	610	1.24	1.45
North West	350	380	460	510	1.21	1.46
Yorkshire and The Humber	350	380	470	510	1.24	1.46
East Midlands	360	400	480	530	1.20	1.47
South East	450	490	630	710	1.29	1.58
London	460	500	680	820	1.36	1.78
All MSOAs	370	410	540	630	1.32	1.70

Source: Office for National Statistics

Map 5.5   **High and low levels of average household net income BHC[1] England and Wales, 2007/08**

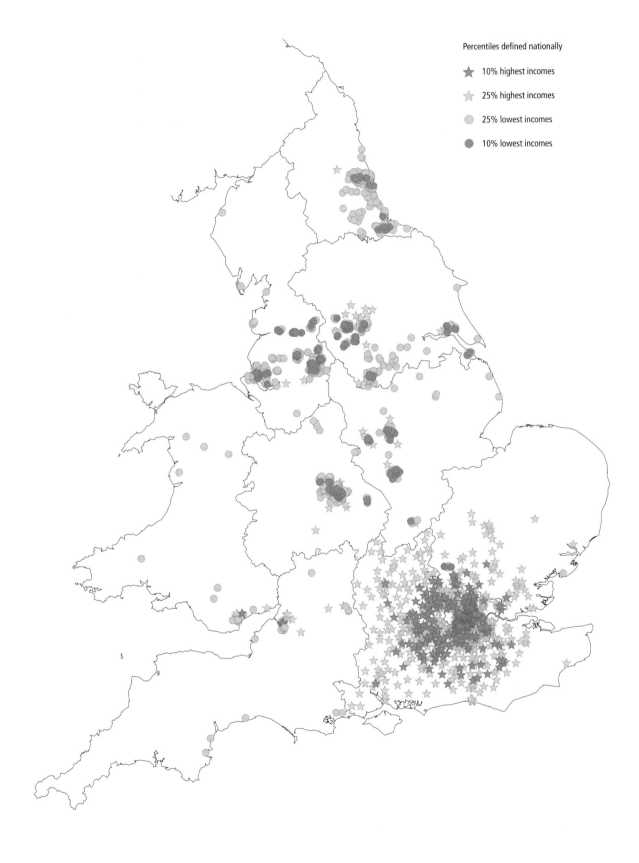

Percentiles defined nationally

★   10% highest incomes

☆   25% highest incomes

◯   25% lowest incomes

⬤   10% lowest incomes

Source: Office for National Statistics

1 Before housing costs.

1

Map 5.6   **High and low levels of average household net income AHC,[1] England and Wales, 2007/08**

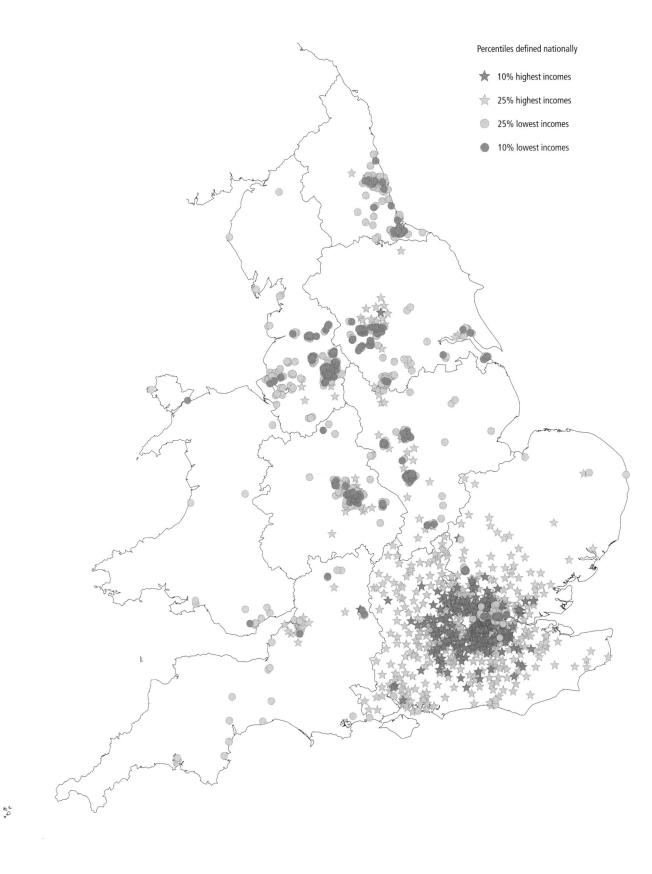

Percentiles defined nationally

★ 10% highest incomes

☆ 25% highest incomes

○ 25% lowest incomes

● 10% lowest incomes

1 After housing costs.

Source: Office for National Statistics

There was also a band of MSOAs towards the southern end of the East of England region with high levels of income, reflecting the influence of the economic prosperity of London in this region. There were two MSOAs with very low levels of income in the south west of the East of England (partially overlapping dark grey circles); these were neighbouring MSOAs located in Luton.

The South West and Wales were interesting due to a lack of MSOAs with very low levels of income, and only one MSOA in each with very high levels of income.

The remaining regions had similar patterns with many MSOAs around the towns and cities having low levels of income, and very few having high levels. Where MSOAs in these regions had high levels of income, they tended to be on the outskirts of a town or city.

Map 5.6 shows the pattern of high and low income levels after housing costs had been removed. It shows the same general pattern of high income in and around London, with low income levels in the midlands and the north of England. However, taking housing costs into consideration shows that there were MSOAs in London and along the South East coast with low and very low levels of income.

Also, AHC income levels in the midlands and the North of England were relatively higher than BHC reflecting the relatively lower

costs of housing. This was shown by a small increase in the number of green stars in these areas. However, for Manchester and Leeds in particular, there was an increase in the number of very low income MSOAs, indicating that housing costs were disproportionately higher in these cities than any increase in income associated with the prosperity that the city generates.

Taking housing costs into consideration, Wales and the South West had more areas with low and very low levels of income.

Focus on London and the influence of housing costs

Map 5.7 shows the distribution of MSOAs in London which had the highest or lowest levels of BHC income, defined using the same national thresholds as Map 5.5.

There was a broad swathe of MSOAs to the west of the city centre, predominantly but not exclusively to the north of the river, that had very high or high average net BHC income levels. Other MSOAs with high income levels were spread around the region, particularly towards its perimeter. There were areas towards Heathrow in the west and in the north east of the region which had few MSOAs with high average income levels.

It is noteworthy that in London there were no MSOAs with average income levels that were below the 10 or 25 per cent thresholds of MSOAs in England and Wales.

Map 5.7   High and low levels of average household net income BHC,[1] London, 2007/08

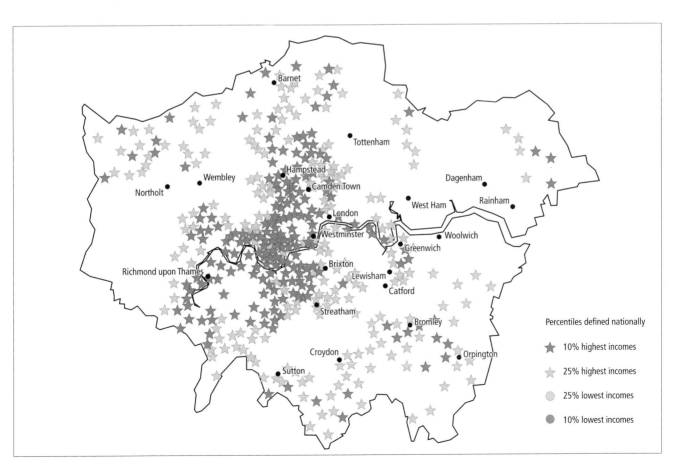

1 Before housing costs.

Map 5.8 **High and low levels of average household net income AHC,[1] London, 2007/08**

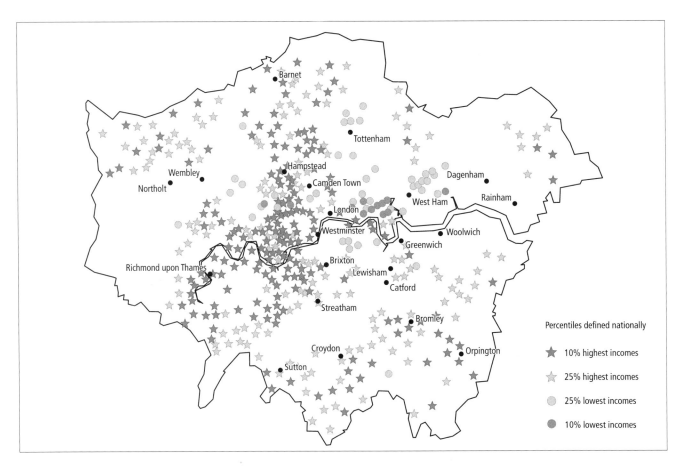

1 After housing costs.

Map 5.9 **High and low levels of average household net income within the North West, 2007/08**

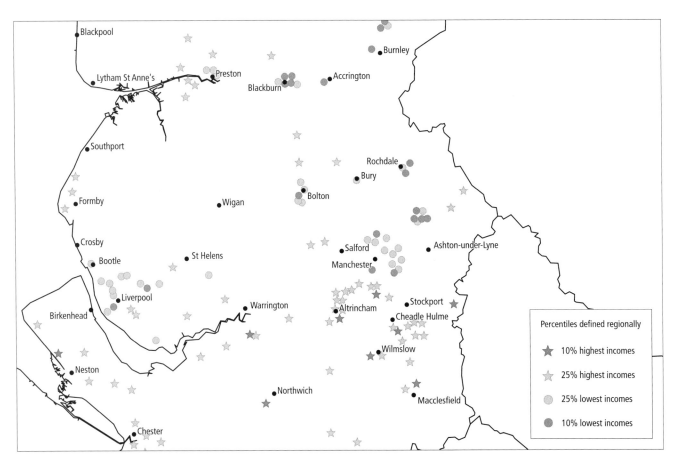

Map 5.8 repeats this analysis for average net income after housing costs (AHC). The pattern of high income was similar to the BHC income levels, albeit with fewer MSOAs with green stars.

The main change was the emergence of MSOAs in London whose income levels after housing costs had been taken into consideration that now lie within the thresholds for the bottom 10 per cent and 25 per cent in England and Wales. The MSOAs whose incomes lay below the P10 threshold were predominantly located in Tower Hamlets, with one each in Barking & Dagenham, Westminster, and Kensington & Chelsea. In addition, local authorities which had more than one MSOA with income below the P25 threshold were: Brent, Havering, Enfield, Newham, Hackney and, to the south of the Thames, Southwark.

Analysis of incomes within a region

As with the regional income spread analysis shown in Table 5.2, this section uses percentiles defined regionally. In this way, analysis of spatial patterns of income within a region is not overly dominated by the high incomes in London and the South East. The important thing to note in this analysis is that the highlighted MSOAs do not represent the same income bands as shown in Map 5.5.

The following section provides an example of within-region analysis, exploring the industrialised band across the centre of the North West region, shown in Map 5.9. The broad pattern was one of low income levels around the major cities and towns (Manchester, Liverpool, Bolton, Burnley, Rochdale, Blackburn and Preston).

MSOAs with income in the top decile or quartile were to be found predominantly to the south of Manchester and away from the main towns and cities.

Local patterns of Income

This analysis drills down to examine income levels within local authorities (LAs). This section highlights the local authorities of Manchester and Liverpool in the North West.

To provide a meaningful comparison between two local authorities in the same region, percentiles based on MSOAs within the region were used to define regional high and low

levels of income. Thus the colours of MSOAs in both parts of Map 5.11 were both based on the same threshold.

Manchester had a swathe of MSOAs to the north and east of the city centre with income levels below the regional P10 and P25 thresholds. There was also one additional MSOA to the south of the city centre whose income lay below the P10 threshold. Further south, there was one MSOA whose income lay above the P90 threshold, and three above the P75 threshold.

Liverpool had only one MSOA whose income was below the regional P10 threshold, and none above the P90. The pattern of MSOAs below the P25 threshold was more spread out than for Manchester.

The spatial patterns shown in Map 5.11 suggest that Manchester had a wider spread of income than Liverpool, and that the areas with very high and low levels of income were more clustered in Manchester than in Liverpool.

Table 5.10 provides basic data for these two local authorities. Manchester and Liverpool are similarly sized LAs containing 53 and 59 MSOAs respectively. Average weekly BHC income for the two was the same at £390 per week.[5] However, the spreads of income were different with Manchester having a lower P10 value and higher P90 value than Liverpool.[6]

This difference in spread was revealed by the P90/P10 ratio. For Manchester, the upper end of the income distribution was 50 per cent higher than the lower. The equivalent for Liverpool was slightly lower at 42 per cent. Thus the data support the messages shown in Map 5.11.

Changes in regional patterns of income

This section looks at how regional income levels in 2007/08, both across regions and within regions, had changed compared with 2004/05.

Table 5.12 provides changes in average net income before housing costs for the English regions and Wales. The largest percentage change occurred in Wales, increasing from £370 to £430 per week, a change of 16 per cent. Next was the South East (14 per cent), which was the region with the biggest actual change of £70 per week. Thus the largest changes

Table 5.10

BHC net income distributions from MSOAs in Manchester and Liverpool, 2007/08

£ per week/ratio

Local Authority	Number of MSOAs	Average BHC income	P10	P90	P90 / P10
Manchester	53	390	322	480	1.49
Liverpool	59	390	330	470	1.42

Source: Office for National Statistics

---

5   Calculated as a household weighted average
6   To explore spread within a local authority, local percentiles are used.

Map 5.11   **Local patterns of average household net income for Manchester[1] and Liverpool[1] by MSOA[2], 2007/08**

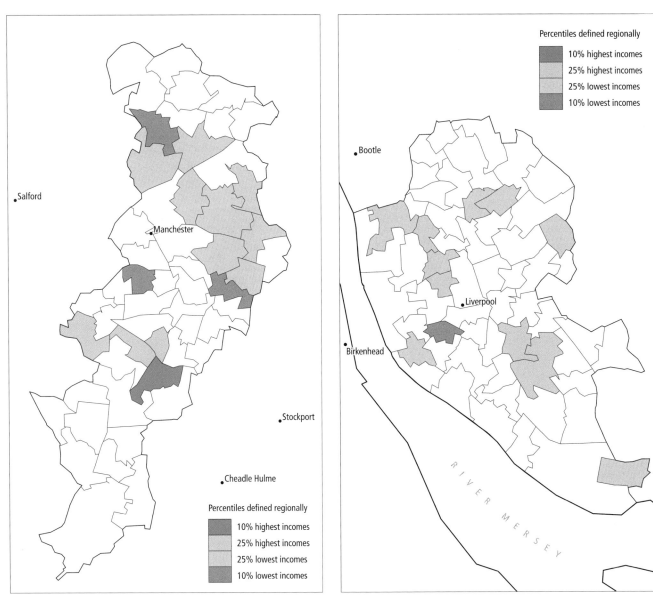

1 These maps represent the local authority districts of Manchester and of Liverpool.
2 Middle Layer Super Output Area.

Table 5.12

Changes in net income before housing costs

Regions	2004/05	2007/08	2004/05–2007/08	2004/05–2007/08
	£ per week	£ per week	£ per week	percentage difference
Wales	370	430	60	16
South East	500	570	70	14
Yorkshire and The Humber	380	430	50	13
East Midlands	390	440	50	13
North East	360	400	40	11
East of England	460	510	50	11
London	560	620	60	11
West Midlands	380	420	40	11
North West	390	420	30	8
South West	430	460	30	7

Source: Office for National Statistics

Figure 5.13

Regional distributions of change in BHC income[1]

Percentages

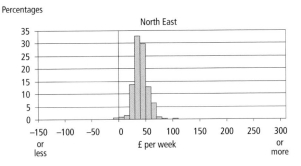

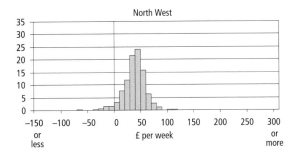

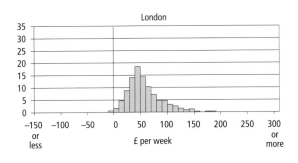

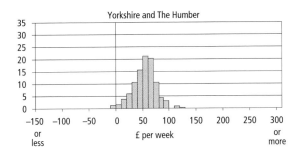

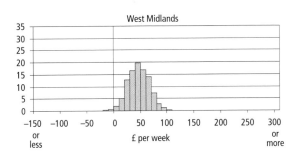

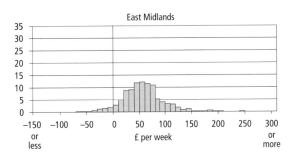

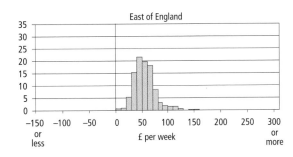

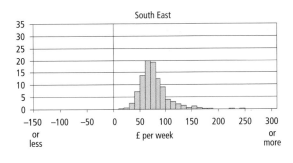

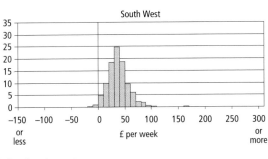

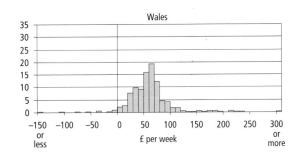

1   Before housing costs.

Figure 5.14

Scatter plot showing MSOA level BHC[1] income in 2004/05 and 2007/08: by region

£ per week

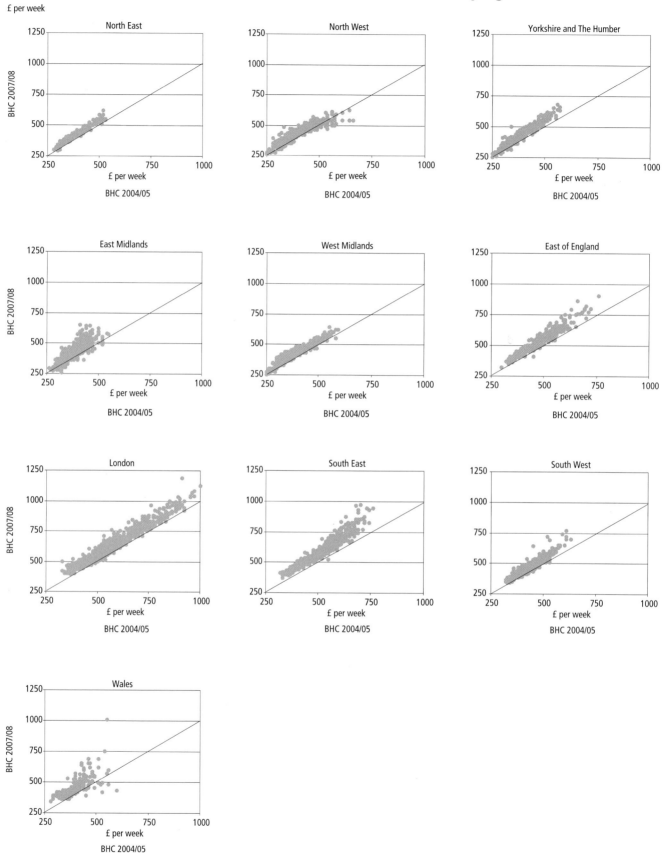

1 Before housing costs.

occurred in regions with one of the highest and one of the lowest levels of income.

In contrast, the South West had the smallest increase of £30 per week, a 7 per cent increase, along with the North West which had an 8 per cent increase.

Variation within each region

This section looks at how change within each region varied, and specifically asks how the gap was changing between MSOAs with the highest levels of income and MSOAs with the lowest levels of income.

Figure 5.13 provides histograms showing the proportions of MSOAs that had different changes in income levels for each region. The black vertical line represents no change in income.

Looking at the spread of income change, the East Midlands and London stand out as having a wider spread than the other regions. The South East, London and Wales have a particularly long 'tail' at the upper end of the distribution, indicating that some of the biggest increases occurred in these regions. Wales also appears to have a long tail at the lower end of the distribution.

The narrowest distribution was in the North East where most MSOAs had very similar changes in income levels, around £40 per week.

Figure 5.14 shows the relationship between income levels in 2004/05 and 2007/08 for each region. Each point on the plot represents the income for a particular MSOA for both years, with the y=x line superimposed. Dots above the line show MSOAs with an increase of income between 2004/05 and 2007/08.

Figure 5.14 shows that Wales in particular has a broader spread of points above and below the line, indicating that more

change in average income was occurring in Wales than the English regions.

To explore these differences in a more methodical way, Table 5.15 shows the changes in the thresholds for P10 and P90 within each region for 2004/05 to 2007/08 (note regions are sorted by increasing P90/P10 threshold – the top region is where the gap between the highest and lowest income MSOAs has reduced the most).

The largest percentage increase in the P10 threshold occurred in Wales where the 2007/08 value was 19 per cent greater than that for 2004/05. Thus the income levels for the MSOAs with the lowest average income levels in Wales increased in percentage terms by more than equivalent MSOAs in any England region.

The region with the second largest increase in P10 threshold was the South East, at 15 per cent, followed by a number of regions that had increases of around 12–14 per cent. The regions with the lowest increases in P10 threshold were the South West (5 per cent), the East Midlands (9 per cent) and the North West (9 per cent).

The largest change in the P90 threshold was in the East Midlands (18 per cent), followed by the South East (16 per cent) and Wales (16 per cent). For these regions, those areas which had the highest levels of income in 2004/05 increased them further.

The change in the P90/P10 ratio provides evidence for changes in the spread of income distributions within the regions. A decrease in the P90/P10 ratio means that the difference between the bottom group of MSOAs and the top group of MSOAs was smaller in 2007/08 than it was in 2004/05. Regions with decreasing P90/P10 ratios had a reduction in the gap between the poorest and the most affluent MSOAs.

Table 5.15

Differences in within-region percentile thresholds and ratio for BHC[1] income, 2004/05 to 2007/08

	Differences				
	P10 (£ per week)	P10 (percentage)	P90 (£ per week)	P90 (percentage)	P90/P10 (ratio)
West Midlands	40	14	30	6	−0.10
North East	40	13	31	7	−0.08
London	50	12	70	9	−0.05
North West	30	9	30	6	−0.04
Wales	60	19	70	16	−0.03
Yorkshire and The Humber	40	13	50	11	−0.03
East of England	50	14	60	11	−0.03
South East	60	15	100	16	0.01
South West	20	5	40	8	0.03
East Midlands	30	9	80	18	0.11
All MSOAs	40	12	70	13	0.01

1   Before housing costs.

The West Midlands had the biggest decrease in the P90/P10 ratio of −0.10. This means that the West Midlands had a 10 percentage point decrease in the income gap between the thresholds defining the top and bottom groups. This decrease can be seen from the percentage changes in the P10 and P90 values, where the P10 value for the West Midlands increased by 14 per cent compared with a smaller increase in the P90 value of 6 per cent.

The North East also saw the gap between the bottom and the top decrease, with a fall of 8 percentage points. The only area to see a large increase in the gap was the East Midlands – the consequence of a fairly small increase in the threshold for the poorest areas and a large increase for the most affluent. Other regions had small increases or decreases in the gap between lowest and highest incomes.

Conclusions

Using the model-based estimates of average income helps understand patterns of income nationally, regionally and locally.

Locally, spatial patterns of neighbourhoods with low income help identify communities that may suffer due to low average income levels. These estimates, therefore, can complement the income domain for the Indices of Multiple Deprivation.[7] The model-based estimates also provide good discrimination at the upper end of the income distribution, locating areas with high average income. Using the before and after housing cost income levels reveals where the high cost of housing causes communities to have low levels of income, once housing costs have been deducted.

Regionally, the model-based estimates permit measures of spread of income to be analysed. This analysis has shown that:

- The North East had the lowest average income and the second narrowest spread behind Wales

- London and the South East had the highest average income and the widest spread

- After taking housing costs into consideration, London and the South East still had the highest average incomes, but they moved much closer to other regions

- The West Midlands, East of England, North West, Yorkshire and The Humber, and the East Midlands all had very similar spreads of average income

- Since 2004/05, Wales has seen the greatest increase in average income, rising 16 per cent over the three-year period

- The lowest regional increases between 2004/05 and 2007/08 were in the North West and South West

- The regions where the gap between the highest and lowest average income closed the most were the West Midlands and the North East. Conversely, the gap increased by 11 percentage points for the East Midlands

At national level, this article has helped to demonstrate the income gap between those areas influenced by London and those that are not. Virtually all the MSOAs which had income levels in the top 10 per cent for England and Wales were in or around London. Equally, virtually all the MSOAs which had income levels in the bottom 10 per cent for England and Wales were in the midlands and the north of England.

Finally, this article has shown some of the insights that are possible using model-based estimates despite the uncertainty in the estimates. It has presented cautions regarding comparisons that should not be attempted, whilst demonstrating the value that these estimates offer in understanding the distribution of average household income throughout the country.

---

7   See 'Understanding patterns of Deprivation' in *Regional Trends* 41, pp 93-114 for more details on the Indices of Multiple Deprivation.

Region and Country Profiles

6.1	North East	97
6.2	North West	98
6.3	Yorkshire and The Humber	99
6.4	East Midlands	100
6.5	West Midlands	101
6.6	East of England	102
6.7	London	103
6.8	South East	104
6.9	South West	105
6.10a	Wales	106
6.10b	Cymru	107
6.11	Scotland	108
6.12	Northern Ireland	109

DATA

Download data by
clicking the online pdf

www.statistics.gov.uk/
regionaltrends42

Statistical Regions of the United Kingdom[1]

SCOTLAND

NORTHERN
IRELAND

NORTH
EAST

ENGLAND

Government
Office Region
boundary

NORTH
WEST

YORKSHIRE
AND THE
HUMBER

EAST
MIDLANDS

WEST
MIDLANDS

EAST

WALES

LONDON

SOUTH EAST

SOUTH WEST

1 For the purposes of statistical analyses, the United Kingdom has been divided into 12 'statistical regions'.

North East

Map 6.1   Population density: by local or unitary authority, 2008

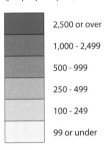

Population density, 2008
(people per sq km)

- 2,500 or over
- 1,000 - 2,499
- 500 - 999
- 250 - 499
- 100 - 249
- 99 or under

1 Wansbeck
2 Blyth Valley
3 North Tyneside
4 South Tyneside
5 Sunderland
6 Newcastle upon Tyne
7 Easington
8 Chester-le-Street
9 Hartlepool UA
10 Stockton-on-Tees UA
11 Middlesbrough UA

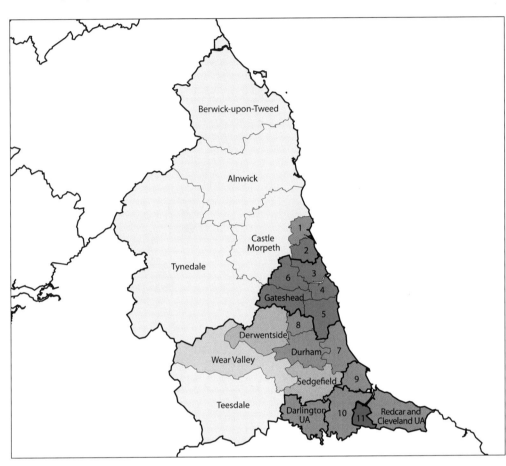

- The North East had a population of 2.6 million in mid-2008, an increase of 1.3 per cent since 2003. This compares with an overall increase of 3.1 per cent for the UK over the same period (Online table 1.2).

- People over state pension age (65 and over for men and 60 and over for women) in the North East in 2008 made up 20.1 per cent of the population, compared with 17.9 per cent for the under-16s. This compares with averages for the UK of 19.2 per cent and 18.8 per cent respectively (Online table 10.3).

- In the North East, men aged 65 in 2006–08 could expect to live another 16.7 years and women 19.3 years. This compares with 17.5 and 20.2 years in the UK as a whole (Online table 6.8).

- In the North East, 44.9 per cent of pupils achieved five or more grades A*–C at GCSE level or equivalent including English and mathematics in 2007/08, compared with 47.7 per cent for the UK as a whole (Online table 4.8).

- The unemployment rate in the North East stood at 9.3 per cent in the fourth quarter of 2009, higher than the UK rate of 7.8 per cent (Online table 1.1).

- The proportion of children living in workless households in the second quarter of 2009 was higher in the North East (21 per cent) than the England average (17 per cent) (Online table 8.6).

- In April 2009, the median gross weekly earnings for full-time employees on adult rates who were resident in the North East was £439, lower than the UK median of £489 (Online table 9.19).

- Labour productivity (gross value added per hour worked) in the North East in 2008 was 9.9 per cent below the UK average (Online table 3.2).

- North East local authorities recycled 28 per cent of household waste in 2007/08 compared with an England average of 35 per cent (Online table 5.11).

North West

Map 6.2   Population density: by local or unitary authority, 2008

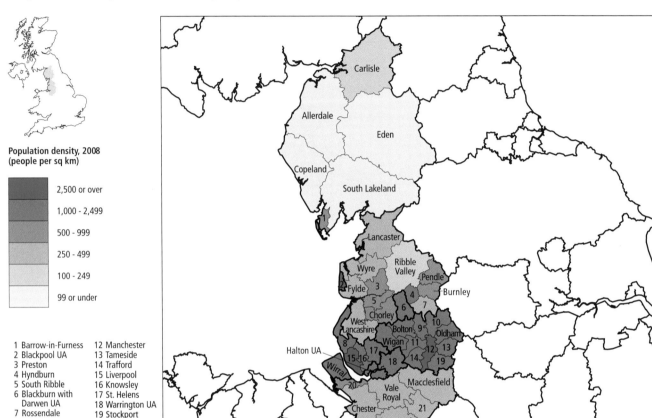

Population density, 2008
(people per sq km)

2,500 or over

1,000 - 2,499

500 - 999

250 - 499

100 - 249

99 or under

1 Barrow-in-Furness
2 Blackpool UA
3 Preston
4 Hyndburn
5 South Ribble
6 Blackburn with
  Darwen UA
7 Rossendale
8 Sefton
9 Bury
10 Rochdale
11 Salford
12 Manchester
13 Tameside
14 Trafford
15 Liverpool
16 Knowsley
17 St. Helens
18 Warrington UA
19 Stockport
20 Ellesmere
   Port & Neston
21 Congleton

- The North West had a population of 6.9 million in mid-2008, an increase of 1.1 per cent since 2003. This compares with an overall increase of 3.1 per cent for the UK over the same period (Online table 1.2).

- People over state pension age (65 and over for men and 60 and over for women) in the North West in 2008 made up 19.4 per cent of the population, compared with 18.9 per cent for the under-16s. This compares with averages for the UK of 19.2 per cent and 18.8 per cent respectively (Online table 10.3).

- In the North West, men aged 65 in 2006–08 could expect to live another 16.8 years and women 19.4 years. This compares with 17.5 and 20.2 years in the UK as a whole. (Online table 6.8).

- In the North West, 47.4 per cent of pupils achieved five or more grades A*–C at GCSE level or equivalent including English and mathematics in 2007/08, compared with 47.7 per cent for the UK as a whole (Online table 4.8).

- The unemployment rate in the North West stood at 8.5 per cent in the fourth quarter of 2009, compared with the UK rate of 7.8 per cent (Online table 1.1).

- The proportion of children living in workless households in the second quarter of 2009 was higher in the North West (19 per cent) than the England average (17 per cent) (Online table 8.6).

- In April 2009, the median gross weekly earnings for full-time employees on adult rates who were resident in the North West was £460, lower than the UK median of £489 (Online table 9.19).

- Labour productivity (gross value added per hour worked) in the North West in 2008 was 12.1 per cent below the UK average (Online table 3.2).

- North West local authorities recycled 33 per cent of household waste in 2007/08 compared with an England average of 35 per cent (Online table 5.11).

Yorkshire and The Humber

Map 6.3   Population density: by local or unitary authority, 2008

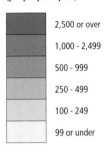

**Population density, 2008
(people per sq km)**

	2,500 or over
	1,000 - 2,499
	500 - 999
	250 - 499
	100 - 249
	99 or under

1 City of Kingston upon Hull UA
2 North Lincolnshire UA
3 North East Lincolnshire UA

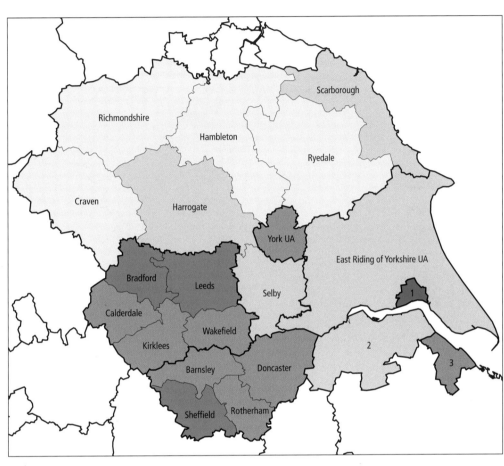

- Yorkshire and The Humber had a population of 5.2 million in mid-2008, an increase of 3.7 per cent since 2003. This compares with an overall increase of 3.1 per cent for the UK over the same period (Online table 1.2).

- People over state pension age (65 and over for men and 60 and over for women) in Yorkshire and The Humber in 2008 made up 19.1 per cent of the population, compared with 18.6 per cent for the under-16s. This compares with averages for the UK of 19.2 per cent and 18.8 per cent respectively (Online table 10.3).

- In Yorkshire and The Humber, men aged 65 in 2006–08 could expect to live another 17.2 years and women 19.8 years. This compares with 17.5 and 20.2 years in the UK as a whole (Online table 6.8).

- In Yorkshire and The Humber, 44.4 per cent of pupils achieved five or more grades A*–C at GCSE level or equivalent including English and mathematics in 2007/08, compared with 47.7 per cent for the UK as a whole (Online table 4.8).

- The unemployment rate in Yorkshire and The Humber stood at 9.1 per cent in the fourth quarter of 2009, higher than the UK rate of 7.8 per cent (Online table 1.1).

- The proportion of children living in workless households in the second quarter of 2009 was higher in Yorkshire and The Humber (18 per cent) than the England average (17 per cent) (Online table 8.6).

- In April 2009, the median gross weekly earnings for full-time employees on adult rates who were resident in Yorkshire and The Humber was £452, lower than the UK median of £489 (Online table 9.19).

- Labour productivity (gross value added per hour worked) in Yorkshire and The Humber in 2008 was 10.8 per cent below the UK average (Online table 3.2).

- Local authorities in Yorkshire and The Humber recycled 31 per cent of household waste in 2007/08 compared with an England average of 35 per cent (Online table 5.11).

East Midlands

Map 6.4   Population density: by local or unitary authority, 2008

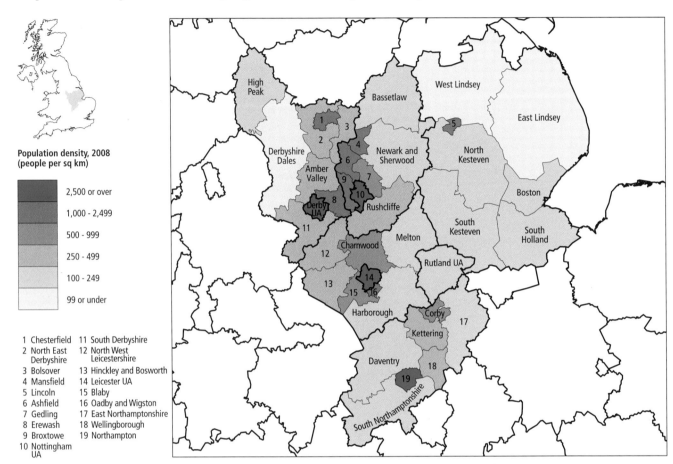

Population density, 2008
(people per sq km)

	2,500 or over
	1,000 - 2,499
	500 - 999
	250 - 499
	100 - 249
	99 or under

1	Chesterfield	11	South Derbyshire
2	North East Derbyshire	12	North West Leicestershire
3	Bolsover	13	Hinckley and Bosworth
4	Mansfield	14	Leicester UA
5	Lincoln	15	Blaby
6	Ashfield	16	Oadby and Wigston
7	Gedling	17	East Northamptonshire
8	Erewash	18	Wellingborough
9	Broxtowe	19	Northampton
10	Nottingham UA		

- The East Midlands had a population of 4.4 million in mid-2008, an increase of 4.2 per cent since 2003. This compares with an overall increase of 3.1 per cent for the UK over the same period (Online table 1.2).

- People over state pension age (65 and over for men and 60 and over for women) in the East Midlands in 2008 made up 19.7 per cent of the population, compared with 18.4 per cent for the under-16s. This compares with averages for the UK of 19.2 per cent and 18.8 per cent respectively (Online table 10.3).

- In the East Midlands, men aged 65 in 2006–08 could expect to live another 17.5 years and women 20.2 years. This is the same as the average for the UK (Online table 6.8).

- In the East Midlands, 47.0 per cent of pupils achieved five or more grades A*–C at GCSE level or equivalent including English and mathematics in 2007/08, compared with 47.7 per cent for the UK as a whole (Online table 4.8).

- The unemployment rate in the East Midlands stood at 7.2 per cent in the fourth quarter of 2009, compared with the UK rate of 7.8 per cent (Online table 1.1).

- A lower proportion of children in the East Midlands (15 per cent) lived in workless households in the second quarter of 2009, than the England average of 17 per cent (Online table 8.6).

- In April 2009, the median gross weekly earnings for full-time employees on adult rates who were resident in the East Midlands was £461, lower than the UK median of £489 (Online table 9.19).

- Labour productivity (gross value added per hour worked) in the East Midlands in 2008 was 7.5 per cent below the UK average (Online table 3.2).

- Local authorities in the East Midlands recycled 42 per cent of household waste in 2007/08 compared with an England average of 35 per cent (Online table 5.11).

West Midlands

Map 6.5   Population density: by local or unitary authority, 2008

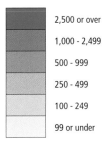

**Population density, 2008
(people per sq km)**

- 2,500 or over
- 1,000 - 2,499
- 500 - 999
- 250 - 499
- 100 - 249
- 99 or under

1 Newcastle-under-Lyme
2 Stoke-on-Trent UA
3 Telford and Wrekin UA
4 Cannock Chase
5 Tamworth
6 Wolverhampton
7 Sandwell
8 Dudley
9 Nuneaton and Bedworth
10 Redditch
11 Worcester

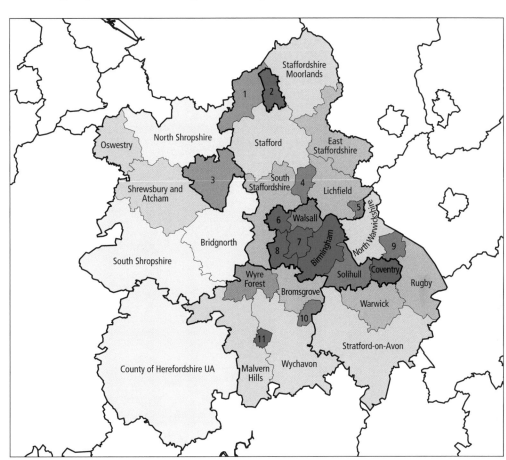

- The West Midlands had a population of 5.4 million in mid-2008, an increase of 1.9 per cent since 2003. This compares with an overall increase of 3.1 per cent for the UK over the same period (Online table 1.2).

- People over state pension age (65 and over for men and 60 and over for women) in the West Midlands in 2008 made up 19.7 per cent of the population, compared with 19.4 per cent for the under-16s. This compares with averages for the UK of 19.2 per cent and 18.8 per cent respectively.(Online table 10.3).

- In the West Midlands, men aged 65 in 2006–08 could expect to live another 17.4 years and women 20.1 years. This compares with 17.5 and 20.2 years in the UK as a whole (Online table 6.8).

- In the West Midlands, 46.1 per cent of pupils achieved five or more grades A*–C at GCSE level or equivalent including English and mathematics in 2007/08, compared with 47.7 per cent for the UK as a whole (Online table 4.8).

- The unemployment rate in the West Midlands stood at 9.4 per cent in the fourth quarter of 2009, higher than the UK rate of 7.8 per cent (Online table 1.1).

- A higher proportion of children in the West Midlands (19 per cent) lived in workless households in the second quarter of 2009, than the England average of 17 per cent (Online table 8.6).

- In April 2009, the median gross weekly earnings for full-time employees on adult rates who were resident in the West Midlands was £457, lower than the UK median of £489 (Online table 9.19).

- Labour productivity (gross value added per hour worked) in the West Midlands in 2008 was 10.4 per cent below the UK average (Online table 3.2).

- Local authorities in the West Midlands recycled 33 per cent of household waste in 2007/08 compared with an England average of 35 per cent (Online table 5.11).

East of England

Map 6.6   Population density: by local or unitary authority, 2008

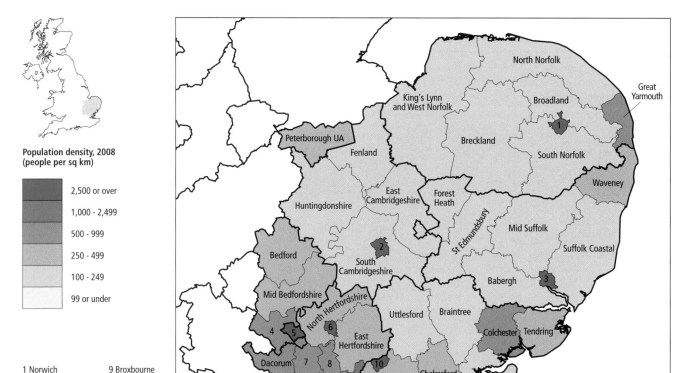

Population density, 2008
(people per sq km)

- 2,500 or over
- 1,000 - 2,499
- 500 - 999
- 250 - 499
- 100 - 249
- 99 or under

1 Norwich
2 Cambridge
3 Ipswich
4 South
  Bedfordshire
5 Luton UA
6 Stevenage
7 St. Albans
8 Welwyn Hatfield
9 Broxbourne
10 Harlow
11 Three Rivers
12 Watford
13 Hertsmere
14 Brentwood
15 Castle Point

- The East had a population of 5.7 million in mid-2008, an increase of 4.6 per cent since 2003. This compares with an overall increase of 3.1 per cent for the UK over the same period (Online table 1.2).

- People over state pension age (65 and over for men and 60 and over for women) in the East in 2008 made up 20.2 per cent of the population, compared with 19.0 per cent for the under-16s. This compares with averages for the UK of 19.2 per cent and 18.8 per cent respectively (Online table 10.3).

- In the East, men aged 65 in 2006–08 could expect to live another 18.2 years and women 20.7 years. This compares with 17.5 and 20.2 years in the UK as a whole (Online table 6.8).

- In the East, 50.3 per cent of pupils achieved five or more grades A*–C at GCSE level or equivalent including English and mathematics in 2007/08, compared with 47.7 per cent for the UK as a whole (Online table 4.8).

- The unemployment rate in the East stood at 6.5 per cent in the fourth quarter of 2009, compared with the UK rate of 7.8 per cent(Online table 1.1).

- A lower proportion of children in the East (12 per cent) lived in workless households in the second quarter of 2009, than the England average of 17 per cent (Online table 8.6).

- In April 2009, the median gross weekly earnings for full-time employees on adult rates who were resident in the East was £509, higher than the UK median of £489 (Online table 9.19).

- Labour productivity (gross value added per hour worked) in the East in 2008 was 0.7 per cent above the UK average (Online table 3.2).

- Local authorities in the East recycled 41 per cent of household waste in 2007/08 compared with an England average of 35 per cent (Online table 5.11).

London

Map 6.7   Population density: by London borough, 2008

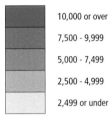

**Population density, 2008
(people per sq km)**

- 10,000 or over
- 7,500 - 9,999
- 5,000 - 7,499
- 2,500 - 4,999
- 2,499 or under

1 Islington
2 Tower Hamlets
3 Barking and Dagenham
4 Hammersmith and Fulham
5 Kensington and Chelsea
6 Westminster
7 City of London
8 Richmond upon Thames
9 Wandsworth
10 Lambeth
11 Southwark
12 Lewisham
13 Kingston upon Thames

- London had a population of 7.6 million in mid-2008, an increase of 3.5 per cent since 2003. This compares with an overall increase of 3.1 per cent for the UK over the same period (Online table 1.2).

- People over state pension age (65 and over for men and 60 and over for women) in London in 2008 made up 13.8 per cent of the population, compared with 19.3 per cent for the under-16s. This compares with averages of 19.2 per cent and 18.8 per cent respectively (Online table 10.3).

- In London, men aged 65 in 2006–08 could expect to live another 18.1 years and women 21.0 years. This compares with 17.5 and 20.2 years in the UK as a whole (Online table 6.8).

- In London, 50.6 per cent of pupils achieved five or more grades A*–C at GCSE level or equivalent including English and mathematics in 2007/08, compared with 47.7 per cent for the UK as a whole (Online table 4.8).

- The unemployment rate in London stood at 9.1 per cent in the fourth quarter of 2009, higher than the UK rate of 7.8 per cent (Online table 1.1).

- A higher proportion of children in London (24 per cent) lived in workless households in the second quarter of 2009, than the England average of 17 per cent (Online table 8.6).

- In April 2009, the median gross weekly earnings for full-time employees on adult rates who were resident in London was £599, higher than the UK median of £489 (Online table 9.19).

- Labour productivity (gross value added per hour worked) in London in 2008 was 32.7 per cent above the UK average (Online table 3.2).

- Local authorities in London recycled 26 per cent of household waste in 2007/08 compared with an England average of 35 per cent (Online table 5.11).

South East

Map 6.8   Population density: by local or unitary authority, 2008

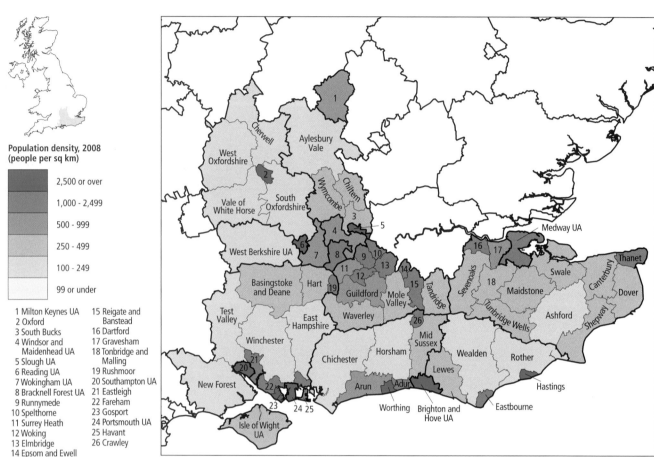

**Population density, 2008
(people per sq km)**

- 2,500 or over
- 1,000 - 2,499
- 500 - 999
- 250 - 499
- 100 - 249
- 99 or under

1 Milton Keynes UA	15 Reigate and
2 Oxford	Banstead
3 South Bucks	16 Dartford
4 Windsor and	17 Gravesham
Maidenhead UA	18 Tonbridge and
5 Slough UA	Malling
6 Reading UA	19 Rushmoor
7 Wokingham UA	20 Southampton UA
8 Bracknell Forest UA	21 Eastleigh
9 Runnymede	22 Fareham
10 Spelthorne	23 Gosport
11 Surrey Heath	24 Portsmouth UA
12 Woking	25 Havant
13 Elmbridge	26 Crawley
14 Epsom and Ewell	

- The South East had a population of 8.4 million in mid-2008, an increase of 3.6 per cent since 2003. This compares with an overall increase of 3.1 per cent for the UK over the same period (Online table 1.2).

- People over state pension age (65 and over for men and 60 and over for women) in the South East in 2008 made up 19.9 per cent of the population, compared with 19.0 per cent for the under-16s. This compares with averages for the UK of 19.2 per cent and 18.8 per cent respectively (Online table 10.3).

- In the South East, men aged 65 in 2006–08 could expect to live another 18.4 years and women 21.0 years. This compares with 17.5 and 20.2 years in the UK as a whole (Online table 6.8).

- In the South East, 51.7 per cent of pupils achieved five or more grades A*–C at GCSE level or equivalent including English and mathematics in 2007/08, compared with 47.7 per cent for the UK as a whole (Online table 4.8).

- The unemployment rate in the South East stood at 6.2 per cent in the fourth quarter of 2009, lower than the UK rate of 7.8 per cent (Online table 1.1).

- A lower proportion of children in the South East (12 per cent) lived in workless households in the second quarter of 2009, than the England average (17 per cent) (Online table 8.6).

- In April 2009, the median gross weekly earnings for full-time employees on adult rates who were resident in the South East was £537, higher than the UK median of £489 (Online table 1.1).

- Labour productivity (gross value added per hour worked) in the South East in 2008 was 3.8 per cent above the UK average (Online table 3.2).

- Local authorities in the South East recycled 36 per cent of household waste in 2007/08 compared with an England average of 35 per cent (Online table 5.11).

South West

2

Map 6.9   Population density: by local or unitary authority, 2008

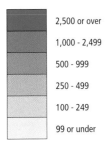

**Population density, 2008
(people per sq km)**

■	2,500 or over
■	1,000 - 2,499
■	500 - 999
■	250 - 499
■	100 - 249
□	99 or under

1 Forest of Dean
2 Tewkesbury
3 Gloucester
4 Cheltenham
5 South Gloucestershire UA
6 Swindon UA
7 City of Bristol UA
8 North Somerset UA
9 Bath and North East Somerset UA
10 West Wiltshire
11 Poole UA
12 Bournemouth UA
13 Christchurch

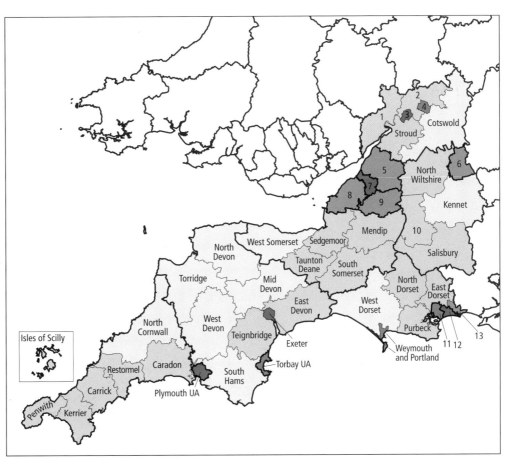

- The South West had a population of 5.2 million in mid-2008, an increase of 4.1 per cent since 2003. This compares with an overall increase of 3.1 per cent for the UK over the same period (Online table 1.2).

- People over state pension age (65 and over for men and 60 and over for women) in the South West in 2008 made up 22.5 per cent of the population, compared with 17.7 per cent for the under-16s. This compares with averages for the UK of 19.2 and 18.8 per cent respectively (Online table 10.3).

- In the South West, men aged 65 in 2006–08 could expect to live another 18.4 years and women 21.2 years. This compares with 17.5 and 20.2 years in the UK as a whole (Online table 6.8).

- In the South West, 49.2 per cent of pupils achieved five or more grades A*–C at GCSE level or equivalent including English and mathematics in 2007/08, compared with 47.7 per cent for the UK as a whole (Online table 4.8).

- The unemployment rate in the South West stood at 6.4 per cent in the fourth quarter of 2009, lower than the UK rate of 7.8 per cent (Online table 1.1).

- A lower proportion of children in the South West (14 per cent) lived in workless households in the second quarter of 2009, than the England average of 17 per cent (Online table 8.6).

- In April 2009, the median gross weekly earnings for full-time employees on adult rates who were resident in the South West was £460, lower than the UK median of £489 (Online table 1.1).

- Labour productivity (gross value added per hour worked) in the South West in 2008 was 6.0 per cent below the UK average (Online table 3.2).

- Local authorities in the South West recycled 40 per cent of household waste in 2007/08 compared with an England average of 35 per cent (Online table 5.11).

105

Wales

Map 6.10a   Population density: by unitary authority, 2008

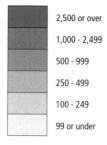

**Population density, 2008
(people per sq km)**

2,500 or over

1,000 - 2,499

500 - 999

250 - 499

100 - 249

99 or under

1 Flintshire UA
2 Wrexham UA
3 Neath Port Talbot UA
4 Bridgend UA
5 Rhondda, Cynon, Taff UA
6 The Vale of Glamorgan UA
7 Merthyr Tydfil UA
8 Cardiff UA
9 Caerphilly UA
10 Blaenau Gwent UA
11 Torfaen UA
12 Newport UA

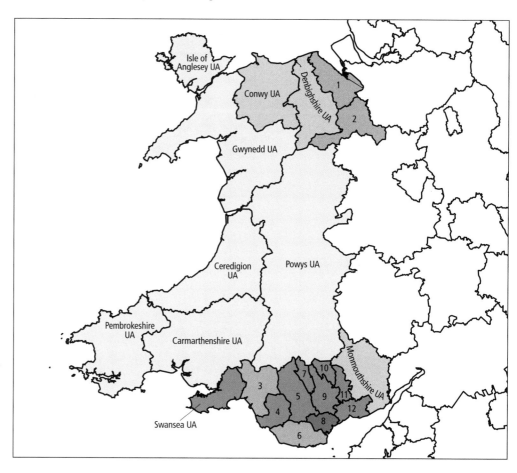

- Wales had a population of 3.0 million in mid-2008, an increase of 2.1 per cent since 2003. This compares with an overall increase of 3.1 per cent for the UK over the same period (Online table 1.2).

- People over state pension age (65 and over for men and 60 and over for women) in Wales in 2008 made up 21.4 per cent of the population, compared with 18.5 per cent for the under-16s. This compares with averages for the UK of 19.2 per cent and 18.8 per cent respectively (Online table 10.3).

- In Wales, men aged 65 in 2006–08 could expect to live another 17.1 years and women 19.8 years. This compares with 17.4 and 20.0 years in the UK as a whole (Online table 6.8).

- In Wales, 45.6 per cent of pupils achieved five or more grades A*–C at GCSE level or equivalent including English or Welsh as a first language and mathematics in 2007/08, compared with 47.7 per cent for the UK as a whole (Online table 4.8).

- The unemployment rate in Wales stood at 8.6 per cent in the fourth quarter of 2009, compared with the UK rate of 7.8 per cent (Online table 1.1).

- A higher proportion of children in Wales (20 per cent) lived in workless households in the second quarter of 2009, than the averages for Northern Ireland (18 per cent), England (17 per cent) and Scotland (16 per cent) (Online table 8.6).

- In April 2009, the median gross weekly earnings for full-time employees on adult rates who were resident in Wales was £445, lower than the UK median of £489 (Online table 9.19).

- Labour productivity (gross value added per hour worked) in Wales in 2008 was 13.6 per cent below the UK average (Online table 3.2).

- Unitary authorities in Wales recycled 32 per cent of household waste in 2007/08 compared with averages for England (35 per cent), Scotland (33 per cent) and Northern Ireland (32 per cent) (Online table 5.11).

Cymru

Map 6.10b   Dwysedd y boblogaeth: yn ol awdurdod unedol, 2008

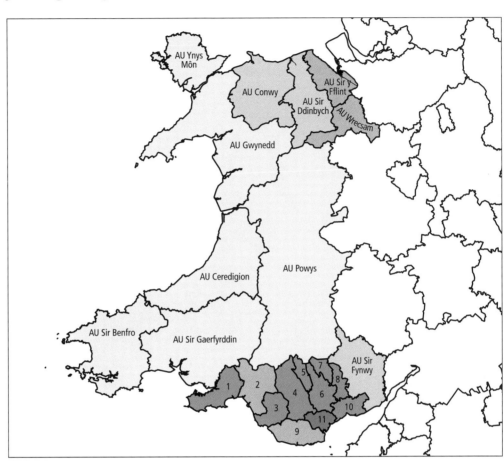

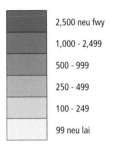

Dwysedd y Boblogaeth, 2008
(pobl fesul km sgwâr)

- 2,500 neu fwy
- 1,000 - 2,499
- 500 - 999
- 250 - 499
- 100 - 249
- 99 neu lai

1 AU Abertawe
2 AU Castell-nedd Port Talbot
3 AU Pen-y-bont ar Ogwr
4 AU Rhondda, Cynon, Taf
5 AU Merthyr Tudful
6 AU Caerffili
7 AU Blaenau Gwent
8 AU Tor-faen
9 AU Bro Morgannwg
10 AU Casnewydd
11 AU Caerdydd

- Roedd gan Gymru boblogaeth o 3.0 miliwn yng nghanol 2008, codiad o 2.1 y cant er 2003. Mae hyn yn cymharu â chodiad cyffredinol o 3.1 y cant ar gyfer y DU yn ystod yr un cyfnod (Tabl ar-lein 1.2).

- Roedd pobl dros oedran pensiwn y wladwriaeth (65 neu'n hŷn i ddynion a 60 neu'n hŷn i fenywod) yng Nghymru yn 2008 yn cyfrif am 21.4 y cant o'r boblogaeth, o'u cymharu â 18.5 y cant i bobl dan 16 oed. Mae hyn yn cymharu â chyfartaleddau'r DU o 19.2 y cant a 18.8 y cant yn y drefn honno (Tabl ar-lein 10.3).

- Yng Nghymru, gallai dynion 65 oed yn 2006-08 ddisgwyl byw 17.1 o flynyddoedd eraill a menywod 19.8 o flynyddoedd. Mae hyn yn cymharu â 17.4 ac 20.0 o flynyddoedd yn y DU yn ei chrynswth (Tabl ar-lein 6.8).

- Yng Nghymru, enillodd 45.6 y cant o ddisgyblion bum neu ragor o raddau A*-C ar lefel TGAU neu lefel gyfatebol gan gynnwys Saesneg neu Gymraeg fel iaith gyntaf a mathemateg yn 2007/08, o'u cymharu â 47.7 y cant i'r DU yn ei chrynswth (Tabl ar-lein 4.8).

- Roedd y gyfradd ddiweithdra yng Nghymru yn 8.6 y cant ym mhedwerydd chwarter 2009, o'i chymharu â chyfradd y DU o 7.8 y cant (Tabl ar-lein 1.1).

- Roedd cyfran uwch o blant yng Nghymru (20 y cant) yn byw mewn cartrefi heb waith yn ail chwarter 2009 na'r cyfartaleddau i Ogledd Iwerddon (18 y cant), Lloegr (17 y cant) a'r Alban (16 y cant) (Tabl ar-lein 8.6).

- Ym mis Ebrill 2009, yr enillion wythnosol gros cymedrig i weithwyr amser llawn ar gyfraddau oedolion a oedd yn preswylio yng Nghymru oedd £445, sy'n is na chymedr y DU o £489 (Tabl ar-lein 9.19).

- Roedd cynhyrchedd llafur (gwerth gros a ychwanegir am bob awr a weithir) yng Nghymru yn 2008 yn 13.6 y cant islaw cyfartaledd y DU (Tabl ar-lein 3.2).

- Ailgylchodd awdurdodau unedol yng Nghymru 32 y cant o wastraff cartrefi yn 2007/08 o'u cymharu â chyfartaleddau Lloegr (35 y cant), yr Alban (33 y cant) a Gogledd Iwerddon (32 y cant) (Tabl ar-lein 5.11).

Scotland

Map 6.11   Population density: by council area, 2008

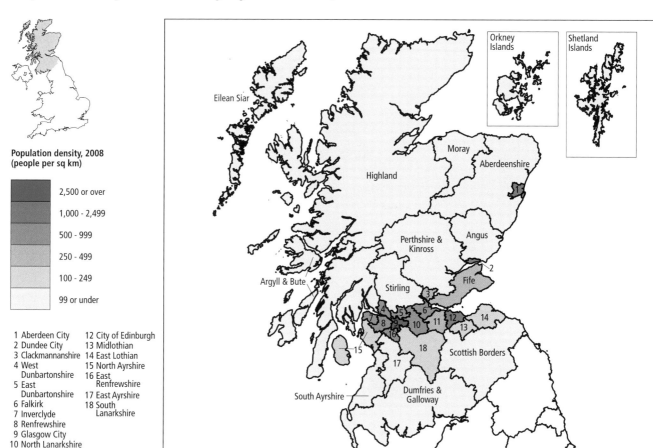

Population density, 2008 (people per sq km)

	2,500 or over
	1,000 - 2,499
	500 - 999
	250 - 499
	100 - 249
	99 or under

1 Aberdeen City
2 Dundee City
3 Clackmannanshire
4 West Dunbartonshire
5 East Dunbartonshire
6 Falkirk
7 Inverclyde
8 Renfrewshire
9 Glasgow City
10 North Lanarkshire
11 West Lothian
12 City of Edinburgh
13 Midlothian
14 East Lothian
15 North Ayrshire
16 East Renfrewshire
17 East Ayrshire
18 South Lanarkshire

- Scotland had a population of 5.2 million in mid-2008, an increase of 2.2 per cent since 2003. This compares with an overall increase of 3.1 per cent for the UK over the same period (Online table 1.2).

- People over state pension age (65 and over for men and 60 and over for women) in Scotland in 2008 made up 19.7 per cent of the population, compared with 17.7 per cent for the under-16s. This compares with averages for the UK of 19.2 per cent and 18.8 per cent respectively (Online table 10.3).

- In Scotland, men aged 65 in 2006–08 could expect to live another 16.2 years and women 18.8 years. This compares with 17.4 and 20.0 years in the UK as a whole (Online table 6.8).

- In Scotland, 46.8 per cent of pupils achieved the equivalent of five or more grades A*–C at GCSE level including English and mathematics in 2007/08, compared with 47.7 per cent for the UK as a whole (Online table 4.8).

- The unemployment rate in Scotland stood at 7.6 per cent in the fourth quarter of 2009, compared with the UK rate of 7.8 per cent (Online table 1.1).

- A lower proportion of children in Scotland (16 per cent) lived in workless households in the second quarter of 2009, than the averages for England (17 per cent), Northern Ireland (18 per cent) and Wales (20 per cent) (Online table 8.6).

- In April 2009, the median gross weekly earnings for full-time employees on adult rates who were resident in Scotland was £472, lower than the UK median of £489 (Online table 9.19).

- Labour productivity (gross value added per hour worked) in Scotland in 2008 was 3.7 per cent below the UK average (Online table 3.2).

- Councils in Scotland recycled 33 per cent of household waste in 2007/08 compared with the averages for England (35 per cent), Northern Ireland (32 per cent) and Wales (32 per cent) (Online table 5.11).

Northern Ireland

Map 6.12   Population density: by district council area, 2008

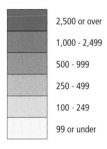

**Population density, 2008
(people per sq km)**

- 2,500 or over
- 1,000 - 2,499
- 500 - 999
- 250 - 499
- 100 - 249
- 99 or under

1 Newtownabbey
2 Carrickfergus
3 Belfast
4 North Down
5 Castlereagh

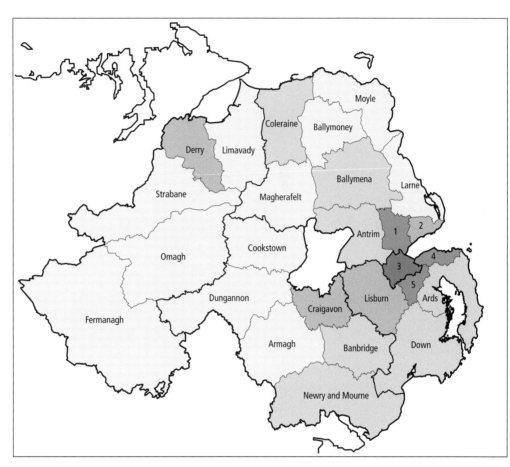

- Northern Ireland had a population of 1.8 million in mid-2008, an increase of 4.3 per cent since 2003. This compares with an overall increase of 3.1 per cent for the UK over the same period (Online table 1.2).

- People over state pension age (65 and over for men and 60 and over for women) in Northern Ireland in 2008 made up 16.7 per cent of the population, compared with 21.5 per cent for the under-16s. This compares with averages for the UK of 19.2 per cent and 18.8 per cent respectively.(Online table 10.3).

- In Northern Ireland, men aged 65 in 2006–08 could expect to live another 16.8 years and women 19.8 years. This compares with 17.4 and 20.0 years in the UK as a whole (Online table 6.8).

- In Northern Ireland, 53.0 per cent of pupils achieved five or more grades A*–C at GCSE level including English and mathematics in 2007/08, compared with 47.7 per cent for the UK as a whole (Online table 4.8).

- The unemployment rate in Northern Ireland stood at 6.0 per cent in the fourth quarter of 2009, lower than the UK rate of 7.8 per cent (Online table 1.1).

- In Northern Ireland (18 per cent) of children lived in workless households in the second quarter of 2009, compared with the averages for Wales (20 per cent), England (17 per cent) and Scotland (16 per cent) (Online table 8.6).

- In April 2009, the median gross weekly earnings for full-time employees on adult rates who were resident in Northern Ireland was £441, lower than the UK median of £489 (Online table 9.19).

- Labour productivity (gross value added per hour worked) in Northern Ireland in 2008 was 18.6 per cent below the UK average (Online table 3.2).

- District councils in Northern Ireland recycled 32 per cent of household waste in 2007/08 compared with the averages for England (35 per cent), Scotland (33 per cent) and Wales (32 per cent) (Online table 5.11).

Data

7   Maps   112

8   Tables   119

9   Directory of Online Tables   124

Section 3

DATA

Download data by
clicking the online pdf

www.statistics.gov.uk/
regionaltrends42

Maps

7.1 Population change: by county or unitary authority, 2003 to 2008   113

7.2 Projected population change: by county or unitary authority, 2006 to 2026   113

7.3 Population density: by county or unitary authority, 2008   114

7.4 Population under 16: by county or unitary authority, 2008   114

7.5 Population of state pension age: by county or unitary authority, 2008   114

7.6 Percentage of the population of working age claiming a key social security benefit: by local authority, August 2009   115

7.7 Unemployment rates: by unitary and local authority, July 2008 to June 2009   116

7.8 Percentage claiming for more than 12 months: by local authority, December 2009   117

7.9 Carbon dioxide emissions per resident: by local authority, 2005 to 2007   118

3

Map 7.1   Population change: by county or unitary authority,[1] 2003 to 2008

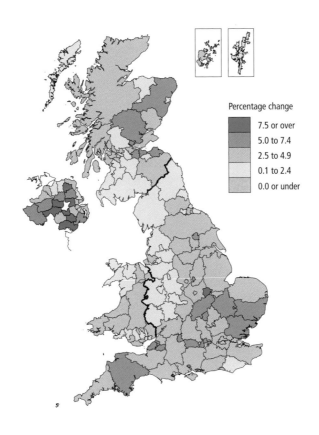

Percentage change

- 7.5 or over
- 5.0 to 7.4
- 2.5 to 4.9
- 0.1 to 2.4
- 0.0 or under

1 Those in effect from 1 April 2009.

Source: Office for National Statistics; General Register Office for Scotland; Northern Ireland Statistics and Research Agency

Map 7.2   Projected population change:[1] by county or unitary authority,[2] 2006 to 2026

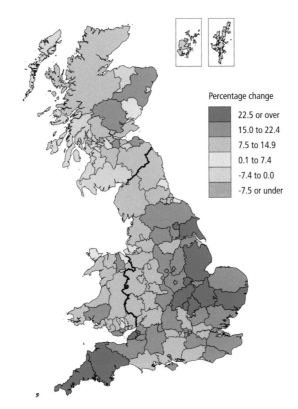

Percentage change

- 22.5 or over
- 15.0 to 22.4
- 7.5 to 14.9
- 0.1 to 7.4
- -7.4 to 0.0
- -7.5 or under

1 2006-based subnational projections. See Glossary.
2 Those in effect from 1 April 2009.

Source: Office for National Statistics; Welsh Assembly Government; General Register Office for Scotland; Northern Ireland Statistics and Research Agency

3

Map 7.3 Population density:[1] by county or unitary authority,[2] 2008

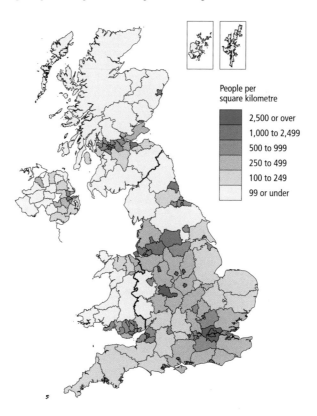

People per
square kilometre

- 2,500 or over
- 1,000 to 2,499
- 500 to 999
- 250 to 499
- 100 to 249
- 99 or under

1 See Notes and Definitions.
2 Those in effect from 1 April 2009.

Source: Office for National Statistics; Welsh Assembly Government; General Register Office for Scotland; Northern Ireland Statistics and Research Agency

Map 7.4 Population under 16: by county or unitary authority,[1] 2008

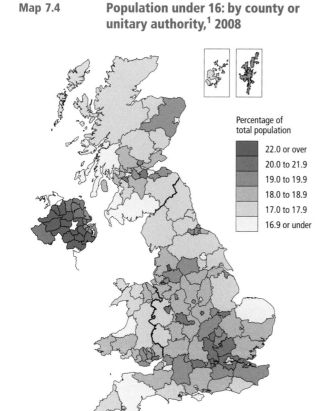

Percentage of
total population

- 22.0 or over
- 20.0 to 21.9
- 19.0 to 19.9
- 18.0 to 18.9
- 17.0 to 17.9
- 16.9 or under

1 Those in effect from 1 April 2009.

Source: Office for National Statistics; General Register Office for Scotland; Northern Ireland Statistics and Research Agency

Map 7.5 Population of state pension age:[1] by county or unitary authority,[2] 2008

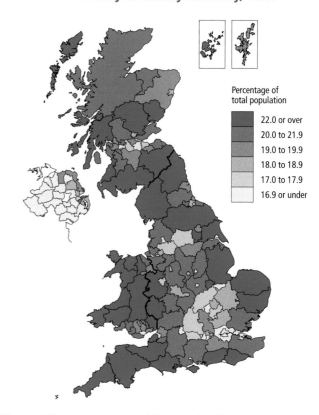

Percentage of
total population

- 22.0 or over
- 20.0 to 21.9
- 19.0 to 19.9
- 18.0 to 18.9
- 17.0 to 17.9
- 16.9 or under

1 Men aged 65 or over, women aged 60 or over. See Glossary.
2 Those in effect from 1 April 2009.

Source: Office for National Statistics; General Register Office for Scotland; Northern Ireland Statistics and Research Agency

Map 7.6 Percentage of the population of working age[1] claiming a key social security benefit:[2] by local authority, August 2009

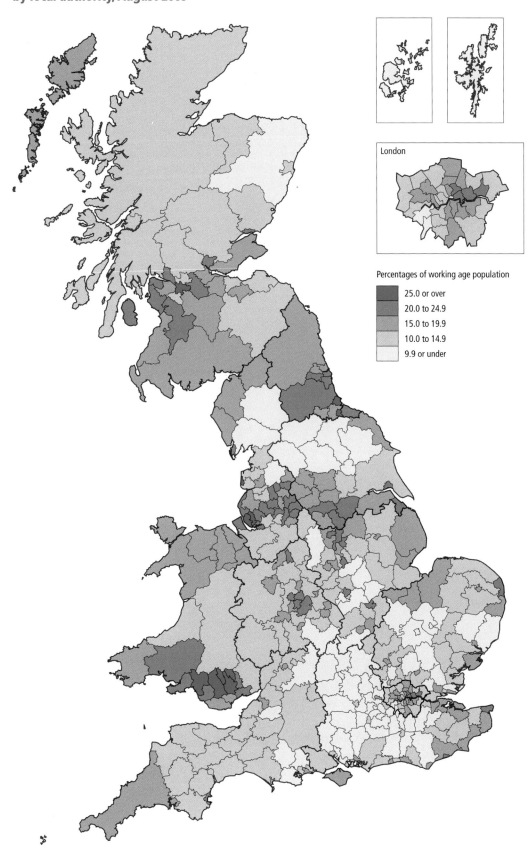

Percentages of working age population

25.0 or over
20.0 to 24.9
15.0 to 19.9
10.0 to 14.9
9.9 or under

1 Men aged 16 to 64 and women aged 16 to 59.
2 Key benefits include claimants of one or more of Jobseeker's Allowance (JSA), Income Support (IS), Incapacity Benefit (IB), Severe Disablement Allowance (SDA), Disability Living Allowance (DLA), Carer's Allowance (CA) and Bereavement Benefit (BB) / Widow's Benefit (WB) for working age claimants (including Pension Credit for males aged 60 to 64).

Source: Work and Pensions Longitudinal Study (WPLS), Department for Work and Pensions

Map 7.7   **Unemployment rates:[1,2] by unitary[3] and local authority, July 2008 to June 2009**

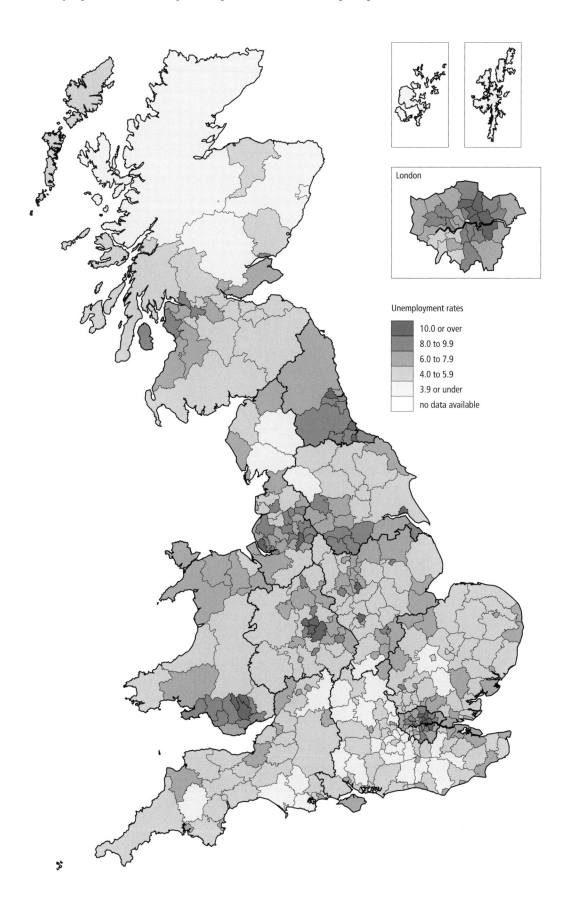

London

Unemployment rates

- 10.0 or over
- 8.0 to 9.9
- 6.0 to 7.9
- 4.0 to 5.9
- 3.9 or under
- no data available

1 Unemployed as a percentage of economically active people aged 16 and over.
2 Model-based estimates of unemployment.
3 Local authorities in England, unitary authorities in Wales, council areas in Scotland.

Source: Office for National Statistics; Labour Force Survey

Map 7.8　Percentage claiming for more than 12 months:[1] by local authority, December 2009

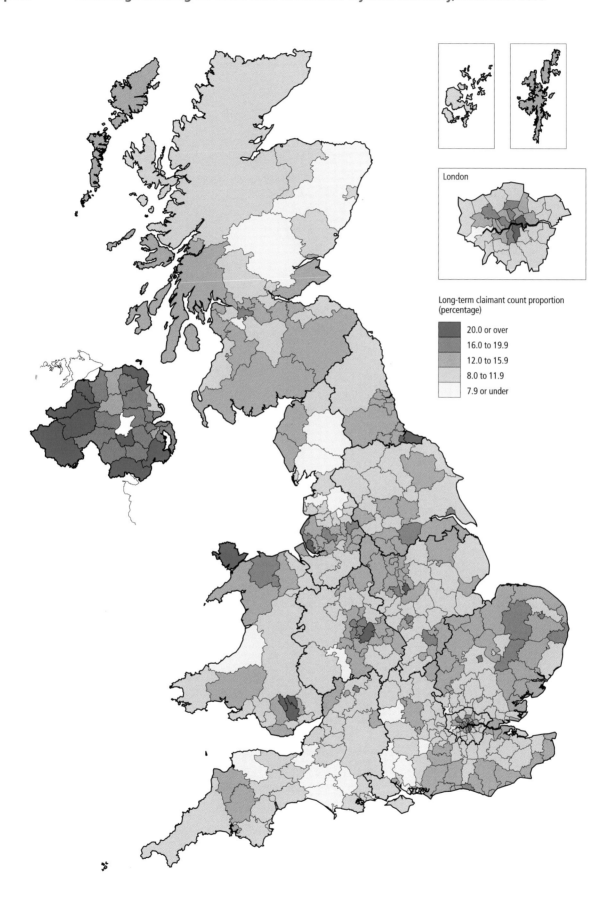

London

Long-term claimant count proportion (percentage)

- 20.0 or over
- 16.0 to 19.9
- 12.0 to 15.9
- 8.0 to 11.9
- 7.9 or under

1 People who have been claiming Jobseeker's Allowance for more than 12 months (computerised claims only), as a percentage of total computerised claimants in each area.

Source: Office for National Statistics

Map 7.9   Carbon dioxide emissions[1,2] per resident: by local authority,[3] 2005 to 2007

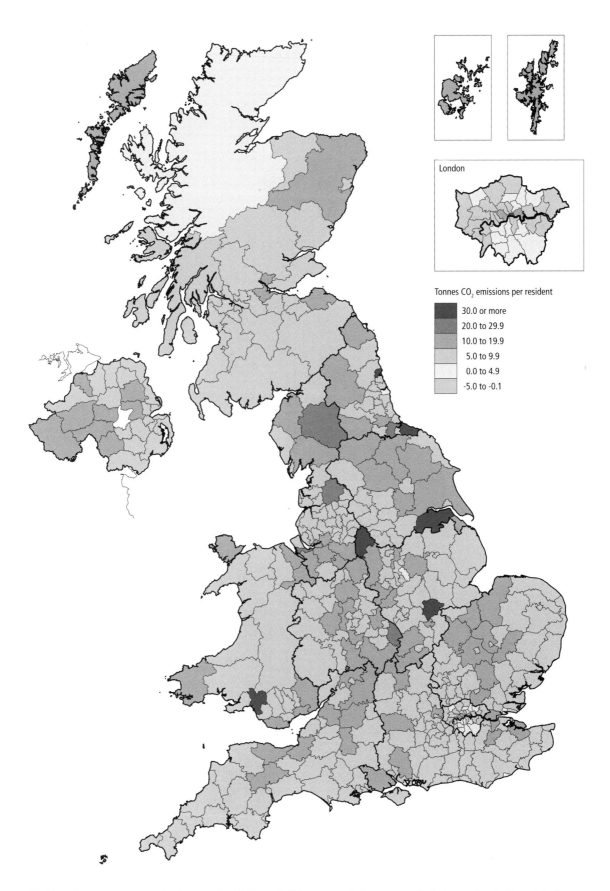

Tonnes CO_2 emissions per resident

- 30.0 or more
- 20.0 to 29.9
- 10.0 to 19.9
- 5.0 to 9.9
- 0.0 to 4.9
- -5.0 to -0.1

London

1 Carbon dioxide emissions are measured by 'end user' not 'at source'. This means emissions are distributed according to the point of energy consumption. See Notes and Definitions online.
2 Negative values indicate removal from the atmosphere.
3 Local authority districts and unitary authorities as defined before April 2009.

Source: Department of Energy and Climate Change

Tables

8.1	Key statistics – population, health and welfare	120
8.2	Key statistics – labour market and education	121
8.3	Key statistics – economy	122
8.4	Key statistics – housing, transport, environment and crime	123

3

Table 8.1   Key statistics – population, health and welfare

	Population 2008[1]			Standardised Mortality Ratio[3] (UK=100) 2008	Percentage of children living in workless households[4] 2009 Q2	Population of working age claiming a key social security benefit[5] August 2009 (percentages)
	Thousands	Percentage aged under 16	Percentage pension age and over[2]			
United Kingdom	**61,383.2**	*18.8*	*19.2*	**100**	...	*15.8*
England	**51,446.2**	*18.8*	*19.1*	*98*	*17*	*16.3*
North East	2,575.5	*17.9*	*20.1*	111	*21*	*20.5*
North West	6,875.7	*18.9*	*19.4*	110	*19*	*19.2*
Yorkshire and The Humber	5,213.2	*18.6*	*19.1*	104	*18*	*16.6*
East Midlands	4,433.0	*18.4*	*19.7*	99	*15*	*14.9*
West Midlands	5,411.1	*19.4*	*19.7*	101	*19*	*18.0*
East	5,728.7	*19.0*	*20.2*	92	*12*	*12.5*
London	7,619.8	*19.3*	*13.8*	92	*24*	*15.3*
South East	8,380.1	*19.0*	*19.9*	90	*13*	*11.4*
South West	5,209.2	*17.7*	*22.5*	91	*14*	*13.1*
Wales	**2,993.4**	*18.5*	*21.4*	**103**	*20*	*20.3*
Scotland	**5,168.5**	*17.7*	*19.7*	**117**	*16*	*17.8*
Northern Ireland	**1,775.0**	*21.5*	*16.7*	**107**	*18*	*..*

1   The estimated mid-year resident population as published in August 2009. See the Notes and Definitions for Population and Migration tables (Topic 10 online).
2   Men aged 65 and over, women aged 60 and over as a percentage of the total population in area. See the Notes and Definitions for Population and Migration tables (Topic 10 online).
3   Standardised Mortality Ratio (SMR) is the ratio of observed deaths to those expected by applying a standard death rate to the regional population. See the Notes and Definitions for Population and Migration tables (Topic 10 online).
4   Children under 16. For definition of a workless household see the Notes and Definitions for Income and Lifestyles (Topic 8 online).
5   Proportion of men aged 16–64 and women aged 16–59 claiming one or more key benefits. Key benefits include Jobseekers's Allowance (JSA), Income Support (IS), Incapacity Benefit (IB), Severe Disablement Allowance (SDA), Disability Living Allowance (DLA), Carer's Allowance (CA) and Bereavement Benefit (BB)/Widow's Benefit (WB) for working age claimants (including Pension Credit for males aged 60 to 64).

Source: Office for National Statistics; General Register Office for Scotland; Northern Ireland Statistics and Research Agency; Department for Work and Pensions

Table 8.2 Key statistics – labour market and education

	Employment rate,[1] 2009 Q4 (percentages)	Unemployment rate,[2] 2009 Q4 (percentages)	Economic inactivity rate,[3] 2009 Q4 (percentages)	Median gross weekly earnings,[4] April 2009 (£)	Percentage of pupils[5] achieving 5 or more grades A*–C[6] GCSE or equivalent qualifications, 2007/08	Percentage of working age[7] population with no qualifications, 2009 Q2
United Kingdom	**72.4**	**7.8**	**21.3**	**488.70**	**64.4**	**11.8**
England	**72.6**	**7.9**	**21.0**	**496.00**	**65.3**	**11.2**
North East	69.0	9.3	23.7	438.80	66.4	14.4
North West	70.4	8.5	22.8	460.20	65.4	12.8
Yorkshire and The Humber	70.7	9.1	21.9	452.40	62.1	11.5
East Midlands	74.6	7.2	19.4	460.50	63.0	11.7
West Midlands	70.5	9.4	21.9	457.40	64.1	14.5
East	76.2	6.5	18.4	509.40	64.7	10.2
London	68.7	9.1	24.2	598.60	65.0	11.8
South East	77.0	6.2	17.7	536.60	66.0	8.4
South West	75.5	6.4	19.1	460.10	63.5	8.1
Wales	**68.9**	**8.6**	**24.3**	**444.90**	**58.0**	**14.3**
Scotland	**73.5**	**7.6**	**20.2**	**472.20**	**58.2**	**13.0**
Northern Ireland	**67.3**	**6.0**	**28.3**	**440.80**	**68.1**	**21.4**

1 Seasonally adjusted data for people of working age (men aged 16-64 and women aged 16-59).
2 Unemployed as a percentage of all economically active people aged 16 and over. Seasonally adjusted.
3 Based on the population of working age. See the Notes and Definitions for Labour Market (Topic 9 online).
4 Residence-based estimates for full-time employees on adult rates whose pay for the survey pay-period was not affected by absence. See the Notes and Definitions for Labour Market (Topic 9 online).
5 GCSE figures for England include all schools, whereas figures for the English regions are Local Authority maintained schools only. Figures for Wales and Northern Ireland include all schools; for Scotland they include publicly funded and independent schools but exclude special schools.
6 Figures for England and Wales include GNVQ equivalents. The England figures also include the wider range of approved pre-16 qualifications. In Scotland, Standard Grade awards at levels 1–3, Intermediate 2 at grades A–C, Intermediate 1 at grade A. See the Notes and Definitions for Education tables (Topic 4 online).
7 Males aged 16 to 64 and females aged 16 to 59.

Source: Office for National Statistics; Department of Enterprise, Trade and Investment, Northern Ireland; Department for Children, Schools and Families; Welsh Assembly Government; Scottish Government; Northern Ireland Department of Education; Department for Innovation, Universities and Skills

Table 8.3   Key statistics – economy

	Gross value added[1] as a percentage of UK,[2] 2008[3]	Labour productivity: gross value added[1] per hour[4] 2008 (UK = 100)	Gross value added[1] per head 2008 (UK = 100)[2]	Gross disposable household income[5] per head 2008 £	Business birth rate[6] 2008	Business death rate[6] 2008[3]
United Kingdom	*100.0*	*100.0*	*100*	*14,872*	*11.6*	*9.4*
England	*85.9*	*101.7*	*102*	*15,090*	*11.8*	*9.5*
North East	*3.2*	*90.1*	*77*	*13,543*	*12.2*	*9.9*
North West	*9.6*	*87.9*	*86*	*13,386*	*11.8*	*9.8*
Yorkshire and The Humber	*7.1*	*89.2*	*83*	*13,115*	*11.3*	*10.2*
East Midlands	*6.3*	*92.5*	*88*	*13,611*	*10.7*	*9.3*
West Midlands	*7.5*	*89.6*	*85*	*13,337*	*10.8*	*9.3*
East	*8.9*	*100.7*	*95*	*15,509*	*11.1*	*9.3*
London	*21.0*	*132.7*	*170*	*19,038*	*15.0*	*10.3*
South East	*14.4*	*103.8*	*106*	*16,792*	*10.9*	*9.0*
South West	*7.8*	*94.0*	*92*	*14,680*	*10.2*	*8.8*
Wales	*3.6*	*86.4*	*74*	*13,073*	*10.1*	*9.5*
Scotland	*8.2*	*96.3*	*98*	*14,301*	*11.0*	*8.7*
Northern Ireland	*2.3*	*81.4*	*79*	*13,260*	*9.5*	*7.3*

1 Workplace based. See the Notes and Definitions for Economy tables (Topic 3 online).
2 UK less Extra-Regio. See the Notes and Definitions for Economy tables (Topic 3 online).
3 Provisional.
4 The annual hours figure used is an average of the four quarters and includes employees, self employed and government supported trainees.
5 Household income covers the income received by households and non-profit institutions serving households. UK figure excludes extra-regio. See the Notes and Definitions for Economy tables (Topic 3 online).
6 Birth and death rates are expressed as a percentage of active enterprises.

Source: Office for National Statistics

Table 8.4   Key statistics – housing, transport, environment and crime

	Housebuilding: permanent dwellings completed by private enterprise[1] 2007/08 (thousands)	Median dwelling price,[2] 2008 (£ thousands)	Traffic[3] increase on major roads[4] between 1998 and 2008 (percentages)	Percentage of household waste recycled, 2007/08	Recorded crime[5,6,7,8] 2008/09 (recorded offences per 100,000 population)	Crimes committed against households[9] 2008/09 (rates per 10,000 households)
United Kingdom	**186.5**	..	..	..	..	..
England	**144.7**	**174**	**8.6**	**34.5**	**8,557**	**2,868**
North East	7.5	120	12.2	28.4	7.975	3.166
North West	19.1	130	10.1	33.4	9,083	3,039
Yorkshire and The Humber	15.2	130	10.4	30.5	9,354	2,837
East Midlands	16.2	138	10.7	41.9	8,676	2,974
West Midlands	12.0	142	9.4	33.0	7,907	2,550
East	18.9	186	8.4	41.2	6,896	2,780
London	14.4	260	-3.9	25.5	11,175	2,965
South East	25.1	215	7.0	36.0	7,741	2,983
South West	16.6	185	14.1	40.3	7,239	2,528
Wales	**8.3**	**135**	**15.2**	**32.3**	**7,905**	**2,203**
Scotland	**21.7**	..	**11.3**	**32.6**	**7,303**	**2,791**
Northern Ireland	**11.8**	..	**23.4**	**31.9**	**6,202**	**1,512**

1 Includes private landlords (persons or companies) and owner-occupiers.
2 Prices of dwellings changing ownership, excluding those bought at non-market prices. See the Notes and Definitions for Housing tables (Topic 7 online).
3 The volume of traffic is expressed as vehicle kilometres, which is calculated by multiplying the Annual Average Daily Flow by the corresponding length of road.
4 Motorways and A roads.
5 Recorded crime statistics broadly cover the more serious offences. See the Notes and Definitions for Crime and Justice tables (Topic 2 online).
6 Crimes recorded by the British Transport police are not included.
7 Figures for Scotland are not comparable with those for England and Wales because of the differences in the legal systems, recording practices and classifications.
8 The Northern Ireland figure includes 'offences against the state' and 'other notifiable offences'.
9 Estimates from the British Crime Survey, Scottish Crime and Justice Survey and Northern Ireland Crime Survey.

Source: Communities and Local Government; Welsh Assembly Government; Scottish Government; Department for Social Development, Northern Ireland; Land Registry; Department for Transport; Department for Regional Development, Northern Ireland; Department for Environment, Food, and Rural Affairs; Northern Ireland Environment Agency; Home Office; Police Service of Northern Ireland; Northern Ireland Office

Directory of Online Tables

Regional data on a wide range of topics can be accessed through the Directory of Online Tables on the ONS website at: www.statistics.gov.uk/regionaltrends/data

The datasets include Notes and Definitions for each topic.

The 'Type' column provides information on the status of the statistics: National Statistics (NS), Non-National Statistics (Non-NS) or Mixed. Statistics accredited as 'National Statistics' are fully compliant with the Code of Practice for Official Statistics and carry the National Statistics kitemark. Statistics labelled as 'Non-National Statistics' follow many of the best practice principles set out in the Code but have not been accredited as fully compliant.

Topic		Type
1: Key Statistics		
1.1a	Key statistics – population, health and welfare	Mixed
1.1b	Key statistics – labour market and education	Mixed
1.1c	Key statistics – economy	Mixed
1.1d	Key statistics – housing, transport, environment and crime	Mixed
1.2	Local authority population and vital statistics	NS
1.3	Local authority education, labour market, benefits and housing	Mixed
2: Crime and Justice		
2.1	Crimes committed against households	Mixed
2.2	Crimes committed against persons	Mixed
2.3	Recorded crimes: by offence group	NS
2.4	Subregional – selected recorded crimes: by Crime and Disorder Reduction Partnership	NS
2.5	Recorded crimes detected by the police: by offence group	NS
2.6	Number of Anti-social Behaviour Orders issued by all courts	Non-NS
2.7	People given a police caution: by type of offence and age	NS
2.8	People found guilty: by type of offence and age	NS
2.9	People aged 18 or over sentenced to immediate imprisonment: by sex and length of sentence imposed for principal offence	Mixed
2.10	People aged 18 or over found guilty of offences: by sex and type of sentence	NS
2.11	Firearms	Non-NS
2.12	Seizures of controlled drugs: by type of drug	Mixed
2.13	Police service strength: by type	Mixed
2.14	Prison population	Mixed

DATA

Hover and click over section of Directory on the online pdf of Regional Trends and you can download tables for the relevant topic into Microsoft Excel. It's as simple as that.

3: Economy

3.1	Workplace-based gross value added (GVA) at current basic prices	NS
3.2	Labour productivity	NS
3.3	Workplace-based gross value added (GVA) per head at current basic prices	NS
3.4	Gross disposable household income	NS
3.5	Subregional – gross value added at current basic prices	NS
3.6	Subregional – gross disposable household income	NS
3.7	Gross value added at current basic prices: by industry groups	NS
3.8	Percentage of gross value added derived from agriculture, industry and services	NS
3.9	Industrial classification of business sites	NS
3.10	Subregional – business sites by industry and services	NS
3.11	Agricultural holdings: by area of crops and grass	NS
3.12	Agricultural holdings: by farm type	NS
3.13	Turnover, expenditure and gross value added in manufacturing	Mixed
3.14	Gross value added in manufacturing: by size of local unit	Mixed
3.15	Construction – contractors' output	NS
3.16	Turnover, expenditure and gross value added in services	Mixed
3.17	Tourism	Mixed
3.18	*Unallocated table number*	
3.19	Business survival rates	Non-NS
3.20	Subregional – business births and deaths	NS
3.21	Export and import trade with EU and non-EU countries	NS
3.22	Expenditure on research and development	NS
3.23	Allocation of EU Structural Funds	Non-NS

4: Education and Training

4.1	Pupils and teachers: by type of school	NS
4.2	Three- and four-year olds: by type of early education provider	NS
4.3	Subregional – education and training	NS
4.4	Class sizes for all classes	NS
4.5	School meal arrangements	NS
4.6	Pupil absence from maintained primary and secondary schools	NS
4.7	Pupils reaching or exceeding expected standards: by Key Stage Teacher Assessment	NS
4.8	Subregional – examination achievements	NS
4.9	Pupils achieving GCSE grades A*–C: by selected subjects and sex	NS
4.10	16- and 17- year-olds participating in post-compulsory education and government-supported training	NS
4.11	Home students in further education in England: by level of course of study	NS
4.12	Home domiciled higher education students: by area of study and domicile	NS
4.13	Destination of full-time first degree graduates	NS
4.14	Population of working age: by highest qualification	NS
4.15	Progress towards achieving National Targets for England for young people and adults	NS
4.16	Employees of working age receiving job-related training: by sex	NS

5: Environment

| 5.1 | Annual rainfall | Non-NS |
| 5.2 | Winter and summer seasonal rainfall | Non-NS |

5.3	Estimated abstractions from non-tidal surface and groundwaters: by purpose	Non-NS
5.4	Estimated household water consumption	Non-NS
5.5	Water quality of rivers and canals	Mixed
5.6	Bathing water standards: by coastal region	Non-NS
5.7	Prosecutions for pollution incidents: by type of prosecution	Non-NS
5.8	Designated areas	Mixed
5.9	Land use	NS
5.10	Previous use of land changing to residential use	NS
5.11	Household waste and recycling	NS
5.12	Recycling of household waste	NS
5.13	Municipal waste disposal: by method	NS
5.14	Percentage change in wild bird indicators	NS
5.15	Subregional – carbon dioxide emissions: by sector	NS

6: Health and Care

6.1	*Unallocated table number*	
6.2	Subregional – live births	NS
6.3	Still births, perinatal mortality and infant mortality	NS
6.4	Age-standardised mortality rates: by cause and sex	NS
6.5	NHS hospital activity: by Strategic Health Authority and region	NS
6.6	General practitioners and dentists: by Strategic Health Authority	NS
6.7	Immunisation uptake	NS
6.8	Subregional – life expectancy at birth and at age 65	NS
6.9	Comparative cancer incidence ratios: selected sites by sex	NS
6.10	Cervical and breast cancer: screening and age-standardised death rates	NS
6.11	Diagnosed HIV-infected patients: by probable route of infection and region of residence	Non-NS
6.12	Notification rates of tuberculosis	Non-NS
6.13	Prescriptions dispensed	NS
6.14	Cigarette smoking among people aged 16 or over: by sex	NS
6.15	Alcohol consumption among people aged 16 or over: by sex	NS
6.16	Drug use among 16- to 24-year-olds	NS
6.17	Council supported residents in care homes	NS
6.18	Children looked after by local authorities	Mixed

7: Housing

7.1	Stock of dwellings	Non-NS
7.2	Housebuilding – permanent dwellings completed: by tenure	NS
7.3	Tenure of dwellings	Mixed
7.4	Subregional – mean and median prices of dwellings changing ownership	Non-NS
7.5	Mortgage advances, income and age of borrowers	Mixed
7.6	Selected housing costs of owner-occupiers	Non-NS
7.7	Average weekly rents: by tenure	Non-NS
7.8	Subregional – dwellings in council tax bands	Non-NS
7.9	County Court mortgage possession orders	NS
7.10	Households accepted as homeless: by reason	NS
7.11	Householders' satisfaction with their area	NS

8: Income and Lifestyles

8.1	Household income: by source	NS
8.2	Distribution of household income	NS
8.3	Income distribution of individuals	NS
8.4	Distribution of income liable to assessment for tax	NS
8.5	Average total income and average income tax payable: by sex	NS
8.6	Working-age households by combined economic activity status of household	NS
8.7	Households in receipt of benefit: by type of benefit	NS
8.8	Subregional – benefits	NS
8.9	Households with different types of saving	NS
8.10	Household expenditure: by commodity and service	NS
8.11	Expenditure on selected foods bought for household consumption and expenditure on eating out	NS
8.12	Expenditure on holidays in the UK and abroad	NS
8.13	Households with selected durable goods	NS
8.14	Households with Internet access	NS
8.15	Participation in the National Lottery	NS
8.16	Library resources and use	Non-NS

9: Labour Market

9.1	Employment and employment rates: by sex	NS
9.2	Labour force: by age	NS
9.3	Employee jobs and self-employment jobs: by sex	NS
9.4	Industrial composition of employee jobs	NS
9.5	Part-time working: by sex and reason	NS
9.6	Distribution of usual weekly hours of work of employees: by sex	NS
9.7	Employees with flexible working patterns: by sex	NS
9.8	People in employment with a second job: by sex	NS
9.9	Employment: by occupation	NS
9.10	Unemployment rates	NS
9.11	Claimant count proportions and rates	NS
9.12	Unemployment rates: by age	NS
9.13	Unemployment: by highest qualification	NS
9.14	Economic activity	NS
9.15	Economic activity and inactivity rates: by sex	NS
9.16	Economic inactivity: by reason	NS
9.17	Redundancy rates	NS
9.18	Subregional – labour market	NS
9.19	Median weekly earnings and hours: by area of residence and sex	NS
9.20	Median and average weekly earnings, workplace based: by industry and sex	NS
9.21	Median and mean gross weekly earnings: by area of residence and sex	NS
9.22	Subregional – earnings distribution	NS

10: Population and Migration

10.1	Resident population: by sex	NS
10.2	Subregional – resident population by age group and sex	NS
10.3	Subregional – resident population by selected age groups	NS
10.4	Resident population estimates by ethnic group (Experimental Statistics)	Non-NS

10.5	Live births, deaths and natural change in population	NS
10.6	Migration	NS
10.7	Inter-regional movements	NS
10.8	Subregional – components of population change	NS
10.9	Age-specific birth rates	NS
10.10	Age-specific death rates: by sex	NS
10.11	Subregional – projected population change	NS
10.12	Conceptions to women aged under 18: by outcome	NS
10.13	Marriages	NS
10.14	Percentage of non-married people aged 16 to 59 cohabiting	NS
10.15	Household numbers and projections	NS
10.16	Households: by type	NS

11: Transport

11.1	Motor cars currently licensed and new registrations	NS
11.2	Households with regular use of a car	NS
11.3	Time taken to walk to nearest bus stop	NS
11.4	Distance travelled per person per year: by mode of transport	NS
11.5	Trips per person per year: by purpose	NS
11.6	Time taken to travel to work: by workplace	NS
11.7	Usual method of travel to work by region of residence	NS
11.8	Trips to and from school: by main mode of transport and length	NS
11.9	Household expenditure on transport	NS
11.10	Public expenditure on roads	NS
11.11	Average daily motor vehicle flows: by type of road	NS
11.12	Traffic increase on major roads	Non-NS
11.13	Road traffic and distribution of accidents on major/minor roads	NS
11.14	Fatal and serious road accidents	NS
11.15	Road casualties: by age and type of road user	NS
11.16	Activity at major airports	Non-NS
11.17	Activity at major seaports	Non-NS
11.18	Bus and light rail passenger journeys	NS

Section 4

Reference

Useful websites   130

Boundary maps   132

Glossary   141

Symbols and conventions   146

DATA

Download data by
clicking the online pdf

www.statistics.gov.uk/
regionaltrends42

Useful websites

Annual Business Inquiry	www.statistics.gov.uk/abi
Annual Population Survey	www.statistics.gov.uk/statbase/Product.asp?vlnk=10855
Annual Survey of Hours and Earnings	www.statistics.gov.uk/statbase/product.asp?vlnk=13101
Business Enterprise Research and Development Expenditure	www.statistics.gov.uk/statbase/Product.asp?vlnk=8206
Communities and Local Government	www.communities.gov.uk
Department for Children, Schools and Families	www.dcsf.gov.uk
Department for Culture, Media and Sport	www.culture.gov.uk
Department of Energy and Climate Change	www.decc.gov.uk/en/content/cms/statistics/statistics.aspx
Department for Environment, Food and Rural Affairs	www.defra.gov.uk
Department for Social Development in Northern Ireland	www.dsdni.gov.uk/
Department for Transport	www.dft.gov.uk/pgr/statistics
Department for Work and Pensions	www.dwp.gov.uk
Department of Enterprise, Trade and Investment, Northern Ireland	www.detini.gov.uk
Department of Education, Northern Ireland	www.deni.gov.uk/
Department of Health	www.dh.gov.uk
Department of the Environment, Northern Ireland	www.doeni.gov.uk/
Designated Areas:	
England	www.defra.gov.uk/evidence/statistics/index.htm
Wales	www.ccw.gov.uk/
Scotland	www.snh.org.uk/
Northern Ireland	www.doeni.gov.uk/
Economic and Labour Market review	www.statistics.gov.uk/elmr
England and Wales Census	www.statistics.gov.uk/census/
Environment Agency	www.environment-agency.gov.uk
General Household Survey	www.statistics.gov.uk/StatBase/Product.asp?vlnk=5756
General LiFestyle Survey	www.statistics.gov.uk/StatBase/Product.asp?vlnk=5756
General Register Office for Scotland	www.gro-scotland.gov.uk
Geography in National Statistics	www.statistics.gov.uk/geography/default.asp
Home Office	www.homeoffice.gov.uk
Index of Multiple Deprivation	www.communities.gov.uk/indices

Labour Force Survey	www.ons.gov.uk/about/who-we-are/our-services/unpublished-data/social-survey-data/lfs/lfs-faqs
Land Registry	www.landregistry.gov.uk
Learning and Skills Council	www.lsc.gov.uk Life
Life Expectancy estimates	www.statistics.gov.uk/statbase/Product.asp?vlnk=8841
Migration statistics	www.statistics.gov.uk/statbase/Product.asp?vlnk=15108
Ministry of Justice	www.justice.gov.uk
Neighbourhood Statistics:	
England and Wales	www.neighbourhood.statistics.gov.uk/
Scotland	www.sns.gov.uk/
Northern Ireland	www.ninis.nisra.gov.uk/
Nomis®	www.nomisweb.co.uk/
Northern Ireland Statistics and Research Agency	www.nisra.gov.uk/
Office for National Statistics	www.ons.gov.uk
Population Estimates by Ethnic Group	www.statistics.gov.uk/StatBase/Product.asp?vlnk=14238
Population Estimates	www.statistics.gov.uk/statbase/Product.asp?vlnk=601&More=N
Publication Hub	
Home Page	www.statistics.gov.uk/hub/index.html
Release Calendar	www.statistics.gov.uk/hub/release-calendar/index.html
Regional Statistics	www.statistics.gov.uk/hub/regional-statistics/index.html
What are National Statistics?	www.statistics.gov.uk/hub/what-are-national-statistics-/index.html
UK Statistics Authority	www.statisticsauthority.gov.uk/
Regional Economic Indicators	www.statistics.gov.uk/StatBase/Product.asp?vlnk=9472
Regional Trends	www.statistics.gov.uk/regionaltrends
Regional Trends – Online Tables (latest data)	www.statistics.gov.uk/regionaltrends/data
Scottish Environment Protection Agency	www.sepa.org.uk
Scottish Government	www.scotland.gov.uk
Scottish Statistics	www.scotland.gov.uk/Topics/Statistics
Statistics for Regions in England:	
North East	www.statistics.gov.uk/cci/nugget.asp?id=1072
North West	www.statistics.gov.uk/cci/nugget.asp?id=1073
Yorkshire and The Humber	www.statistics.gov.uk/cci/nugget.asp?id=1074
East Midlands	www.statistics.gov.uk/cci/nugget.asp?id=1075
West Midlands	www.statistics.gov.uk/cci/nugget.asp?id=1076
East of England	www.statistics.gov.uk/cci/nugget.asp?id=1077
London	www.statistics.gov.uk/cci/nugget.asp?id=1078
South East	www.statistics.gov.uk/cci/nugget.asp?id=1079
South West	www.statistics.gov.uk/cci/nugget.asp?id=1080
Subnational Population Estimates for England	www.statistics.gov.uk/statbase/Product.asp?vlnk=997
The NHS Information Centre for health and social care	www.ic.nhs.uk
Welsh Assembly Government	www.wales.gov.uk

4

Boundary maps

Counties and unitary authorities in England, 1998 and 2009   133

NUTS levels 1, 2 and 3 in England, 2008   134

Unitary authorities in Wales, 2005/Awdurdodau unedol yng Nghymru, 2005   135

NUTS levels 1, 2 and 3 in Wales, 2008/NUTS lefelau 1, 2 a 3 yng Nghymru, 2008   135

Councils in Scotland, 1996   136

NUTS levels 1, 2 and 3 in Scotland, 2008   136

Geographical classifications in Northern Ireland   137

Police areas, United Kingdom   138

Health areas, England, 2006   139

Environment Agency regions, England and Wales, 1996   139

Regions of the National Rivers Authority, England   139

Education authorities in England   140

4

Counties and unitary authorities in England, 1998[1] and 2009[2]

1   Hartlepool
2   Middlesbrough
3   Redcar and Cleveland
4   Stockton-on-Tees
5   Darlington
6   Halton
7   Warrington
8   Blackburn with Darwen
9   Blackpool
10 East Riding of Yorkshire
11 City of Kingston upon Hull
12 North East Lincolnshire
13 North Lincolnshire
14 York
15 Derby
16 Leicester
17 Rutland
18 Nottingham
19 County of Herefordshire
20 Telford and Wrekin
21 Stoke-on-Trent
22 Luton
23 Peterborough
24 Southend-on-Sea
25 Thurrock
26 Bracknell Forest
27 Reading
28 Slough
29 West Berkshire
30 Windsor and Maidenhead
31 Wokingham
32 Milton Keynes
33 Brighton and Hove
34 Portsmouth
35 Southampton
36 Isle of Wight
37 Medway
38 Bath and North East Somerset
39 City of Bristol
40 North Somerset
41 South Gloucestershire
42 Plymouth
43 Torbay
44 Bournemouth
45 Poole
46 Swindon

Local government structure post
April 2009[2]

County Durham

A Cheshire West and Chester
B Cheshire East

A Bedford
B Central Bedfordshire

Cornwall
Isles of Scilly

1 Local government structure as at April 1998. See Notes and Definitions online.

2 Areas affected by changes on 1st April 2009 are shaded grey. Four areas: Durham, Cheshire, Bedfordshire, Cornwall and Isles of Scilly had boundary/
name changes at this level and insets show the current structure. The remainder: Northumberland, Shropshire and Wiltshire changed from county to
unitary authority status but were otherwise unchanged, these are not inset. Local authority districts as at April 1998 are shown on the maps in the
Region and Country Profiles (Section 2).

NUTS levels 1, 2 and 3 in England,[1] 2008

NUTS level 3 areas

1 Tyneside
2 Sunderland
3 Darlington
4 Hartlepool and Stockton-on-Tees
5 South Teeside
6 Blackpool
7 Blackburn with Darwen
8 Sefton
9 Liverpool
10 East Merseyside
11 Greater Manchester North
12 Greater Manchester South
13 York
14 Bradford
15 Calderdale, Kirklees and Wakefield
16 East Riding of Yorkshire
17 Kingston upon Hull, City of
18 North and North East Lincolnshire
19 Barnsley, Doncaster and Rotherham
20 Sheffield
21 East Derbyshire
22 North Nottinghamshire
23 Derby
24 Nottingham
25 South Nottinghamshire
26 South and West Derbyshire
27 Wirral
28 Halton and Warrington
29 Telford and Wrekin
30 Stoke-on-Trent
31 Walsall and Wolverhampton
32 Dudley and Sandwell
33 Birmingham
34 Solihull
35 Coventry
36 Leicestershire CC and
   Rutland
37 Leicester
38 Northamptonshire
39 Peterborough
40 Milton Keynes
41 Buckinghamshire CC
42 Bedfordshire CC
43 Luton
44 Outer London - West and North West
45 Inner London - West
46 Inner London - East
47 Outer London - East and North East
48 Outer London - South
49 Thurrock
50 Southend-on-Sea
51 Medway

52 Bristol, City of
53 Bath and North East Somerset,
   North Somerset and South Gloucestershire
54 Swindon
55 Plymouth
56 Torbay
57 Bournemouth and Poole
58 Southampton
59 Portsmouth
60 Brighton and Hove

1 NUTS (Nomenclature of Units for Territorial Statistics) is a hierarchical classification of areas that provides a breakdown of the EU's economic territory. See Notes and Definitions online.

Unitary authorities in Wales, 2005
Awdurdodau unedol yng Nghymru

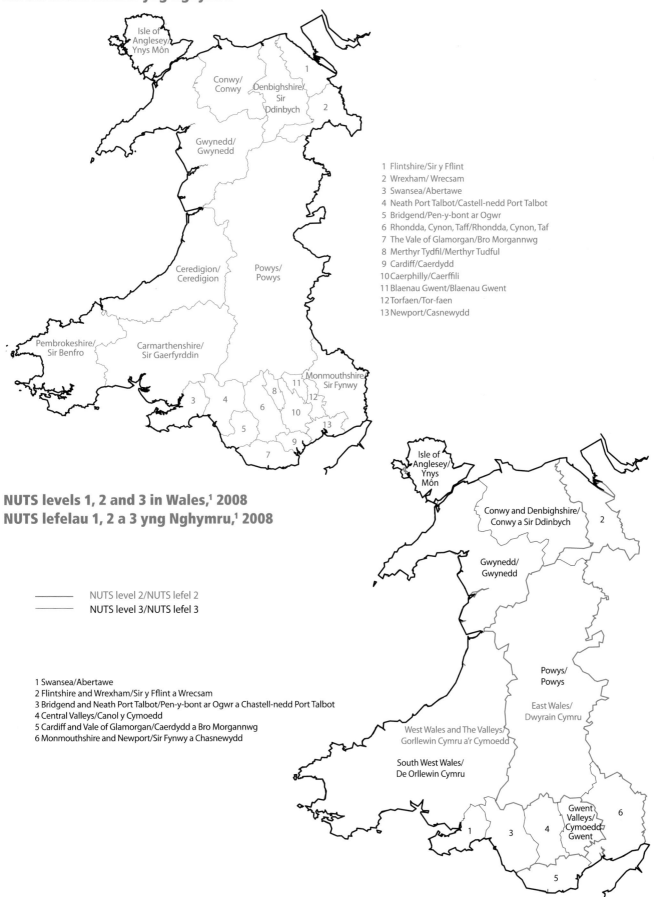

1 Flintshire/Sir y Fflint
2 Wrexham/ Wrecsam
3 Swansea/Abertawe
4 Neath Port Talbot/Castell-nedd Port Talbot
5 Bridgend/Pen-y-bont ar Ogwr
6 Rhondda, Cynon, Taff/Rhondda, Cynon, Taf
7 The Vale of Glamorgan/Bro Morgannwg
8 Merthyr Tydfil/Merthyr Tudful
9 Cardiff/Caerdydd
10 Caerphilly/Caerffili
11 Blaenau Gwent/Blaenau Gwent
12 Torfaen/Tor-faen
13 Newport/Casnewydd

NUTS levels 1, 2 and 3 in Wales,[1] 2008
NUTS lefelau 1, 2 a 3 yng Nghymru,[1] 2008

——— NUTS level 2/NUTS lefel 2
——— NUTS level 3/NUTS lefel 3

1 Swansea/Abertawe
2 Flintshire and Wrexham/Sir y Fflint a Wrecsam
3 Bridgend and Neath Port Talbot/Pen-y-bont ar Ogwr a Chastell-nedd Port Talbot
4 Central Valleys/Canol y Cymoedd
5 Cardiff and Vale of Glamorgan/Caerdydd a Bro Morgannwg
6 Monmouthshire and Newport/Sir Fynwy a Chasnewydd

1 NUTS (Nomenclature of Units for Territorial Statistics) is a hierarchical classification of areas that provides a breakdown of the EU's economic territory. The NUTS level 1 area is the whole country. See Notes and Definitions online.
Mae NUTS (Enwau Unedau Tiriogaethol at Ddibenion Ystadegaeth) yn ddosbarthiad hierarchaidd o ardaloedd sy'n darparu dadansoddiad o diriogaeth economaidd yr UE. Yr ardal NUTS lefel 1 yw'r wlad gyfan. Gweler y Nodiadau a'r Diffiniadau ar-lein.

Councils in Scotland, 1996

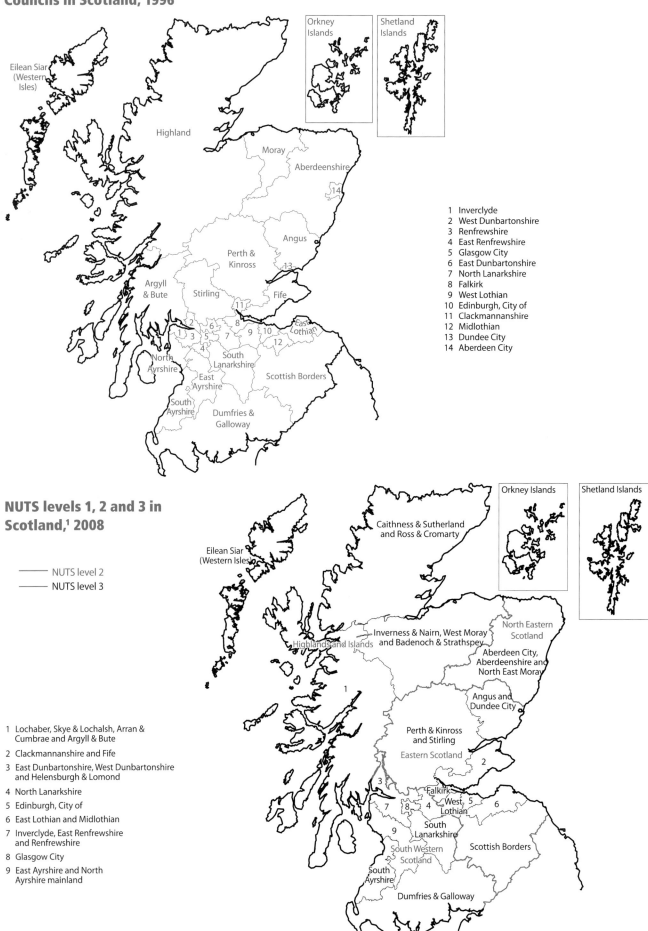

1 Inverclyde
2 West Dunbartonshire
3 Renfrewshire
4 East Renfrewshire
5 Glasgow City
6 East Dunbartonshire
7 North Lanarkshire
8 Falkirk
9 West Lothian
10 Edinburgh, City of
11 Clackmannanshire
12 Midlothian
13 Dundee City
14 Aberdeen City

NUTS levels 1, 2 and 3 in Scotland,[1] 2008

NUTS level 2
NUTS level 3

1 Lochaber, Skye & Lochalsh, Arran & Cumbrae and Argyll & Bute
2 Clackmannanshire and Fife
3 East Dunbartonshire, West Dunbartonshire and Helensburgh & Lomond
4 North Lanarkshire
5 Edinburgh, City of
6 East Lothian and Midlothian
7 Inverclyde, East Renfrewshire and Renfrewshire
8 Glasgow City
9 East Ayrshire and North Ayrshire mainland

1 NUTS (Nomenclature of Units for Territorial Statistics) is a hierarchical classification of areas that provides a breakdown of the EU's economic territory. The NUTS level 1 area is the whole country. See Notes and Definitions online.

Geographical classifications[1] in Northern Ireland

Education and Library Boards, 1992

Health and Social Services Boards, 2003 [2]

District Councils, 1992

NUTS levels 1, 2 and 3 in Northern Ireland, 2008

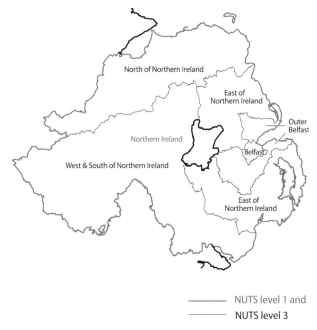

1 COLERAINE
2 BALLYMONEY
3 NEWTOWNABBEY
4 CARRICKFERGUS
5 BELFAST
6 CASTLEREAGH
7 NORTH DOWN
8 CRAIGAVON

———— NUTS level 1 and
———— NUTS level 3

1 See Notes and Definitions online.
2 The structure of health administration in Northern Ireland changed from 1 April 2009. A single Health and Social Care Board (HSCB) replaced the 4 Health and Social Services Boards

Police areas, United Kingdom

Northern

Grampian

Tayside

Fife

Central

Strathclyde

Lothian &
Borders

Dumfries
& Galloway

Northumbria

Police Service of
Northern Ireland

Durham

Cleveland

Cumbria

North Yorkshire

Lancashire

Humberside

W. Yorks

G.M.P.¹

S. Yorks

Merseyside

Cheshire

Derbys

Lincolnshire

Notts

North Wales

Staffs

Leicester

Norfolk

West
Mercia

W.Mids

Northants

Cambs

Suffolk

Dyfed-Powys

Warks

Beds

Gloucs

Thames
Valley

Herts

Essex

Gwent

South Wales

Met²

City

Wiltshire

Surrey

Kent

Avon
and Somerset

Hampshire

Sussex

Devon and
Cornwall

Dorset

——— Police force area
boundary

1 Greater Manchester Police.
2 Metropolitan Police.

Health areas, England, 2006

Strategic Health Authority boundary

North East

Yorkshire and The Humber

North West

East Midlands

West Midlands

East of England

South Central

London

South West

South East Coast

Environment Agency regions, England and Wales, 1996

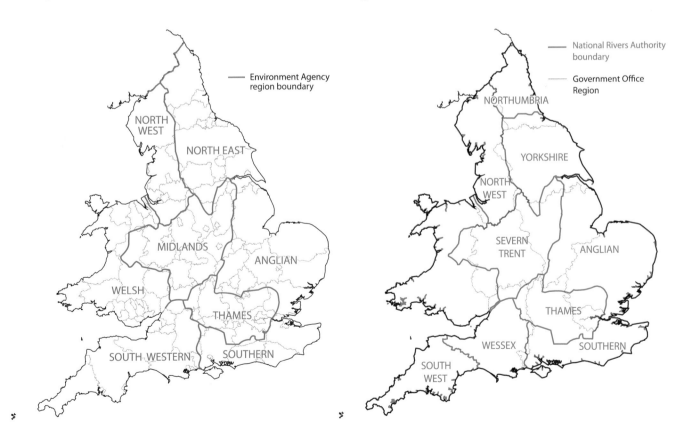

Environment Agency region boundary

NORTH WEST

NORTH EAST

MIDLANDS

ANGLIAN

WELSH

THAMES

SOUTH WESTERN

SOUTHERN

Regions of the National Rivers Authority,[1] England

National Rivers Authority boundary

Government Office Region

NORTHUMBRIA

YORKSHIRE

NORTH WEST

SEVERN TRENT

ANGLIAN

THAMES

WESSEX

SOUTHERN

SOUTH WEST

1 The nine original regions as used for rainfall data. The NRA became part of the Environment Agency upon its creation in 1996.

Education authorities in England

1 North Tyneside
2 Newcastle upon Tyne
3 Gateshead
4 South Tyneside
5 Sunderland
6 Hartlepool
7 Stockton-on-Tees
8 Darlington
9 Middlesbrough
10 Redcar and Cleveland
11 Kingston upon Hull
12 North Lincolnshire
13 North East Lincolnshire
14 Calderdale
15 Kirklees
16 Wakefield
17 Barnsley
18 Sheffield
19 Rotherham
20 Doncaster
21 Derby
22 Nottingham
23 Leicester
24 Rochdale
25 Oldham
26 Tameside
27 Stockport
28 Manchester
29 Bury
30 Blackburn with Darwen
31 Bolton
32 Wigan
33 Salford
34 Trafford
35 Warrington
36 St Helens

37 Knowsley
38 Sefton
39 Liverpool
40 Wirral
41 Halton
42 Telford and Wrekin
43 Stoke-on-Trent
44 Wolverhampton
45 Walsall
46 Dudley
47 Sandwell
48 Birmingham
49 Solihull

50 Coventry
51 Peterborough
52 Luton
53 South Gloucestershire
54 Bristol
55 North Somerset
56 Bath and North East Somers
57 Swindon
58 West Berkshire
59 Reading
60 Wokingham
61 Bracknell Forest
62 Windsor and Maidenhead
63 Slough
64 Thurrock
65 Medway
66 Southend on Sea
67 Southampton
68 Portsmouth
69 Brighton and Hove
70 Poole
71 Bournemouth
72 Milton Keynes

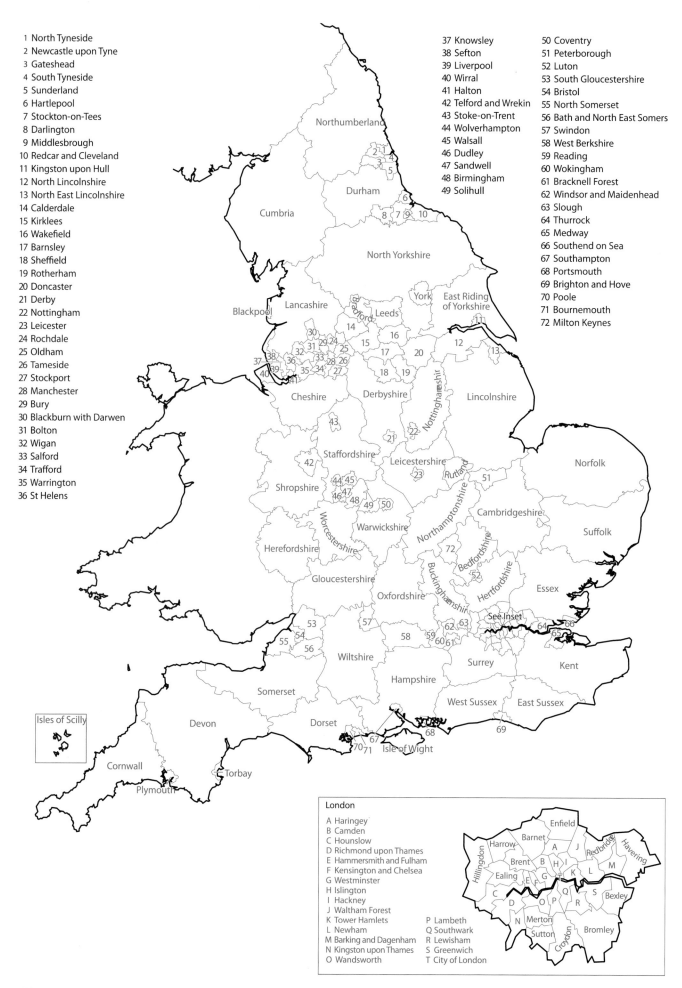

London

A Haringey
B Camden
C Hounslow
D Richmond upon Thames
E Hammersmith and Fulham
F Kensington and Chelsea
G Westminster
H Islington
I Hackney
J Waltham Forest
K Tower Hamlets
L Newham
M Barking and Dagenham
N Kingston upon Thames
O Wandsworth

P Lambeth
Q Southwark
R Lewisham
S Greenwich
T City of London

Glossary

Age-standardised mortality rates	A statistical measure to allow more precise comparisons between two or more populations by eliminating the effects in age structure by using a 'standard population'.
Annual Business Inquiry (ABI)	A sample survey of businesses in Great Britain that collects information on employee jobs and output. See online **Notes and Definitions** for **Labour Market** (Topic 9 online) and **Economy** tables (Topic 3 online).
Annual Population Survey (APS)	A sample survey providing data for local authority districts. It comprises the quarterly Labour Force Survey (LFS), plus data from the annual LLFS (Annual Local Area LFS) boosts for England (2004 and 2005 only), Scotland and Wales.
Areas of Outstanding Natural Beauty	A precious landscape whose distinctive character and natural beauty are so outstanding that it is in the nation's interest to safeguard them.
Average dwelling price	Average price for house sales registered in a particular period. See **Notes and Definitions** for **Housing** tables (Topic 7 online). Two measures are used – **mean** and **median** (see separate entries).
Billion	One thousand million.
Birth rate	The number of live births per 1,000 of the mid-year resident population.
British Crime Survey	A sample survey measuring crimes experienced by respondents in England and Wales. **Scottish Crime and Victimisation Survey** in Scotland and **Northern Ireland Crime Survey** collect similar information. See **Notes and Definitions** for **Crime and Justice** tables (Topic 2 online).
BCS comparator offences	The BCS comparator includes recorded theft of and theft from a vehicle, vehicle interference and tampering, domestic burglary, theft or unauthorised taking of a pedal cycle, theft from the person, criminal damage, common assault, wounding and robbery.
Business births	Newly created enterprises. See **Notes and Definitions** for **Economy** tables (Topic 3 online).
Business deaths	Enterprises that have ceased trading. See **Notes and Definitions** for **Economy** tables (Topic 3 online).
Cause of death	Corresponds to the **International Classification of Diseases** (10th Revision) codes (ICD10). See **Notes and Definitions** for **Population and Migration** tables (Topic 10 online).
Claimant count	A count, derived from administrative sources, of those who are claiming unemployment-related benefits at Jobcentre Plus local offices, primarily Jobseeker's Allowance.
Claimant count proportion	Number of claimants as a proportion of the resident working-age population of the area.
Claimant count rate	Number of claimants as a percentage of the estimated total workforce of the area.
Cohort	A group of people who are observed over time, usually defined by date of birth or date of attaining some other status. For example, a sample of people born in 1965 would form a birth cohort.
Compulsory education	Education is compulsory for all children in the UK between the ages of 5 (4 in Northern Ireland) and 16.
Conception	A pregnancy which leads to either a maternity or an abortion.
CO_2 emissions	Carbon dioxide emissions are measured by 'end user' not 'at source'. This means emissions are distributed according to the point of energy consumption. See **Notes and Definitions** for **Environment** tables (Topic 5 online).

Daily traffic flows	Calculated as annual traffic divided by road length and divided by the number of days per year.
Death rate	Total deaths registered per 1,000 of the mid-year **resident population**.
Dependent children	Children aged under 16, or aged 16 to 18 in full-time education and never married.
Dwelling	A self-contained unit of accommodation with all the rooms behind a door, which only that household can use.
Economically active	People who are in **employment** plus the unemployed.
Economically inactive	People who are neither in employment nor unemployed. This includes those looking after a home, retired or permanently unable to work.
Employees	A household survey-based measure of people aged 16 or over who regard themselves as paid employees.
Employee jobs	A measure of jobs held by civilians based on employer surveys. The term refers to the number of jobs rather than the number of persons with jobs. For example, a person holding both a full-time job and a part-time job, or someone with two part-time jobs, will be counted twice.
Employment	People aged 16 or over who did some paid work in the reference week (whether as an employee or self-employed); those who had a job that they were temporarily away from (on holiday, for example); those on government-supported training and employment programmes; and those doing unpaid work in a family business.
Employment rate	The proportion of any given population group who are in **employment.** The main presentation of employment rates is the proportion of the population of working age who are in employment.
Ethnic groups	The classification of ethnic groups is broadly the same as used in the 2001 Census. See **Notes and Definitions** for **Population and Migration** tables (Topic 10 online).
Experimental statistics	ONS Statistics that are in the testing phase and are not fully developed. See **Notes and Definitions** for **Population and Migration** tables (Topic 10 online).
Extra-Regio	Accounts for business activity that cannot be assigned to a specific region. For the UK this consists mainly of offshore oil and gas extraction and activities of UK embassies and forces overseas.
Filled jobs	See **workforce jobs**.
Full-time employees	In the **Annual Survey of Hours and Earnings** data this refers to **employees** who were paid for more than 30 hours per week.
GCSE grades A*–C or equivalent	Equivalent to level 2 qualifications, see separate entry in Glossary. In Scotland, Standard Grade awards at levels 1–3, Intermediate 2 at grades A–C, Intermediate 1 at grade A.
Government-supported training	People aged 16 and over participating in one of the Government's employment and training programmes administered by the **Learning and Skills Councils** in England, the **National Council for Education and Training** (ELWa) in Wales, local enterprise companies in Scotland, or the **Training and Employment Agency** in Northern Ireland.
Gross disposable household income (GDHI)	Total household income less certain cost items such as tax payments and social security contributions. In essence, this is the value of the resources that the household sector has available to spend.
Grossing	See **Weighting**.
Gross Value Added (GVA)	Regional GVA is a measure of the economic contribution of an area, measured as the sum of incomes earned from the production of goods and services in the region. Unless stated this is **workplace-based GVA**. See **Notes and Definitions** for **Economy** tables (Topic 3 online).
Gross weekly earnings	Measured before tax, National Insurance or other deductions. Gross weekly earnings includes overtime pay, bonuses and other additions to basic pay but excludes any payments for earlier periods (for example, back pay), income in kind, tips and gratuities.
GVA per filled job	A **workplace-based** measure of **labour productivity** that takes account of employment rates.
GVA per head	Divides output of those working in a region by everyone living in that region. This should not be used as a measure of productivity. See **Notes and Definitions** for **Economy** tables (Topic 3 online).

GVA per hour worked	A **workplace-based** measure of **labour productivity** that takes account of the variety of hours worked by employees.
Household	Defined as a single person or a group of people living at the same address as their only or main residence who share either one main meal a day or the living accommodation, or both.
Household projections	Household projections are trend-based; they illustrate what would happen if past trends in household formation were to continue into the future. See **Notes and Definitions** for **Population and Migration** tables (Topic 10 online).
Housing completions	Newly built permanent dwellings. A dwelling is regarded as completed when it becomes ready for occupation, whether it is occupied or not. See **Notes and Definitions** for **Housing** tables (Topic 7 online).
Index of Multiple Deprivation (IMD)	A summary measure of relative deprivation at **Lower Layer Super Output Area** (LSOA) level in England.
Infant mortality rate	Deaths of infants under one year of age per 1,000 live births.
International migration	A long-term international migrant is defined as someone who changes his or her country of usual residence for a period of at least a year. See **Notes and Definitions** for **Population and Migration** tables (Topic 10 online).
Inter-regional migration	Internal population movements based on the movement of NHS doctors' patients between former Health Authorities (HAs) in England and Wales and Area Health Boards (AHBs) in Scotland and Northern Ireland. See **Notes and Definitions** for **Population and Migration** tables (Topic 10 online).
Jobs density	The number of filled jobs in an area divided by the number of people of working age resident in that area.
Key Stage 4	Pupils aged between 14 and 16 (year groups 10 and 11) in England and Wales. Attainment is measured through **National Qualification Framework (NQF) level 2 qualifications**.
Labour productivity	**GVA per filled job** and **GVA per hour worked** are measures of labour productivity.
Labour Force Survey (LFS)	A quarterly sample survey that provides the main labour market data for the UK.
Life expectancy	The average number of years that a person would live if he or she experienced the specific mortality rates of that area for the specified time period throughout the rest of his or her life. Estimates for the UK and the four countries – England, Wales, Scotland and Northern Ireland – are taken from the National Interim Life Tables. The subnational estimates are calculated using abridged life tables and comparable UK figures are provided which differ from the official national estimates.
Lower Layer Super Output Area (LSOA)	Small areas defined for England and Wales that are designed to be homogeneous and also roughly equal in population size. LSOA's have an average population of 1,500.
Lower quartile	The 25th **percentile**; the level below which 25 per cent of values fall.
Maintained schools	Schools funded through local authorities.
Mean, or Average	The sum of the values divided by the number of values.
Median	Statistical term for the value for which half the data are above and half are below. An alternative measure of the average, which is less affected by extreme values than the mean.
Middle Layer Super Output Area (MSOA)	Middle Layer Super Output Areas are built from groups of contiguous **Lower Layer Super Output Areas**. The minimum population is 5,000 and the mean is 7,200.
Modelled unemployment rates	See **unemployment rates**. A statistical model is used to improve the annual **APS** estimates of unemployment for small areas – by using supplementary information – mainly the numbers of claimants of Jobseeker's Allowance (**the claimant count**).
National Parks	In the UK, there are 15 National Parks which are protected areas because of their beautiful countryside, wildlife and cultural heritage.
National Qualification Framework (NQF) level 2 qualifications	Equivalent to GCSE grades A* to C. See **Notes and Definitions** for **Education** tables (Topic 4 online).
National Qualification Framework (NQF) level 3 qualifications	Equivalent to A levels. See **Notes and Definitions** for **Education** tables (Topic 4 online).

4

National Qualification Framework (NQF) level 4 qualifications	Equivalent to a first degree or other higher education qualification below a higher degree. See **Notes and Definitions** for **Education** tables (Topic 4 online).
Natural change	The difference between births and deaths. More births than deaths results in the population experiencing a natural increase, while more deaths than births in a natural decline.
Net migration	The difference between migration into the area and migration out of the area.
Net migration and other changes	Changes in population due to internal and international civilian migration and changes in the number of armed forces (both UK and non-UK) and their dependants resident in the UK.
NUTS (Nomenclature of Territorial Statistics) area classification	NUTS is a hierarchical classification of areas that provides a breakdown of the EU's economic territory for regional statistics that are comparable across the European Union. See **Geography Notes and Definitions** in the **Regional Trends Directory of Online Tables.**
Online tables	Regional and sub-regional data tables in the **Regional Trends Directory of Online Tables** at www.statistics.gov.uk/regionaltrends/data.
Percentiles	One of the values of a variable that divides the distribution of the variable into 100 groups having equal frequencies. The median is equivalent to the 50th percentile.
Population density	Population per square kilometre.
Population projections	Based on mid-year estimates of the population and a set of demographic trend-based assumptions about the future. See **Notes and Definitions** for **Population and Migration** tables (Topic 10 online).
Recorded crime	Statistics compiled from police returns that broadly cover the more serious offences. See **Notes and Definitions** for **Crime** and **Justice** tables (Topic 2 online). See also **BCS comparator offences**.
Residence-based GVA	Residence-based GVA allocates the income from employment to individuals' place of residence. See entry for GVA and **Notes and Definitions** for **Economy tables** (Topic 3 online).
Resident population	The estimated resident population of an area includes all people who usually live there, whatever their nationality. Members of UK and non-UK armed forces stationed in the UK are included and UK forces stationed outside the UK are excluded. Students are taken to be resident at their term-time address. See **Notes and Definitions** for **Population and Migration** tables (Topic 10 online).
Residual household waste	Household waste that is not re-used, recycled or composted.
Rural/Urban definition	A classification of LSOAs in England and Wales based on settlement size and relative population density in different areas. For more information see www.statistics.gov.uk/ geography/nrudp.asp.
Seasonally adjusted	A series of monthly or quarterly data that have been adjusted using a statistical method to expose the underlying trend.
Service industries	Service Industries include the following sections of the **Standard Industrial Classification (SIC)** 2003: wholesale and retail trade, repair of motor vehicles, motorcycles and personal and household goods; hotels and restaurants; transport, storage and communications; financial intermediation; real estate, renting and business activities; public administration and defence, compulsory social security; education; health and social work and other community, social and personal service activities.
Standard Industrial Classification (SIC)	For most tables, the industrial breakdown used is the Standard Industrial Classification Revised 2003 (SIC2003); certain tables now use SIC2007. For further information see **Notes and Definitions** for **Economy** tables (Topic 3 online).
Standardised Mortality Ratio (SMR)	The standardised mortality ratio (SMR) compares overall mortality in a region with that for the UK. The ratio expresses the actual number of deaths in a region as a percentage of the hypothetical number that would have occurred if the region's population had experienced the sex/age-specific rates of the UK that year.

4

State pension age	The age at which people are normally able to claim the state pension. Up to 2009, this was 65 for men and 60 for women. From 2010, the pension age for women is being gradually increased to 65 by 2020.
Stock of dwellings	Number of dwellings including vacant dwellings and temporary dwellings occupied as a normal place of residence. Estimates of the stock in England, Wales and Scotland are based on data from the 2001 Census and projected forward annually.
Total Fertility Rate (TFR)	A measure of the average number of live children that a group of women would bear if they experienced the age-specific fertility rates of the calendar year in question throughout their childbearing lifespan. See **Notes and Definitions** for **Population and Migration** tables (Topic 10 online).
Unemployment rate	The proportion of the **economically active** who are unemployed. The main presentation of unemployment rates is the proportion of the **economically active** population aged 16 or over who are unemployed.
Weighting	Sample survey data relates only to the units in the sample. Therefore the estimates need to be inflated to represent the whole population of interest. Each sample observation is assigned a 'weight' that reflects the population that the sample observation represents. The estimation process that calculates these weights is referred to as **weighting** or **grossing up**.
Workforce jobs	A measure of **employee** jobs, self-employment jobs, all HM Forces and government-supported trainees.
Working age	Currently men aged 16 to 64 and women aged 16 to 59.
Workless household	No adults (men aged 16–64, women aged 16–59) in the household are in **employment**.
Workplace-based GVA	Workplace GVA allocates the income from employment to individuals' place of work. See entry for **GVA** and **Notes and Definitions** for **Economy** tables (Topic 3 online).
Work-based learning	Work-based learning for young people (aged 16–24) in England covers **Advanced Modern Apprenticeships** (AMA), **Foundation Modern Apprenticeships** (FMA) and **Entry to Employment**.

4

Symbols and conventions

Geography	Where possible *Regional Trends* uses data for the whole of the UK. When data from the constituent countries of the UK are not comparable, data for Great Britain or the constituent countries are used. Constituent countries can advise where data are available that are equivalent but not directly comparable with those of the other constituent countries.
Provisional and estimated data	Some data for the latest year (and occasionally for earlier years) are provisional or estimated. To keep footnotes to a minimum, these have not been indicated; source departments will be able to advise if revised data are available.
Q	Specific quarter of a year (Q2 = second quarter).
Rounding of figures	In tables where figures have been rounded to the nearest final digit, there may be an apparent discrepancy between the sum of the constituent items and the total as shown.
Seasonal adjustment	Unless otherwise stated, unadjusted data have been used.
Sources	Sources are usually listed as the name by which the source is currently known.
Survey data	Many of the tables, maps and figures in *Regional Trends* present the results of household surveys that can be subject to large sampling errors. Care should therefore be taken in drawing conclusions about regional differences, and especially with subnational changes over time.
Symbols	The following symbols have been used throughout *Regional Trends*:
	.. not available
	. not applicable
	- negligible (less than half the first digit shown)
	0 nil
Units	Figures are shown in italics when they represent percentages.
Years	
Reference years	Where a choice of years has to be made, the most recent year or a run of recent years is shown. In some cases a particular reference year may be included, for example, a past population census years (1991, 2001 etc.) or the mid-points between census years (1996 etc.) Other years may be added if they represent a peak or trough in the series or relate to a specific benchmark or target.
Academic year	For example, September 2006 to July 2007 would be shown as 2006/07.
Financial year	For example, 1 April 2006 to 31 March 2007 would be shown as 2006/07.
Non-calendar years	Data covering more than one year, for example 1998, 1999 and 2000 would be shown as 1998–2000.

4